THE GLORY OF THE VIOLIN

The Glory of the Violin

JOSEPH WECHSBERG

The Viking Press ❧ New York

Gratefully, to the great violinists I've heard

First published in 1973 by The Viking Press, Inc.
625 Madison Avenue, New York, N.Y. 10022
Published simultaneously in Canada by
The Macmillan Company of Canada Limited
SBN 670-34266-1
Library of Congress catalog card number: 72-78999
Printed in U.S.A. by Vail-Ballou Press, Inc.

Portions of this book were first published in somewhat
different form in *The New Yorker*
and *Esquire*

*Illustrations courtesy of
Rembert Wurlitzer, Inc.*

Contents

Interlude: The Mystery of Violin Sound

The Wonderful Art of Violin-Playing

Illustrations follow p. 154

THE GLORY OF THE VIOLIN

 *Introduction*

I FIRST WANTED TO WRITE THIS BOOK when I fell in love with the violin some forty years ago. I'm glad I didn't, because I knew little about the subject. I still don't consider myself a self-appointed expert. That would be very foolish.

There are perhaps no more than a score of violin experts on earth —people who can pass judgment on the authenticity and merits of fine old violins and make their judgments stick. Even some of these admit that they are not infallible and don't know everything. The Hill brothers, great experts, wrote in 1902, in the preface to their standard work on Antonio Stradivari, "Much of absorbing interest to violin-lovers yet remains to be written."

Almost any intelligent person with a reasonable amount of discernment and taste can become a connoisseur of furniture, paintings, sculptures, or china by study and experience, but no one can become an expert on the subject of old violins by reading books about them, or by playing them. It takes more. An expert on violins must have not only an extensive academic knowledge of them but also an eye and an instinct for the instrument, and, if possible, the experience of a life-time. Nothing less will do. Like great mathematicians or great wine experts, violin experts are born with a special, unanalyzable talent. Sydney Beck of the New York Public Library's Music Division calls it "a kind of composite perception of men whose combined talents and interests and common background enabled them to set down in clear language the innermost secrets of the violin-maker's art, . . ." The great experts approach the violin with this kind of perception and a feel for it, not just with the cold appraiser's look. Though the violin is a masterpiece of art and science, it is also a miracle, not to be judged only scientifically. There are few amateurs among the small clique of celebrated experts; this is no occupation for dilettantes. Most experts are dealers of international renown and unquestioned integrity, and their word is usually accepted as gospel.

Fortunately, and this is where we come in, most of them are not professional writers. They don't always present the subject with the fascination it deserves. Some of their books read like the papers by cel-ebrated physicists that are understood only by fellow physicists. Not surprisingly, perhaps, because the violin is a great achievement of physics and acoustics. Once perfection had been attained by Stradivari more than two hundred and fifty years ago—his most celebrated vio-lin, called "The Messiah," was made in 1716—no better violin was ever made. The achievements of Stradivari and the other great Cre-monese makers were not surpassed.

The golden age of violin-making lasted less than two hundred years. Almost all great violins are at least two hundred years old. Since Ni-colò Amati, Antonio Stradivari, and Guarneri del Gesù made their masterpieces, no one seems to have succeeded in surpassing them. Fine violins are still being made by gifted artists, but how will they sound in two hundred years? Only time will tell. The scientists tell us that some of the new violins sound as well as the old ones, and "prove" it with statistics, figures, and experiments (such as different violins being played behind a curtain). And we—violinists, collectors, and violin-lovers generally—listen to the scientists and tell them you-know-what. Because even the finest-sounding new violin cannot compete with the old-age charm and beauty, sonority and sweetness, of a rare Italian fiddle.

Every year the number of the rare old instruments gets smaller, owing to wear and tear, wars and revolution, accidents and catastrophes, and particularly mistreatment by their temporary possessors. No one can tell how long our great violins will live and sound well. The oldest instruments known, made over four hundred years ago, show no trace of senility. But a violin is a piece of varnished wood, not of granite. Future generations may not hear live the unforgettable sound of a fine violin from Cremona. Some violins may survive in museums, kept under glass, scientifically protected from the hazards of climate and the ravages of time. Stradivari's "Messiah" was bequeathed by the Hill brothers to the Ashmolean Museum in Oxford; and the Library of Congress in Washington also has a quintet of beautiful Stradivari instruments, which are regularly played there. There will always be violins, of course; the violin continues to be the most important instrument in orchestral music. But future generations will have to get used to the new violins. Some day the glory of Cremona will be only a memory.

I started out, as an eight-year-old boy, with a cheap, three-quarter "factory fiddle" which cost the equivalent of three dollars and was hardly worth it. I worked my way up in the violin world; now I am the proud possessor of a Stradivari made in 1730. Such luck obliges: writing this book was a subject of enthusiasm and a labor of love, but also a project of thorough research and a matter of hard study. My lifelong enthusiasm about the violin was always matched by my curiosity. Most violin-lovers never get tired of finding out more about their favorite instrument.

This is not easy. The violin is surrounded by mysteries, and *mystique*, perhaps more than are other works of art. Scientists have put down in mathematical terms the designs and acoustical properties of the old Italian fiddles. The curvature has been defined precisely. Exact blueprints of famous violins exist: anyone could copy them, and many did. But even the finest copyists—noted artists in their own right— were not certain about the exact relationship between the wood the old masters used and the tone color they achieved. Men have walked on the moon, but are still unable exactly to reproduce the varnish of the great Cremonese makers, though its composition is *no* secret (as is so often believed). The experts do not agree about the exact influence of the varnish on the tone of the instrument, though a degree of influence is admitted by everybody.

In fact, experts disagree on nearly everything that concerns the violin—its evolution, history, development. The encyclopedic standard works on the violin contain bewildering inconsistencies on many violin data. Makers' names are variously spelled, dates of birth and death vary, brothers become cousins and uncles become brothers. (Enrico Ceruti, generally considered the last of the Cremonese masters, who died as recently as 1883, is called Cerruti, Cerutti, or Cerrutti, though he spelled it "Ceruti" on his own labels.) Many facts can no longer be checked about the violin, but few experts will admit this: "A sort of Gresham's law seems to prevail in violin literature, with every author's mistakes copied a dozen times more frequently than his accurate statements," writes Arnold Gingrich.

The violin happens to be unique as a work of art because it is appreciated most fully by persons practicing its art. One may become a knowledgeable collector of paintings, sculptures, or rare manuscripts without being a sculptor, painter, or writer. But to enjoy fully a rare old violin, one has to be able to play it. Looking at it isn't enough. (Henry Ford collected old violins, but didn't play the instrument. He admired it for its technical perfection.) A rare old violin resembles a rare old bottle of wine that is fully enjoyed only by people who have had years of testing, tasting, and trying. The beauty of a violin doesn't communicate itself as easily as the beauty of a painting. You are fascinated by a fine violin or you aren't. But for those of us who love violins the sight of a beautiful old fiddle is as rewarding as a great painting. The mysterious inner fire that seems to set in motion the interplay of the waves of the varnish on the back of a fine Stradivari is as exciting to us as the mysterious smile around the mouth of the Mona Lisa.

Of all musicians, string players have the most intimate relationship with their instruments, and fiddlers have an anthropomorphic attitude toward their violins. We feel they are almost human, members of our family. We are closer to a violin we cherish than to another of greater fame and value. No mature man leaves his wife for the first beautiful starlet he sees, and that's how a mature fiddler feels about his fiddle. Stories are told of noted artists who switch instruments often, always trying to find one that "suits" them better. Exactly as some do with their women. The fault is more often with the man, or the violinist, than with the woman, or the violin.

Pianists can be casual about their instrument; though they appreciate a fine piano, they can rarely travel with their own, unless they are in the Paderewski-Rubinstein class. They are able to play well on any good instrument. Other musicians take pains to keep their instruments in good shape—think of the poor oboe players sitting up nights, making their own reeds—but they rarely talk about their instruments the way we string players do. They wouldn't claim, as we do, that it is almost alive. A French horn isn't alive, though it may become so when played by a fine performer. But when I play my Stradivari it sings out with an almost human voice, the sort of voice I like in a woman. In such moments I feel my violin is alive.

Violins often behave as capriciously as women do. They can be sweet or bored or temperamental. On some days they sound better than on others. They may lovingly respond to your efforts or angrily reject you. They want to be wooed; if you make a mistake, they scream. On damp days they are depressed. When you bring them out of the cold into a warm room, they need a while to get acclimatized. The most minute change—a lowering of the bridge by the fraction of a millimeter—will give them several bad weeks of adjustment. I once owned a lovely Antonius and Hieronymus Amati, made in 1608, that disliked bright lights. But one must make allowances in the presence of a lady over three hundred and fifty years old with a lovely body and a bewitching voice. My Stradivari was born when its maker was eighty-six. You wouldn't know it, though, when you look at its youthful charm and its brown-red varnish, soft and translucent. My Stradivari is allergic to smoke, especially cigar smoke. It doesn't like protracted fog. It sounds best when there is sunshine outside. This will not surprise other owners of rare old violins. David Laurie, the nineteenth-century English expert who once took a beautiful Stradivari from Paris to London, wrote in his *Reminiscences,*

> I knew . . . its tone would be affected by the sea air in crossing the Channel. It will seem curious to many readers that violins should be susceptible to *mal-de-mer* . . . but long experience has taught me that it is so, and the finer the instrument, the more susceptible it is. Most of them do not recover properly themselves for at least a fortnight.

The truth is that, unlike pianists and trumpeters, who merely play their instruments, we fiddlers live with ours. The very thought of an assembly line for violins like the assembly line for snare drums and slide trombones gives us the horrors. There is one important thing to be said about attractive fiddles (and attractive women): they are never dull.

In this book I've tried to separate facts from fiction and evidence from legends, whenever possible. It isn't always possible. No one knows exactly when or where Antonio Stradivari was born. But, frankly, does it matter, as long as we have his violins? We don't know where Mozart is buried, but that doesn't bother me when I play his "Dissonance" String Quartet, or listen to his "Jupiter" Symphony. I won't let my enthusiasm interfere with my job as a student, researcher, and writer, but I didn't set out to write another cold compilation of often retold facts and anecdotes. The violin is the most personal musical instrument of all, and toward the end of the twentieth century our feelings have changed about it, as about everything else. I have long been interested in both the physiology and the psychology of the violin. This book is neither an encyclopedia of the violin nor a how-to manual. Instead I tried to write a book for violin-lovers today—musicians and collectors, amateurs and professionals. Such a book ought to contain all available facts and findings and also reflect one's feelings and fascination. Difficult, but the only way is to try.

"Eight hundred guineas seems a long price for a dealer to give," Charles Reade, novelist and violin-lover, wrote in 1878 to the editor of the London *Globe.* "But after all, here is a Violin, a picture, and a miracle in one; and big diamonds increase in number; but these spoils of time are limited for ever now, and, indeed, can only decrease by shipwreck, accident, and the tooth of time." The violin is, at the same time, a work of art to be looked at and a musical instrument to be played on. It appeals to more of the human senses than any other work of art. Therefore, a book on the mystery of the violin wouldn't be complete without discussing the "mystery" of violin-playing that transcends technical problems. (Many fine works exist on technical and musical problems, from Locatelli's *L'Arte di Violino* and Leopold Mozart's *A Treatise on the Fundamental Principles of Violin Playing* in the eighteenth century, to Carl Flesch's *The Art of Violin Playing,* Szigeti's *A Violinist's Notebook,* and Ivan Galamian's *Principles of Violin Playing and Teaching* today.)

Great violin-playing encompasses more than technique, the mere ability to play many notes fast and accurately. It boldly struggles to bring out the essence of the music, and to create the very special throb of soul and heart that touches the listener's soul and heart.

No one can determine by analysis how great playing is achieved, and almost no one can teach it. Its attainment concerns the great violinist as much as the amateur chamber-music fiddler. In principle, both strive for the same thing: to make the music come alive. It is the amateur's untiring devotion to the violin that has kept the instrument alive and eternally young, and kept the virtuoso in business. Few musical instruments that are three and four hundred years old are still being played, and none of them enjoys the worldwide appeal of the violin. Many violinists admit that they secretly adore the cello for its serene beauty and masculine sonority. But the violin, so close to the human voice, remains widely beloved. People have always loved to sing. Playing the violin is almost like singing.

To write yet another book about the violin seems almost absurd, for hundreds of books about the violin have been published, but most of them were written for small groups of subscribers. Violin-lovers never get tired of reading about great violins—where they are today, the pedigrees and myths and legends, the names of the lucky owners. Other enthusiasts always hope to find the answer to some other "secret"—the varnish of Stradivari, or the tone color of Guarneri del Gesù. Violin literature ranges from histories of the master violin-makers to biographies of the celebrated violinists, from manuals on how to build your own violin to books on the manifold aspects of the art of violin-playing. Some books cover special points of technique, claiming astonishing shortcuts to virtuosity. Others offer facile analyses of masterpieces, with apparently infallible advice to the student. Many seem based on the premise that when the necessary technique is acquired, the rest will follow: musicianship, taste, style, and the ability to grasp the spiritual content of the music. Unfortunately, it doesn't work out that way. The violin is a complex instrument. Playing it is even more complex. "The violin has . . . at one and the same time a soul and a mind," wrote Eugène Ysaÿe, one of the greatest late-nineteenth-century violinists. To play it well, one needs not only soul and mind, but heart as well.

For when all is said and written, there remains one thing to remember: music should be made, performed, listened to, and written about by people who *love* music. Nowadays many people write music (or about music) in order to get rid of their aggressions. But among all the arts, music is the most universal and the most emotional. It asks to be loved. So does the violin, the instrument so close to the human voice and better suited to express the emotional and spiritual content of the music than any other instrument. Once I had decided to write this book on the violin, the only way to write it was with love of music and love of the instrument.

The Violin—

All the Facts

(and Some Legends, to Be Sure)

Who Created the Violin?

Of all musical instruments made by the hand of man, none is more mysterious than the violin (and the viola, the cello, and the double bass, also made by violin-makers). Little is known about its beginning. "The origin of all stringed instruments is lost in the mists of time, and despite the most patient and laborious research on the part of famous savants, no positive information has as yet been furnished regarding this point," wrote Alberto Bachmann in 1925 in his *Encyclopedia of the Violin,* and the intervening years of research have added little further knowledge. The predecessors of the violin are known: the Arabian *rabab;* the pear-shaped *rebec,* also from the Orient, which was popular in Spain and France in the fifteenth century; the Gothic *fidula* (fiddle); the French *vielle;* the English *crwth;* the Italian *viola.* These instruments were played with bows but otherwise they have little in common with our violin, which was an incredible improvement over all predecessors. Incredible, because the violin wasn't developed gradually, as are almost all other works of art: it emerged, almost at its beginning, in its final perfect form. There were no "primitive" violins. No one has ever been able to explain that.

There is much disagreement among the historians concerning the evolution of the violin. Even its sex is enigmatic. The Italians call it *il violino* and the French *le violon;* both use the masculine gender. To the Germans (*die Geige, die Violine*) the violin is a she. In the second edition of his *Musica instrumentalis deutsch,* published in 1545 in Wittenberg, M. Agricola speaks of a Polish "Geige." In 1533, G. M. Lanfranco, in *Scintille di musica,* published in Brescia, describes "a small viol without frets." Philibert Jambe de Fer, in *Epitôme musical* (printed in Lyon in 1556) makes a distinction between viols, which were used by *"gens du vertù,"* people of taste, while violins were used "for dances and weddings." One of the earliest paintings showing a violin was made by Gaudenzio Ferrari, who worked in towns around Milan between 1530 and 1540. Andrea Amati, who is now considered the creator of our violin—on that nearly all experts agree—was born in Cremona, probably before 1510. The first mention in print of *il violino* is in Italy in 1551. By 1560 Andrea Amati was so famous that he received an order to make an entire set of thirty-eight string instruments for the court of King Charles IX of France. Four violins still exist; one of them, dated 1566, is now in a private collection in America.

The meaning of Agricola's expression "Polish 'Geige' " was never convincingly explained. It may point toward the violin's early appearance in the Baltic and Scandinavian countries. The Poles had nothing to do with the early evolution of the instrument.

For a long time it was generally believed that the violin was directly developed from the older viol, which had a flat top. This was denied by Arnold Dolmetsch and Alexander Hajdecki, at the turn of our century. Both reached the same conclusion independently.

The violin was not created by artisans. It is indubitably the work of genius—of one, or perhaps more than one working at the same time. The great innovations (compared to earlier instruments) are the curvature of its top and back, and its characteristic f-holes. The curved top spreads the vibrations. Without the sound holes, this spread would be hindered. The violin's architectural design is beautifully balanced. Its construction is dominated by laws of physics and acoustics. Nothing about the violin can be changed without seriously disturbing its equilibrium as a work of art and as a musical instrument. Romantic-minded historians connected the f-shaped sound holes with King François I of France, a patron of Leonardo da Vinci—the inventor, artist, and musician, and certainly a genius. There is no proof, though. Leonardo da Vinci left many drawings of his inventions, from military fortresses to flying machines, but none were of the violin with the brilliant innovation of the fretless fingerboard.

Although the violin is generally considered a child of Italy, even Italian historians admit that some bowed instruments, still unknown in Italy in the thirteenth century, had been made in Germany. The Italians caught up with the barbarians, however, when their lute-makers and guitar-makers began experimenting with various forms of viols.

The true violin was created in the Italian Renaissance. By the early sixteenth century some intruments of the Gothic era had been discarded—the psaltery, the bagpipe, the medieval *vielle* of the French troubadours. The new polyphony demanded the church organ, the lute, and other instruments with stronger, more dynamic string tone. Gradually the more flexible string orchestra replaced the former, heavier wind orchestra with its cornets, trombones, and bombards. Early chamber music was written for the more intimate sounds of strings and keyboard instruments. They had a more variable and more pleasant tone than the older wind instruments, and could produce chromatic tones. Claudio Monteverdi, another genius from Cremona and the creator of opera, called the new instrument *violino ordinario da braccio* to distinguish it from the *violino piccolo alla francese,* tuned a fourth higher. (The word *braccio,* "arm," reappears in the German word *Bratsche,* viola, the alto member of the violin family.) Leopold Mozart in 1756 mentions "concertos written for these small violins." The smallest violin was the *pochette* (*Taschengeige*), a tiny instrument tuned an octave above the violin; it was used by dance masters who carried it in their coat pockets.

The Renaissance was a time of change, and everybody was experimenting with new tools, new inventions, new instruments. In the Bavarian village of Füssen, some lute-makers created instruments that are now forgotten. One Bavarian family is often mentioned, however, the

Tieffenbrucker; they worked in Padua, Venice, and Lyon. Their most famous member was Caspar Tieffenbrucker (c. 1514–1571), whose name was later Gallicized into Gaspard Duiffoprugcar. At one time many historians believed that he was an early master who actively participated in the gradual metamorphosis from the viol to the violin. Roquefort, a French writer, mentions him in his biographical dictionary. According to Roquefort, Gaspard (or Caspar, or Gasparo) was born in the late fifteenth century in the South Tyrol, worked in Bologna, was invited to Paris by King François I, and finally moved to Lyon. A French scientist, Henry Coutagne, admits that Gaspard's name was originally Tieffenbrucker, that he was born in Bavaria, perhaps in Füssen, in 1514, and that he worked in Lyon around 1550. An engraving of 1562 by Pierre Woeriot shows a Teutonic-looking bearded man ("Gaspar Duiffoprugcar") surrounded by some instruments. Among them is an alto violin and, half hidden below, what seems to be a true violin. Perhaps Woeriot hid it because he had never seen one. A bass viol attributed to Tieffenbrucker is now at the Museum of the Brussels Conservatory. He bought a vineyard near Lyon in 1556, built a house there, and was made a citizen of Lyon by royal decree. A document exists that gives his birth place as "Fessin," which has been interpreted either as Füssen, in the Allgäu, or Freising, near Munich, also in Bavaria. He died in 1571. Louis-Antoine Vidal, the nineteenth-century French historian, claims that Duiffoprugcar made fine bass viols but that all so-called Tieffenbrucker violins are spurious.

Tieffenbrucker, claimed by several countries, certainly existed and must have been a very gifted instrument-maker. But he probably had little or nothing to do with the creation of the violin. The first violins that survive today were made by Andrea Amati, in Cremona. Later, Gasparo da Salò, a viol-maker in Brescia, began making violins and violas.

His family name was Gasparo Bertolotti. Most authorities claim that he was born in 1542 in Salò, at the southern end of Lake Garda in Northern Italy and he called himself Gasparo da Salò when he went as a young man to the nearby town of Brescia, already famous for its viol- and lute-makers. An Italian historian, A. M. Mucchi, has written that Gasparo was born on May 20, 1540, in the small village of Polpenazze, and that he studied music with his uncle, Agostino Bertolotti

(1510–1584), chapel master at the Cathedral of Sale. Gasparo seems to have arrived in Brescia in 1562 or the following year. His name is registered for the first time in the parish of Santa Agatha on March 23, 1565, when his son Francesco was born there. Gasparo first worked with the lute-maker Girolamo Virchi. In 1580 he was established as a maker of viols and violins in Contrada (section) del Palazzo Vecchio. Eight years later, he bought a house in Contrada de la Cocere. Gasparo died in Brescia, probably around 1609. Few of his violins and violas have survived, and a number are now believed to be spurious, among them four cellos. The study of his instruments proves beyond doubt that he was a great maker who went his own way. He must have known the early violins of Andrea Amati, but he did not copy them. Andrea Amati made instruments with a sweet but rather small tone, Gasparo was interested in instruments with a big, sonorous tone. His violins have a dark, haunting timbre, almost an alto tone. Actually, he was not primarily a maker of violins. Dario d'Attili, the great expert, knows less than half a dozen of his violins, among them one undersized and two rather large ones, 14¼ inches long. Their outline is not elegant, the dimensions are large, the varnish is amber or reddish brown. Gasparo's development is as fascinating as Andrea Amati's. He began with viols that had a small tone and wound up making large violins with a powerful tone, and throughout his life he kept his individuality. Many historians consider him the founder of the school of Brescia, but in the strict sense of the word this honor should go to Pellegrino, called Zanetto da Montechiaro, who was born in 1522, preceding Gasparo by eighteen years. But doubtless there was an important school of Brescia; Andrea Amati founded the school of Cremona, which survived that of Brescia. Andrea's grandson, Nicolò Amati, later influenced Stradivari, the champion violin-maker. Gasparo da Salò and his pupil, Giovanni Paolo Maggini, later had great influence on Guarneri del Gesù, Stradivari's challenger. The old argument of whether Andrea Amati or Gasparo da Salò created the first violin is academic and useless. Both masters were giants in the history of violin-making, and each contributed to it in his own way. They were the first generation: the "inventors." To our way of thinking, Gasparo da Salò, prophetically searching for the powerful, sonorous violin tone of the future, emerges as a "modern" master.

One of his most famous violins is now at the town museum in Bergen, Norway, a gift from Ole Bull, the great virtuoso, who was born there. It is beautifully decorated with ivory and bronze, and a neck painted with red, blue, and gold arabesques. Instead of a scroll it has a small angel's head, and underneath a carved mermaid whose fish-body is covered with green and gold scales. According to contemporary gossip (which may be true), the violin's first owner, Cardinal Aldobrandini, sent it to Benvenuto Cellini in Florence for a special ornamenting job. The violin was made after 1560, and Cellini died in 1572; with Cellini or no, the violin remains one of the oldest that survive.

Gasparo da Salò's later violins were always well built, on the sturdy side. The backs were made of fine maple, there were low ribs and rather large sound holes; the varnish was dark brown but translucent. The tone is nearly always sonorous and powerful. One of his violins, made in the 1570s, is now in America, owned by Hugh W. Long. (It was selected as one of the fifteen violins played in 1963 by Ruggiero Ricci on the comparison record to *The Glory of Cremona*. Its tone is dark, veiled, and beautiful.) Another famous instrument is the double bass he made for the Monastery of San Marco in Venice. It was later played by Domenico Dragonetti (1763–1846), the famous Venetian double bass virtuoso, who gave concerts all over Europe. It is smaller than most double basses and its tone is soft and warm; the high notes sound as on a very fine cello. Dragonetti gratefully bequeathed the instrument to the city of Venice, where it remains.

Gasparo da Salò's most important assistant and disciple, Giovanni Paolo Maggini, was born in Botticini in 1580. He took over Gasparo's workshop after his teacher's death in 1609. Maggini was a great master and experimenter and did much for the fame of the Brescia school of violin-making. (Dario d'Attili calls him "the first true maker of *violins* in Brescia.") Both the Brescians and the Cremonese decided early to make two different models of the violin—a small one, about 13½ inches long, and a larger one, about 14 inches. There was demand for both models; Gasparo da Salò, Maggini, and Andrea Amati all knew what their customers wanted. A number of Maggini's violins survive today and some have been much appreciated by performings artists. Charles Auguste de Bériot (1802–1870), who established the Belgian school of violin-playing, owned two Maggini violins. Maggini's violins have large dimensions and a powerful tone. The sound holes are long and pointed, and the arching of the top is considerable. The varnish varies between light yellow and dark brown. Today the "Brescian" tone means dark and veiled, somewhat haunted. The instruments are not used by modern performers but have great artistic and historical value.

For centuries violin historians and experts have argued whether Gasparo da Salò or Andrea Amati "invented" the violin. (Tieffenbrucker is out of the running today.) It doesn't really matter, historically or geographically: the distance between Brescia and Cremona is only thirty-one miles. If Andrea Amati was born around or after 1510, he would be older than Gasparo. The patrician family of the Amatis in Cremona has been traced back to 1007. Andrea was the first member of the family who made musical instruments. On his labels, he used the Latinized Amadus (in Latin "amatus" means "the beloved one"). Occasionally one finds the spelling "Amadi" on fake labels of German origin.

The violin was created during the first part of the sixteenth century in the uninspiring region between Brescia and Cremona, in the Italian province of Lombardy. Andrea Amati began as a maker of lutes and viols. He may have studied with Marco del Busseto, a Cremonese lute-maker. He may even have been for a time in nearby Brescia. Some experts see in the sloping edges and the f-holes of his early violins the influence of the Brescians: such readings are narrow-minded and useless. Andrea Amati soon developed his own design for the violin.

Much that concerns the creation of the violin remains speculation and detection, intuition and experience. But the contribution of Andrea Amati is a fact, demonstrated by his violins. Obviously, the idea was in the early-sixteenth-century air. The violin was needed and thus it was created.

To formulate ideas that exist but have not yet been expressed, that is the poet's task. Andrea Amati and Gasparo da Salò—and perhaps even Tieffenbrucker—were the early poets of the violin. They succeeded in expressing the idea in a design which gloriously survives to this day. Specifically, it was Andrea Amati's model which was later used by members of his family, by Nicolò Amati's most famous pupil, Antonio Stradivari, and by most Italian makers in Cremona and elsewhere. He freed himself from the heritage of the older viol and the different set of acoustic laws on which it was based. Within three or four decades he had become a prime mover in the evolution from the old viol to the modern violin. Andrea Amati's best violins were already so well made that even Stradivari, unquestionably the greatest maker of all, could not improve the basic design. Nowadays the word "genius" is often used when "talent" would be appropriate. "Doing easily what others find difficult is talent, doing what is impossible for talent is genius," wrote the Swiss critic Henri-Frédéric Amiel. Andrea Amati was the first genius of the violin.

The exact dates of his birth and death are not known. For a long time it was assumed that he was born in 1535 and died in 1612. Recent research by Carlo Bonetti and others has established that he was born between 1500 and 1510, probably around 1510. By 1526 he was established as *liutaio* (instrument-maker) in Cremona's parish of Santa Helena. In 1538 he leased, and later bought, the house in San Faustino where for the next two hundred years several generations of Amatis lived and created some of the greatest instruments. The birth of his first daughter, Apollinaria, was registered in 1535. Four other children were born, two daughters, Elizabeth and Valeria, and the two sons, Antonio and Girolamo, who became famous violin-makers. The sons are named Andrea's heirs in a notarized deed signed January 2, 1580, which would indicate that Andrea had died a short while before. Consequently, all labels bearing a later date seem false.

After the middle of the sixteenth century the violins made by Andrea Amati became famous all over Europe. In 1555, the Marshal de Brissac brought several violinists to the Court of France. Their leader was Balthazar de Beaujoyeux, "the best violinist in Christendom." The following year, Philibert Jambe de Fer described the violin in his *Epitôme musical*, "Contrary to the viol, the violin has only four strings, tuned in fifths . . ." In 1559 Pierre Lupo from Antwerp sold to the magistrate of Utrecht "five violins with their cases" for 72 pounds. All these instruments seem to refer to Andrea Amati because they predate the first violin made by Gasparo da Salò probably in 1562.

In his *Carteggio* (Diary) Count Ignazio Alessandro Cozio di Salabue

(1755–1840), the Piedmontese nobleman who was the first important expert, collector, and dealer in violins, and at one time or another saw nearly all the celebrated violins, describes a violin made by Andrea Amati in 1546 that belonged to the abbé Venini of Sant' Ambrogio in Milan: "Its back is slightly flattened toward the edges. The top is well gradated though high. The sound holes are longish, the varnish has a chestnut shade. The violin has a clear and penetrating tone." This reads like the authentic description of one of the earliest existing violins.

The oldest surviving violins made by Andrea Amati were perhaps made after 1550. They were rather small, especially when compared to Gasparo da Salò's instruments, with strongly curved tops, and with a thick translucent varnish. Andrea originally used dark reddish colors and later switched to light brown and dark yellow, almost golden, shades which remain typical for all members of the Amati family. The oldest Andrea Amati now in the United States was probably made in 1566. You can hear it, too, on the recording *The Glory of Cremona* (discussed below in the interlude, "The Mystery of Violin Sound"). The Andrea Amati has a full, round tone, dark and mellow. There is not a trace of old age in its sound, though it is over four hundred years old.

Seniority alone wouldn't establish the position of Andrea Amati in the violin world. But the Amati family did more than anyone else to establish and develop the Cremonese school of violin-making. "Andrea Amati deserves the credit for the design of the modern violin," writes Edmund H. Fellowes; "Except for small improvements in detail which Antonio Stradivari introduced more than a century later, the violin of Andrea Amati is virtually the violin of today." This is correct but doesn't diminish the great contribution of the Brescians, Gasparo da Salò and Paolo Maggini. At one time during his career, Stradivari was known to experiment with a model which would combine the beauty of sound and easy response of the best Cremonese violins with the power and sonority of the Brescians.

Around 1540, when Andrea Amati made his early violins, Michelangelo was sixty-five and Benvenuto Cellini was forty. By 1700 Bernini had been dead twenty years and Stradivari had begun making his greatest violins, never surpassed by anyone else. He died in 1737. Giu-

seppe Guarneri del Gesù, today considered Stradivari's only competitor, died in 1744. Fine violins have been made since then, but never
one that was better. Men have learned to split the atom and to trans-
plant the human heart, but not to surpasss the Cremonese violins. It is
a bewildering and also a comforting thought. Apparently man's imagination and skill are not unlimited, as some of us believe in moments
of exhilaration.

No one knows exactly how many fine violins were made in Cremona. Dario d'Attili, one of today's top experts, believes that perhaps
ten thousand stringed instruments were produced in Cremona between
1550, when Andrea Amati reached his prime, and 1883, when Enrico
Ceruti died. Perhaps half of these are still in existence. "The Cremona
violin was expensive even while the maker was still alive, and therefore was more appreciated and cared for." The mortality rate among
instruments from the less renowned schools—Brescia, Venice, Milan,
Turin, Naples, etc.—was considerably higher. More than half of all
Cremonese instruments are now in the United States.

Some day a great old violin will be even more of a rarity than it is
now. Violas, cellos, and double basses will be the most scarce because
the celebrated violin-makers made relatively few of them; only eleven
Stradivari violas exist today.

If the violin-making school of Cremona lasted in all from 1550 until
1883, the "golden age" was shorter, only over a hundred and fifty
years. By 1744, after the glorious trinity (Nicolò Amati, Stradivari,
Guarneri del Gesù) was gone, there were still fine makers in town:
Francesco Ruggieri, Carlo Bergonzi, Lorenzo Storioni. Elsewhere there
were Domenico Montagnana, Santo Seraphin, Matteo Goffriller, the
Guadagninis, Francesco Gobetti, Carlo Tononi, the Grancino and
Gagliano families. But Cremona had reached the end of its glory.

The city was not otherwise historically important during the era of
the violin-makers. It had been free and independent from 1082 to
1335, when the beautiful Romanesque and Gothic buildings were created. Cremona lost its independence in 1344, when it became part of
the duchy of Milan; after 1535, Milan belonged to Spain. Cremona
had a modest school of painting during the Renaissance. In the early
sixteenth century, when Andrea Amati was born, Cremona was a

sleepy provincial town on the left bank of the Po River. It was well known for its noble palaces and beautiful squares, the old cathedral with its Lombard Romanesque façade, and the four-hundred-foot-high Gothic Torrazzo, "Italy's highest bell tower." Even the proudest Cremonese wouldn't claim that their town could compare with Florence, Venice, Rome, or half a dozen other Italian cities, but the citizens were surrounded by beautiful buildings, beautiful colors, beautiful sounds. Nature and man seemed in harmonious synthesis.

The center of public life in Cremona was the piazza around the Duomo. A couple of hundred yards away was Piazza San Domenico, with the Church and the Convent of San Domenico; Number 5 was the comfortable house of Stradivari (it has now been renamed the Piazza Roma, and the old houses have disappeared). Through a side street one reached the parish of San Faustino, with the patrician house of the Amati family. Even closer to Stradivari's home, also in today's Piazza Roma, was San Matteo parish, in which was Andrea Guarneri's more modest house. Walking past the north side of the Duomo one came to the parish of San Prospero, where Giuseppe del Gesù lived in a rather run-down place, less than five minutes from Stradivari. Nearby was Carlo Bergonzi's large house and the smaller one owned by Francesco Ruggieri. Most of the world's great violins have come from this relatively small section in Cremona, and most of them were made within less than two hundred years. That's another mystery no one can explain about the violin.

With the decline of the Renaissance princes in Italian cities certain academies had been established, societies of noblemen who were trying to keep intact the country's cultural heritage. There was not much cultural life in Cremona at the time the first violins were made. The Academy of the *Animosi* was founded in 1560, about when Andrea Amati's violins became famous. (He was not invited to join.) Membership was restricted to the city's aristocratic families. In 1607 the Academy performed a concert selection from *Orfeo,* the new opera written by Claudio Monteverdi, a Cremonese. He had gone to nearby Mantua, where the dynasty of the Gonzaga did for opera and music what the Medici in Florence had earlier done for painting and sculpture.

Opera was not popular in Cremona. A theater had been built by the wealthy Ariberti family, but Leone Allacci's *Drammaturgia* mentions no opera performance in Cremona before 1755, a pretty late date. Francesco Arisi (1657–1743), the author of *Cremona Litterata,* writes much about local literature and philosophy but takes a dim view of music in the town. The great violin-makers were discovered in France, Spain, Austria, and England before they were esteemed in their home town. Not until 1819, did a local chronicler named Lancetti write with pride in his *Biografia Cremonese* about the great violin-makers. He remembered that when the French armies had passed through Cremona, in 1795, their commanding general wanted to buy an Amati or a Stradivari. There were none for sale, though. Most had been sold elsewhere, and the few people in town who had good instruments wouldn't part with them. Since then Cremona has done little to preserve its treasures. When I came to Cremona one day in 1948, there was not a single violin in town made by the Amatis, Stradivari, or the Guarneris.

 # The Bow

Unlike the violin, which emerged from the beginning almost as we know it today and underwent no major changes, the bow passed through many phases before it became the forceful and graceful implement we now take for granted. The importance of the bow can hardly be overstated. Some violinists spend a great deal of effort (and money) on the violin and a disproportionately small amount on the bow.

The bow is to a string player what breath is to a singer. A good singer knows the importance of breath-control which preserves the voice and prolongs its life span. Even the greatest larynx cannot be fully used without technically correct breathing. And violinists have another, related problem: "In my opinion," Alberto Bachmann wrote, "every violinist who reaches a certain age should learn how to breathe properly . . . it is very difficult to play the violin when the player's breath is labored." A nervous player, Bachmann made it a practice to inhale deeply as he began to perform on the stage. He noticed that his performance gained in calmness and equality. If you sit close to the platform, you may see many celebrated violinists taking—probably unconsciously—a deep breath before they start the difficult cadenza in a violin concerto.

The best breathing of the singing artist, like the violinist's best bowing, will not be noticed by the listener. One only notices it when something is wrong. Great violinists agree that proficiency of the left hand is easier to acquire than a good bowing technique in the right. Eugène Ysaÿe used to say that any fool could manipulate the fingers of the left hand, but "the right hand is the artist."

Originally, the bow was just a bent stick with an incision at either end through which the hair was tied. In the fifteenth century, the nosed tip and the frog at the heel end (the block to which the hair is attached) were introduced. Then the frog was refined. It was secured to the stick by a wire and furnished with a toothed metal clamp at the back, to give the hair the needed tension. The stick still curved upward, however, though it gradually became somewhat flatter, as we know from Corelli's bow. Corelli and other early performers could play only *forte* or *piano;* they were unable to achieve dynamic modifications in between. The Cremonese makers made their own bows but none has survived—another minor mystery. Count Cozio di Salabue's collection of relics from Stradivari's original workshop, purchased from the master's heirs, also contained designs for the heads and nuts of the type of bow then made.

Tartini was the first virtuoso who suggested improvements. He became the creator of the modern bow technique. The bow was made of lighter wood, and the stick lost its upward curve, becoming straight and elastic. Tartini's bow was further improved by Giovanni Battista Viotti, who was famous for his elegant bowing and sweet *cantilene.* Viotti designed the bow more or less as we now know it, and had them made by the Tourte family in Paris. Fançois Tourte (1747–1835) perfected the balance of the bow and became the Stradivari of bowmakers. He was born ten years after the death of Stradivari, who would have been fascinated to hear the subtle dynamic shadings that can be achieved on his violins with Tourte's bow.

Like Stradivari, François Tourte had a long and fruitful life. He worked until he died at eighty-eight. He had begun as a watchmaker, and became interested in physics. After eight years he gave up watch-making and joined his father and brother, who were already making violin bows. His sharp eye, sense of accuracy, and watchmakers' training enabled him to make rapid progress. He practiced by making bow sticks from the staves of old barrels because he couldn't afford expensive wood. Later he began experimenting with various types of wood. He discovered that Pernambuco wood from Brazil would be the most suitable because it was hard, yet flexible. A fine bow must remain straight and elastic; only a healthy piece of wood with a very straight grain will do that. When Tourte began making his famous bows around 1780, he often couldn't get enough Pernambuco wood, owing to the sea wars between France and England, and had to use other kinds of wood. He would examine a hundred blocks of wood before selecting a piece that was cut straight with the fibers running through the block, and with no knots.

Tourte's measurements are still accepted everywhere; no one has since made better bows. He determined the ideal length of the violin bow, from end to end, between 28½ and 29⅛ inches (about 73 centimeters). His bows for viola and cello were somewhat shorter. He solved the problem of where to put the greatest weight of the cylindrical or prismatic stick to achieve an essential balance: he increased the weight of the lower end of his bows, which had a higher head than the earlier bows, and thus brought the point of greatest weight closer to the hand. He fixed the point of maximum weight at 19 centimeters (7½ inches) from the frog. The diameter of his stick was 8.6 millimeters (⅝ inch) at the lower end, decreasing evenly to 3.3 millimeters at the tip. Other famous bow-makers later experimented with different measurements. They always came back to Tourte, though, who seems to have determined the gradual reduction of the diameter with mathematical accuracy. Tourte even specified the selection, thickness, and number of hairs, from 150 to 250. He was the first maker who fixed the hair to the frog by a wedge, which he covered with a small blade of mother-of-pearl. His frogs are often made of silver, gold-mounted ebony, or tortoise shell. He used only white horsehair, and only the finest, roundest hairs are selected; never flat or uneven hairs. Jean-Baptiste Vuillaume (1798–1875), who studied François Tourte's bows all his life, wrote about the difficulty of arranging the hairs so that they form a perfectly flat ribbon along their entire length.

Prominent violinists have their preference (or idiosyncrasy) for special kinds of horsehair, as for everything else. Some fiddlers from the west buy their hairs in Moscow; some famous Russian artists buy them in New York. The best horsehair now comes from the western provinces of Canada, where large herds of horses are raised. The hairs must be carefully treated. Horsehair has tiny identations which make the strings sound. The hairs should be hung in such a way that one hair goes upside down and the next goes right side up. Few specialists can do this job well. Years ago Canadian horsehair was sent to Japan for this special treatment and shipped back by way of Siberia, arriving as "Russian horsehair" in New York.

François Tourte didn't varnish his bows, he polished them with powdered pumice and oil. Though he was said to be unable to read or write, he worked with unfailing accuracy and made his bows the most delicate instruments of breathing. He didn't have to wait to be discovered. His bows were immediately recognized as the best, and he was unable to fill all his orders because he would not do second-class work. In this respect he resembled, and even surpassed, Stradivari. He destroyed every bow that wasn't up to his strict standards. In the beginning he charged only 20 or 30 *sous* for a bow. Later, he got up to 15 *louis d'or*. Toward the end of his life, people would pay 500 francs for a Tourte bow. Today it is worth several thousand dollars. Prices of fine bows have gone up even faster in recent years than those of fine violins. There is a fine François Tourte bow in the Wurlitzer Collection in New York, which Mrs. Lee Wurlitzer Roth has refused to sell for "more than $10,000." Thomas Jefferson, violin-player as well as President, used a François Tourte bow with a gold-mounted frog that had an American eagle and the initials "T J" on its gold ferrule, and was spangled with thirteen stars. Tourte didn't brand his sticks. Some bows have tiny labels ("*Cet archet a été fait par Tourte en 1824*") glued at the bottom of the trench at the lower end of the stick, but there is no proof of the rumor that they were written by his daughter.

François Tourte remains unique, but his English contemporary, John Dodd, came close to him. Dodd was born in Stirling, Surrey, in 1752, and died in Richmond in 1839, four years after Tourte's death. Dodd's bows are fine and elegant though somewhat shorter than Tourte's. He worked hard and got good prices, but he was improvident and died in an asylum at the age of eighty-seven—bow-making seems as healthy a profession as violin-making. Dodd refused to train apprentices and once turned down an offer of 1000 pounds for a copy of his pattern. He was quite a character: he visited his favorite pubs four times a day, ordering "purl," a mixture of beer and gin; when asked whether he was Catholic or Protestant he would say, "A little of both." He has been called "the English Tourte," but ought to be remembered simply as John Dodd; he marked his bows DODD. Another great name in English bow-making is the Tubbs family, four generations of conscientious artists. The best was James Tubbs (1835–1919), who was assisted by his son, Alfred. They made some five thousand bows, all of high quality.

If no other bow-maker reached the eminence of François Tourte and John Dodd, there were still some first-rate artists. François Lupot II (1774–1837) was one of the finest French bow-makers. He was one of the pupils of Vuillaume, who remains the most gifted copyist of great violins. Vuillaume wrote down the rules of Tourte's discoveries and saved them from getting lost. (Unfortunately he was born too late to record for posterity the formula of Cremonese varnish.) Joseph François Fétis, the musicologist, published in 1856 the Tourte-Vuillaume formula for the gradual reduction of the diameter of the bow stick.

Another celebrated French bow-maker was Dominique Peccatte (or Peccate), 1810–1864, from Mirecourt, who began as a *luthier* but later specialized in bows. He worked as an apprentice for Vuillaume and then took over the firm of François Lupot. Peccatte's finest bows are considered almost the equals of Tourte's. They are rarely signed and can be authenticated only by experts. His son Charles (1850–1920) continued his father's tradition. One of Dominique Peccatte's best pupils was Joseph Fonclauze (1800–1864).

Other good bow-makers came from Mirecourt. François Nicolas Voirin (1833–1885) came to Paris in 1855 and worked with Vuillaume for fifteen years. He too began making violins but later switched to bows and established himself as an independent *archetier*. Paris remains the Cremona of bows. Voirin signed his elegant bows "F. N. Voirin." His best pupil was Alfred Joseph Lamy, also from Mirecourt (1850–1919), who was succeeded by his son, Alfred, who died in 1944.

And Eugène Sartory (born in Mirecourt in 1851) worked with Charles Peccatte and Alfred Joseph Lamy until establishing himself in the Boulevard Bonne-Nouvelle, where he died in 1946; he signed his fine bows "Sartory."

Nineteenth-century German bow-makers deserve special mention. Hermann Richard Pfretschmer worked along the models of Tourte and Voirin, while Franz Albert Nürnberger II followed Tourte and Vuillaume. The best German bow-makers, Ludwig Bausch (1805–1871) and Henri Knopf (middle nineteenth century), are as good as the good French—though the eminence of Tourte has never been challenged.

⤳ The Perfect Structure

Spiritually the violin is a creation of the Renaissance; architecturally it is a child of the Baroque. It doesn't have the clear, serene, straight lines of Classicism and the Renaissance. Its curves and convexities resemble the shapes of the angels and saints in Baroque sculpture. Baroque art was created by passionate, exultant artists who believed in God and the glory of the Church. The violin, too, was invented by artists who were passionate, exultant, and devout in their beliefs. Princes of the Church as well as worldly rulers were among the patrons of the Amatis and Stradivari.

The violin is a marvel of science—mathematics, physics, chemistry, acoustics—and also the miracle of a passion, the love of music. It is that rare mixture, the synthesis of emotion and intellect, of passion and science. Passion came first, but was subdued by adherence to the strict laws of science—otherwise the violin would have been a failure as a musical instrument.

The viol, softer and less expressive, was the most important chamber-music instrument during the Renaissance. In the Baroque the violin replaced the viol and became the most important instrument in Italian schools and conservatories, and in the opera houses of Mantua, Venice, and Rome. Composers also frequently wrote for the strings alone. A hundred years after Corelli discovered the violin as a solo instrument, Johann Sebastian Bach wrote his violin sonatas and partitas, the greatest polyphonic music for the solo violin. The center of the musical world shifted to Vienna after Joseph Haydn created the string quartet, and the rise of the orchestral symphony began. Noted instrumentalists from Bohemia and Germany went to Vienna to work. Around 1750, a few years after the death of Antonio Stradivari and Guarneri del Gesù, the hegemony of the violin within the orchestra was well established.

It was never challenged. The tone color of the violin (and related string instruments) makes it the most important, most adaptable element of modern instrumental music. Gottfried von Einem, the modern Austrian composer, calls it the *"Grundfarbe"* (basic tone color) of the orchestra. A few modern composers, especially those writing esoteric microtonal experiments, have tried to change the function of the strings, but they are exceptions. "Many students of modern music instinctively react against such innovations," says Von Einem. "Just as instinctively they need the melody-making family of string instruments because they are closest to the human voice. Modern music slowly turns away from the symptoms of aggression. The violin cannot be used to express aggression."

For the past three hundred years, most composers gave to the violin the dominant voice in their orchestral music. The string section of the modern symphony orchestra is numerically the largest and is always seated in front. The singing qualities of the violin, the viola, and the cello often carry the principal melody. No other group of instruments offers the richness, softness, and depth of the strings. Trends come and go in music, but the violin remains *primus inter pares* in the modern orchestra.

The fundamental characteristics of the violin are its flat-box resonator with an arched top; its four strings, tuned in intervals of a fifth; its highly arched bridge; and its unfretted fingerboard, which forces (and

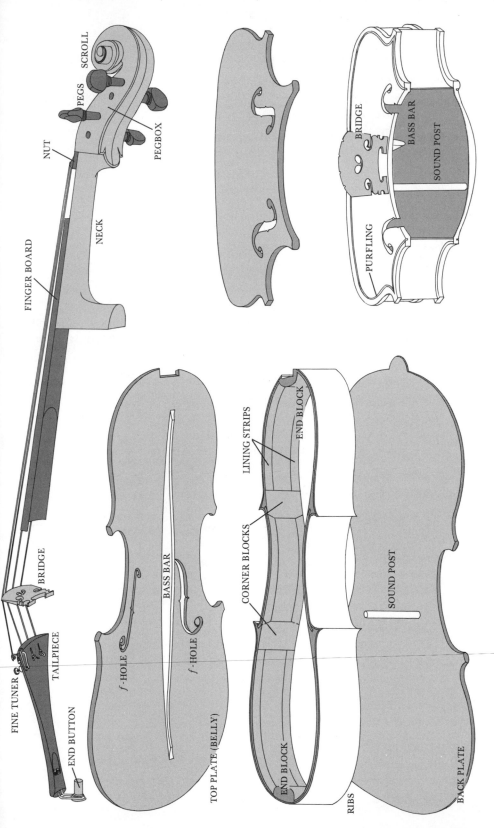

SCROLL

PEGS

PEGBOX

NUT

NECK

FINGER BOARD

FINE TUNER

BRIDGE

TAILPIECE

END BUTTON

f-HOLE

BASS BAR

f-HOLE

TOP PLATE (BELLY)

LINING STRIPS

END BLOCK

CORNER BLOCKS

END BLOCK

RIBS

SOUND POST

BACK PLATE

BRIDGE

BASS BAR

SOUND POST

PURFLING

enables) the player to create the tone. There is no mathematical exactness about it. The great makers were flexible, knowing that extreme precision might restrain their creative power; they used their eyesight and instinct rather than rules and formulas. They knew that a fine violin embodies a delicate interplay of forces and ideas, that its inner harmony is more important than its measurements. Nicolò Amati, Antonio Stradivari, Guarneri del Gesù were able to create that inner harmony. They divined an optimum relation between the principles concerned in the structure of the violin and its materials. Structurally, the violin—even a cheap factory fiddle—is a miracle of construction. Once invented, it was never basically changed. It is perfect. Perfection cannot be improved.

Students and experts have often wondered why Stradivari continually changed the thickness of his tops and backs during his life. He varied the thickness of these parts according to the quality of the wood and the attempted curve. Perhaps his intuitive sense of acoustics had something to do with it. Generally he made "thicker" violins when he was young and "thinner" ones as he grew old, but there were exceptions. Had he checked and measured with control instruments at every moment his violins would not have their wonderful expression of freedom. Nothing is standardized about them. He was probably able to touch the back of a violin with two fingers and feel its thickness down to $\frac{1}{64}$th of an inch. The center back of a Stradivari violin varies from $\frac{14}{64}$ths of an inch in 1672, to only $\frac{9}{64}$ths in 1733. It has been claimed that some of his late violins were made too "thin," perhaps because his eyes were failing, but it is a fact that some of these late "thin" violins have a very beautiful tone.

Stradivari was human and fallible but he rarely made basic errors. When he gradually switched from "thick" to "thin" backs and tops he also adjusted the other dimensions of his models and preserved the correct proportions within the entire structure of the instrument; this included the quality of the wood, and the mixture and application of the varnish. The late instruments may be somewhat different from the earlier ones, but the inner harmony is always there. Stradivari handled the various parts of the violin as a great composer handles the elements of a score. The composer may use stronger string sound, or stronger sound of the woodwinds, the brass, the percussion instruments—anything as long as he succeeds in creating the music he set out to create. What the greatest composers have achieved with only four voices in a string quartet is no more miraculous than what the greatest violin-makers did with several pieces of wood and some varnish.

The music which a composer writes is only possible as the sum of all music he heard previously. In its way, this must also be true of the makers of string instruments. No one can explain how the violin emerged in a perfect state from the beginning, but doubtless each maker knew and studied the work of his predecessors. Yet each asserted his originality. The basic pattern of the violin was given; but a maker created his individual outline as soon as he had found his artistic personality. To the untrained eye many fine violins seem similar in form. To the expert they instantly reveal the *spirit* of the maker. The experts can guess the maker's ideas, his character, and his artistic beliefs from the way he formed his violins, cut his f-holes, and carved the scroll. All makers understood that anything went, so long as the balance and harmony were kept; perhaps the violin should be called a scientific compromise rather than a masterpiece of precision. The greatest makers combined sound knowledge with artistic intuition. This spiritual freedom sets the members of the violin family apart from all other musical instruments.

Basically the violin consists of the hollow body and of various parts belonging to it. Visible are the neck with the peg box, the pegs, and the carved scroll; the fingerboard, and the strings stretched across the bridge; the tailpiece at the bottom of the body. Depending on how one counts the purfling (inlaid border) and some other features, the violin has from 70 to 90 parts. Several varieties of wood are used: hard maple for back, neck, ribs, and bridge; soft pine (spruce) for top, corner blocks, linings, and such invisible parts as bass bar and sound post; ebony or rosewood for fingerboard, nuts, pegs, tailpiece, and tailpiece button. Back and top are shaped by chisels, planes, and knives. Ribs and linings are planed to thickness and bent with a hot iron; the linings are sometimes wet before bending. All this information is elementary, to be found in many manuals for amateur makers.

The other string instruments are made in the same manner as the violin, the proportions being increased. The viola, tuned five tones lower than the violin, is approximately one-seventh larger than the fiddle; it is the alto voice of the orchestra. The violoncello, its strings tuned one octave below the viola, is the baritone voice; it has twice the dimensions of the violin. The double bass, twice the size of the cello, has a flat back and sloping shoulders, resembling the old viol. The strings are tuned in fourths, and they sound an octave lower than the music written for them.

The back of the violin body has the same size and shape as the upper part, the top (also called table or belly). The back consists of one part, or of two parts glued together lengthwise along the joint. The decision whether to make a one-part back or a two-part back depends on the best piece of wood available. The tone of the instrument is not altered in either case because the hardwood back does not vibrate on its own accord; that is the function of the softwood top. Visually, however, the back is very important. Many experts and collectors often look at it first. A handsome piece of maple, its striking pattern brought out by a soft, beautiful, translucent varnish, seems like a great painting. Sometimes the back gave the violin its name, as in the case of the "Dolphin" Stradivari, made in 1714: its two-piece back shows the changing, iridescent colors of a dolphin. The back of the "Dolphin" came from the same tree which had given the back to the "Boissier" Stradivari in 1713. Not wanting to repeat himself, Stradivari placed the curls of the "Boissier" back slanting down, and those of the "Dolphin" slanting up. Some people love the harmony of two matching pieces, others prefer a one-piece back. The French describe the play of light on the curls of the back as *les ondes,* suggesting the waves of the sea.

Both back and top have narrower upper bouts (ribs) and wider lower bouts. The waists on either side of back and top are cut in the form of a C. The back is carved, with the help of a gouge and a small plane, out of a maple board so that the outside becomes convex and the inside concave; the degree of curvature may depend on the size and shape of the board. Toward either side the curvature flattens out into the chamfer near the edges. The curvature of the back and especially of the top has considerable influence upon the character and strength of the violin's tone. A highly curved instrument has a sweeter but softer tone, a flatter instrument has a stronger but harder tone.

Jacob Stainer and the Amatis made violins with a high curvature; these had a sweet, dulcet tone, and they were extremely popular during the seventeenth and eighteenth centuries. Stradivari followed the Amati model in the early "Amatisé" violins that he made until 1690.

In the eighteenth century the flat, robust models of the Brescian school—by Gasparo da Salò and Giovanni Paolo Maggini—were less appreciated. In the early nineteenth century taste gradually changed in their direction. Paganini and famous violinists after him felt they needed instruments with more tonal power and greater sonority. Stradivari's flat models, especially those made after 1710, and the beautifully sonorous violins made by Guarneri del Gesù became much admired. Today there is sometimes a tendency to admire exaggerated flatness, and some instruments by Nicolò Amati and Stradivari are criticized for their curvature. But the arching must never be considered by itself, but in relation to the height of the sides, the dimensions of the bouts, the appearance and appeal of the instrument. Does the whole breathe an inner harmony? The violin is a work of art and must be judged in its entirety, including the graining of the wood and the shade of the varnish.

The top usually consists of two parts of soft pine, exceptionally one part; two-part tops are better acoustically. Pine (or spruce or fir) is harder to handle than maple because it breaks easily. It is hard to find a piece of pine with an upright, even grain and no stains of resin or other shortcomings, and any such piece is usually smaller than nine inches wide. Thus violin makers usually make a top from two pieces, each 4½ inches wide. The piece of wood is split down the center and the two halves joined side by side. At its upper part the top has an indentation for fastening the neck, and at the lower for fixing the saddle and the tailpiece. Fitted to the highest point of the top is the bridge. Two f-shaped sound holes are cut on either side of the bridge.

Top and back are held together by the bouts (ribs) which are made of thin maple: two upper, two middle, and two lower bouts. Mere gluing wouldn't be sufficient to hold all these together, the bouts must have linings inside the body. The linings are supported by four corner blocks, placed inside the corners of the C curves at the waist. The Amatis used pine for their corner blocks and willow for their linings; Stradivari used willow for both blocks and linings: willow is light but strong. A top block supports the neck. Stradivari inserted three nails in the top block in order to fasten the neck securely, other masters used from one to four nails. The nails have been removed later from most violins, but sometimes their traces can still be seen. The lower block has two functions: to prevent the lower bouts which meet there from shifting position, and to relieve the tension of the violin's top.

The edges all around the top and back are bordered by a narrow channel with the inlaid purfling inserted. The purfling is both ornamental and structural, strengthening the violin against damage along the edges. Usually, there are three separate strips of purfling, two outer black ones and a white one between. The purfling, as it follows the outline of the instrument, emphasizes the accuracy and elegance of the contours, the sweep of the curves. Modern makers often insert the purfling right after cutting the outlines of top and back, but many Cremonese makers did not even cut the grooves until after the body of the violin had been glued together. Before inserting the purfling they could carefully survey the outlines and correct any minute inequality. Then the grooves were cut: this made the outline final. Certain makers, especially Stradivari, were admired for the pronounced individuality of their purfling. Stradivari was able to vary the thickness of the grooves and their distance from the outer edges. His mitres were not pointed toward the centers of the corners but rather toward their inner points, downward in the upper corners, and upward in the lower ones, giving a striking effect. (One sees it clearly on the top of the "Messiah," Stradivari's most famous violin.) At certain moments in a Mozart string quartet a sound of genius will suddenly occur in the middle voices (not in the melody) that makes the phrase a miracle of perfection; such a hardly noticeable sound is exactly comparable to one of Stradivari's subtle touches of perfection.

There is more to the violin than meets the eye. Its interior is often more fascinating than its outside. "The interior of Stradivari's instruments serves to this day as our guide, and no modern maker of real ability has departed from it," wrote the Hills. The most interesting feature of the interior is the bass bar, a narrow ledge of pine wood that is fitted and glued to the curve of the top underneath the bass side where the G string is stretched. The left foot of the bridge stands right over it. The function of the bass bar is mainly to support the top at the left side. It is not certain how it came into being. The earliest viols made in Brescia had no separate bar; for acoustical reasons the bellies were thicker on the bass side, forming a sort of ridge. Perhaps some viol-makers noticed that they had made the belly too thin and tried to correct the mistake by adding an extra piece of pine wood instead of throwing it all away. Then they may have realized that one could improve the tone of the instrument by exactly determining the size of the bass bar. The earliest bass bars glued to the inside of the top are found in the instruments of Gasparo da Salò, Paolo Maggini, and Andrea Amati. Later, the bass bar became one of the most important parts of the violin. Its most minute imperfection can ruin the tone of the instrument.

The bass bar is one of the few parts of the violin that had to be slightly altered to bring the violin up to modern tonal requirements. Stradivari's bars were shorter, lower, and narrower than those used today. Charles Reade, the nineteenth-century novelist, who knew a lot about violins, once talked to John Lott, the assistant to the famous French violin-maker J. B. Vuillaume. In 1859 Lott had opened the "Betts" Stradivari of 1704, at Vuillaume's request. Lott was astonished to discover in it the original bass bar. "It was very low and very short, and quite unequal to support the tension of the strings at our concert pitch," Lott later told Reade, who writes wistfully that "the true tone of this violin can never have been heard in England before it fell into Vuillaume's hands." But then, no music for strings can be heard as it was at the time it was written. Bach's unaccompanied sonatas and partitas, the greatest music written for the solo violin, sounded quite different from today when played by Bach and his eighteenth-century fellow musicians. The common pitch was perhaps as much as half a tone below today's A. Consequently the strings were under less tension, and the violin of Bach's time had a lighter, thinner, less intense tone. Steel strings (naturally, unknown in Cremona) exert a twenty-five-per-cent stronger pressure than gut strings.

The lower arch of the bridge made it easier to play the devilish double chords that make Bach's solo works an ordeal for the performer, but the lower bridge also required greater accuracy of bowing. In his excellent *Treatise on the Fundamental Principles of Violin Playing*, Leopold Mozart wrote in 1756, "Merry and playful passages must be played with light, short and lifted strokes, happily and rapidly, just as in slow passages one performs with long strokes of the bow, simply and tenderly." The advice remains excellent. Leopold Mozart disliked the attack from the air: "The strike must necessarily be started gently with a certain moderation, without the bow being lifted, played with such smooth connexion that even the strongest strike touches the already vibrating string quite imperceptibly." The early violinists played easily and naturally. They didn't "dig in," and it was considered bad taste to create robust sound; they used no vibrato, and little bow. Clarity, purity, and transparency were more important than strength and passion. It was the texture of a piece that had to be heard, rather than its emotion.

Today there is a tendency toward hard "metallic" sound rather than the mellow, warm tone of aged wood. Electric amplifiers, high-fidelity stereo recordings, high-frequency radios make our sense of hearing more discerning—and more prejudiced. We've learned to hear new tonal nuances and musical colors, but this deeper truth isn't always an advantage because the microphone is merciless. I have often liked a violinist in concert but have had second thoughts when a radio transmission of his performance makes me notice small shortcomings which I hadn't noticed earlier.

The violins of the great Cremonese makers were made for the tonal requirements of their time, not for today's. A Stradivari that hasn't been touched since it left the master's workshop in the 1720s would not satisfy a concert performer now. Yet the prophetic genius of the great makers enabled their violins to suit the most demanding soloist today, after minor alterations are made. These alterations concern the bass bar, and lengthening the neck and fingerboard.

The modern bass bar is about 10¾ inches long, $7/16$ths of an inch high at its center, and ¼ inch thick. By comparison, many Stradivari bars were 9½ inches long, $4/16$ or $5/16$ths of an inch high, and $3/16$ths of an inch thick. The longest bass bars were inserted by Carlo Bergonzi and the members of the Gagliano family, whose instruments were noted for power. But such instruments were then not very popular. Most players were satisfied with the smaller, sweeter tone of violins having smaller bass bars. The first "modern" bass bars were put in at the beginning of the nineteenth century when music began to demand a stronger tone. (By that time François Tourte had created the "modern" bow, which enables us to play the many dynamic shades between *piano* and *forte*.

Only a truly skilled violin-maker is able to insert a bass bar having the right dimensions in relation to the sound of that violin. Size, shape, and position—all are important: in this case artisanship becomes art. A thorough knowledge and a certain intuition are indispensable. The life span of a modern bass bar ranges from ten to twenty years, but it may last up to forty years; a high built instrument normally needs a new bar earlier than a flat one.

Also inside the violin is the second important part, the sound post —a small, cylindrical rod made also of pine, that is forced into the body between the top and the back, just underneath the right foot of the bridge. The sound post transmits the lengthwise long-wave vibrations of the softwood top to the hardwood back. A violin without a sound post would have a hollow, muted tone; it wouldn't carry far. Even a fraction-of-a-millimeter shift of the sound post might change the violin's tone. There is no mathematical rule for placing the sound post. It is a matter of sensitivity—the Germans call it *Fingerspitzengefühl*, to feel with your fingertips—and the violin-maker must, so to speak, feel the exact position of the sound post. The instruments of the violin family are the only ones with, literally, a "soul," for *"l'âme"* is what the often-logical French call the sound post. The violin has often fascinated scientists, who see it as a product of physics *and* metaphysics. Albert Einstein, for example, who didn't play the violin very well, admitted to me that he loved it though he didn't profess to understand it.

Unlike the invisible bass bar and sound post, the sound holes (or f-holes) are quite visible, even conspicuous: they are in the face of a violin what the eyes are in a human face. They also express the character of the maker and can be read like his signature. "It is difficult to meet with two specimens of Stradivari's work having sound holes of identical design," the Hills wrote, after seeing most of the surviving Stradivari instruments: the sound holes may differ in infinitesimal ways that are perceptible only after years of study, but they always betray Stradivari's identity (just as the signatures of one man, no matter how they differ, are recognizable to an experienced bank teller). Each important maker has his artistic identity. All of them placed the sound holes in the position that was the only possible one—but this position, like everything else about violins, is flexible.

Scientists have codified the mathematical rules governing the designs of Stradivari and other great makers, but that doesn't mean that anyone can make a fine violin by following these rules exactly. The sound holes are a good case in point. They can be copied with almost photographic accuracy, yet an expert can tell the difference. A copied sound hole is dead; a Stradivari sound hole is alive, it "breathes" the master's personality. Stradivari used the method of his famous predecessors: he relied on his eyes rather than on a pattern. Most of the great violinmakers were accomplished draftsmen and designers, as well as fine cutters and carvers; they understood the theory and knew the practice. An amateur would probably trace the entire sound hole on the top before cutting it. The great masters fixed exact positions only for the top and bottom holes. They might place a small templet between the holes; a point at each end would hold it. They might make a rough sketch of the "f"—but then they would take the knife and start cutting. Thus the curves are characteristic for the maker's design and for his mood at the moment. On one day an artist would make more beautiful sound holes than on another one. In general, the important makers kept their signature: Maggini, Stainer, Nicolò Amati, and Stradivari had their personal designs, which even a nonexpert can see. The most difficult maker to recognize is Giuseppe Guarneri del Gesù because he was an erratic artist. Sometimes his sound holes are beautifully done; sometimes they are sloppy; yet even these sound holes reflect the artist's personality, never dominated by a sense of order and self-discipline. Stradivari often placed the right sound hole slightly higher than the left one, especially on violins made after 1720, when he was in his seventies, approaching the last period of his work. The irregularity was caused by worn, defective molds for the top that had been used for dozens of instruments. Stradivari must have known this but the irregularity didn't seem to bother him much.

Most violin-players are apt to underrate the importance of the "secondary" parts of the violin. Next to the stronger, longer bass bar, the most visible change in the "modern" violin is the longer neck and the altered position of the scroll. At the time of the Amatis, Stainer, and Stradivari, the player would rarely go beyond the third or fourth position. The violins had shorter necks, varying from $4\frac{3}{4}$ to $4\frac{7}{8}$ inches long. Today the length of the neck is from $5\frac{1}{16}$ to $5\frac{1}{8}$ inches. The modern neck is $\frac{1}{4}$ or $\frac{3}{8}$ of an inch longer and about $\frac{1}{8}$ of an inch narrower. It is not true that a thin neck "makes playing easier": the neck must be just right—neither too thin nor too thick.

The fingerboard must also have the correct form and shape. Its height above the body depends on the curvature of the violin's top. It must be wide enough to enable the violinist to play single and double notes. The angle of neck and fingerboard in relation to the top of the violin was also changed to facilitate playing in the highest positions; adjustments were inevitable when Paganini and other virtuoso composers began to extend the technique of violin-playing, writing solo passages that went all the way up the fingerboard. Stradivari's fingerboards varied in length from $7\frac{1}{2}$ to $8\frac{1}{2}$ inches; modern fingerboards are exactly 27 centimeters long, $10\frac{5}{8}$ inches. During the eighteenth century Pietro Giovanni Mantegazza and his brothers in Milan specialized in lengthening the necks of violins.

At the top of the fingerboard is the nut, a slight elevation notched for the strings. Above the nut is the peg box, with holes for the four pegs, made of ebony or rosewood. The pegs should have slender stems that fit accurately; they must not give way while one is playing. The peg box is crowned by the scroll (the head). Together with the sound holes, the scroll gives the instrument its signature. It has no influence on the tone of the violin but adds a sculptural element, "the all-important part of the instrument from an artistic point of view" (Hill). Andrea Amati in Cremona and Paolo Maggini in Brescia first gave the scroll its character and beauty. They early realized that it enabled its maker to add a dimension to his art, to express his imagination and originality. The earlier Amatis treated the scroll as an artistic unit *per se;* Nicolò Amati and Stradivari and the later makers considered the scroll in relation to the outline of the violin, as part of the whole work of art.

In a well-made scroll each side is the counterpart of the other, as in a mirror. Stradivari carefully designed both sides before he started carving the scroll; probably he used templates too. His scrolls are famous for their accuracy and graceful sweep. A fine Stradivari scroll seems to vibrate with music; it is music written in wood.

Each important violin-maker had his own method of making the scroll. Some used markings around the tip to help toward absolute symmetry. Others used a compass so that the line between the fluting would be in the exact center. But all did not work with such accuracy. Guarneri del Gesù, the great nonconformist, rarely made perfect scrolls, but even his imperfect ones have great charm. Probably he made one side first, worked at something else in between, and did the other side on a day when he was in the mood. Often the second side is not the mirror image of the first. He knew this, but didn't care—after all, the scroll didn't influence the tone of the instrument, and it was the tone that interested him. Some makers would carve a number of scrolls, and later select the one that seemed to fit the wood of a certain violin. Thus the scroll may be older than the body of the violin.

The bridge is another minor part of the violin that is nonetheless important and often neglected. Ancient bridges often had ornamental designs which added to the beauty of the violin. Modern bridges are less decorative, and somewhat more raised and arched; the present design has been scientifically developed to let the vibrations of the strings go through the bridge into the top of the violin, and by way of the sound post below into the back. The bridge must be neither too low (the strings must not touch the fingerboard) nor too high (this would make playing difficult). Bridges are now made of carefully selected maple, medium hard and with a horizontal grain. The feet of the bridge must fit the curve of the top, with no hollow space between feet and top. Only a skilled violin-maker can adjust a bridge accurately.

The tailpiece, made of ebony or rosewood, is fixed with a short loop to the tail pin (end button) at the bottom of the instrument. The tail pin is located in the center of the rib between back and top, where the lower bouts meet, and pierces the bottom block. It may be taken out if a repairer wants to look into the interior of the violin, perhaps to check the position of the sound post. The top of the violin should be taken off only when absolutely necessary; every time a violin is opened it loses a little precious wood and irreplaceable varnish.

The chin rest, a secondary but unfortunately necessary part, is often made of ebony wood, plate-shaped. Some people say it blocks the intimate connection between the player's body and the sound body of the violin. The greatest violinist of all, Paganini, probably used no chin rest. His most famous violin, Guarneri del Gesù's "Cannon" made in or about 1742 and now exhibited under glass in the Council Room of the Municipal Palace in Genoa, shows traces of a chin rest; perhaps one was used by a previous owner. The varnish has worn off both sides of the tailpiece since the violin was often held by the chin on the treble side of the top during the eighteenth century. Paganini, according to contemporary records, would push out forward his left shoulder and rest the violin on his collarbone. Not many violinists have a physique that enables them to follow Paganini's method.

The connection between the player's body and the violin should doubtless be as close as possible. The player creates and determines the personal timbre of the tone, which is filtered and amplified by a good violin. It is a fallacy to believe that the sweet tone of Kreisler, the warm tone of David Oistrakh, or the sensuous tone of Heifetz is due to their violins. The tone is of course created by the violinist; the instrument merely beautifies and amplifies the player's tone. The same violin played by several violinists sounds different in the hands of each player. No wonder prominent artists are not pleased to be told, "Your violin sounds beautiful." Rightly, they should be told that *they* sound beautiful.

The tone of all string instruments is produced by vibrations of the strings. Bad strings produce tones of inferior quality even on a rare, fine violin. Yet most violinists know little about strings, despite their importance; they take good strings for granted, and use the best they can afford. They know, of course, that strings "are made of gut" but don't want further details, instinctively avoiding accurate knowledge about how the small intestines of sheep help to make beautiful violin music.

Accordingly, I'll describe briefly the recipe for good strings without going too much into their background. A good string should have a soft texture and cylindrical form, and it should be flexible, sensitive, and true to a "perfect fifth." It should respond easily, with no false overtones, producing a rich, warm, pure tone which is vibrant with life. And it should be durable enough to stand some wear and tear. This is certainly a lot to ask from the small intestines of a sheep, and no string can be better than the gut it is made of. The manufacture of strings is based on long experience, constant observation, continued tests, and the highest standards of production; the best raw material is processed in the best possible way.

A sheep gut consists of three membranes: external, internal, and a fibrous membrane enclosed between the two others. Only this middle membrane is used to make violin strings. (Catgut, incidentally, is never used.) The intestines are cleansed, soaked, and scraped until they are reduced to the fibrous middle membrane, which has about one-twentieth of the gut's original volume. These, in turn, are scraped, then sorted and classified according to whiteness and length, and divided into long threads which are twisted, sulphured, thinned, polished, and finished. This is the old European process, a slow, laborious method; the more modern "American method" uses mechanization and special machines that spin and polish the strings. Their color, incidentally, has no relation to strength and trueness of tone. White, glassy strings may be obtained by bleaching. Sometimes dark strings last longer. Covered strings consist of gut wound with silver, copper, or aluminum wire.

The prominent string-makers claim to have their "secrets," a convenient expression for the accumulated experience of centuries. If the greatest violins have come from Cremona and the finest bows from Paris, the best strings were originally made in Rome. After the death of David Tecchler (c. 1666–1748) and his assistant Michael Platner, Roman violin-makers began specializing in strings instead. In 1793, Giorgio Pirazzi, a master string-maker from Rome, emigrated to Offenbach in Germany, where he was sure to get first-rate gut from German sheep. He had the knowledge, devotion, and zeal of a Renaissance craftsman, and he made fine-quality strings of the Italian type. The annals of the House of Pirazzi registered with pardonable pride the fact that Nicolò Paganini used Pirazzi strings, including the G strings on which he performed his astonishing miracles.

Since its founding, the firm has produced some of the world's best strings. In 1875 Gustav Pirazzi, the founder's grandson, took over; when the old factory burned down ten years later, he built a new one and announced the first strings to be known as "perfect fifth" quality. They were named "Elite," and were used by the elite of the late nine-teenth-century virtuosos. Even Joachim had high praise for them. After Theodor Stroebel, Gastav Pirazzi's friend, became a partner, the firm changed its name to Pirastro (PIRAzzi and STRObel), and the "Elite" strings were renamed "Wondertone." The firm, now managed by Hermann Pirazzi, the fourth-generation master string-maker, is still producing fine strings.

Nearly everybody agrees that a gut E string sounds better than steel on a fine violin, but gut strings are rarely used because they don't last long. The elasticity, pressure, and stretch of a steel E string is four and one-half times greater than that of a gut string, and the heavier weight of the steel string has an unfavorable effect on the violin's acoustical properties. Still, most professionals and many amateurs use the more reliable steel strings. The Pirastro firm now makes a golden-steel E string of high quality.

Despite its delicate appearance, a fine violin is a robust work of art, and the larger members of the violin family are even stronger. David Laurie, the English collector and dealer, writes in *The Reminiscences of a Fiddle Dealer* about N. F. Vuillaume, the younger brother of the celebrated violin-maker J. B. Vuillaume. One day N. F. showed Laurie the broken remnants of an Andrea Amati cello that had been made for the chapel of King Charles IX of France, and was ornamented with armorial bearings and gold designs. "It was terribly broken up when he got it, but he found all the original pieces and had the pa-tience to restore it. This was certainly a labor of love; for the pieces numbered hundreds and they were so well inserted that, at the first glance, the cello seemed quite sound, even to an experienced eye."

(Laurie unfortunately doesn't say how the Amati cello sounded.) Many violin-makers have had similar experiences. If the pieces of an instrument exist—the wood and the varnish—they can be put together by a skilled maker. After proper restoration, the instrument may sound as well as before. But I don't suggest that the owner of a rare old fiddle submit his instrument to the ultimate tone test of partition and reassembly!

❧ The Great Amati Dynasty

The violins of Andrea Amati (c. 1510–c. 1580) became famous in Italy and all over Europe because they were beautiful to look at and sounded well. Unlike the Brescian violin-makers, Andrea understood that the beauty of a violin enhanced its value, and he knew that the delicacy of its detail contributed to its beauty. This was a new principle and became respected by all prominent makers in Cremona (except perhaps for Guarneri del Gesù, who was primarily interested in beautiful sound and sonority).

Andrea Amati's masterpieces were the instruments—twenty-four violins, six violas, and eight cellos—that were ordered in 1560 for the court of King Charles IX of France and long preserved in the Royal Chapel at Versailles. One of the four surviving violins is illustrated in the book about the Henry Hottinger Collection, published by Rembert Wurlitzer, Inc. The violin has the monarch's coat of arms on the back, and his motto *Pietas et Justitia Unito Propugno* (With piety and justice I go forth unarmed) is lettered in gold on the sides. Some of the instruments may have been studded with precious stones. During the French Revolution the instruments disappeared from Versailles; a few later turned up in England.

Andrea Amati and all Amatis after him made violins of two different sizes, smaller and larger. Both sizes follow the same graceful design, with a higher curvature toward the center; margins are narrow and beautifully finished. The purfling is well made, the scroll is elegant, and the sound holes are sometimes a little archaic and stiff in the case of Andrea, but always characteristic. Nicolò made them less open, with more linear charm than his grandfather's. The varnish nearly always has yellow shades, from gold to gold-brown; sometimes it is amber.

The Amatis were artists but practical-minded businessmen as well. There was a demand for smaller and larger instruments and they made both. People with smaller hands find it easier to play a smaller instrument. (Switching from my Antonius and Hieronymus Amati, made in 1608, to my Stradivari, made in 1730, was almost as difficult as switching from a violin to a viola. It isn't a question of length, but of width of the upper bouts. Stradivari's are $6\frac{5}{8}$ inches while the upper bouts of the Amati were $6\frac{3}{16}$—a difference of almost half an inch.)

Andrea Amati became a rich man, and traveled and shopped for the best materials. He would go to Venice to buy the ingredients for his varnish: amber, resins, dyes. He was very careful to buy fine wood. He would use the best maple—for the backs, ribs, necks—that he could find in Italy. (Others used maple which the Venetians imported from Dalmatia.) He preferred fine pine for the tops, sound posts, and bass bars. Legend tells us he would walk through the forests of the South Tyrol looking for pieces of "resonant" pine. When he saw a tree he liked he would knock on the trunk with a small wooden mallet to hear whether it sounded clear and pure.

The violins made by all the members of the Amati family have the characteristic Amati tone—lovely and sweet, "silvery," sometimes compared to the "nightingale sound." It is quite different from the mellow, rich oboe sound of a Stradivari, or the sonorous, French horn-like sound of a fine Guarneri del Gesù. Sound is created by physical characteristics. Most Amati violins have a strongly curved top. Andrea's sons developed their father's model, and Nicolò, a grandson who worked at fifteen in his grandfather's shop, early learned to admire the old man's violins.

Amati violins as well as those made by Jacob Stainer, the greatest non-Italian maker from Tyrol, fetched top prices until 1790; at that time Giovanni Battista Viotti, then the most celebrated virtuoso, switched from Amati to Stradivari because he found its fuller, richer tone more rewarding. (On some Amati violins the G string is relatively weak.) Suddenly everybody began to "discover" Stradivari's violins. And after Paganini's example, when soloists needed instruments with strong sonority to compete against larger orchestras in larger halls, they began to discover the long-neglected masterpieces of Guarneri del Gesù.

Andrea Amati had two gifted sons. Antonio was born in Cremona in 1538; in 1556 his name appears in the parish register of San Faustino, listed as his father's assistant. Later he was closely associated with his brother Girolamo, also born in Cremona, probably in 1561. Both lived and died in Cremona. The "Brothers Amati" made and signed many of their instruments together. On their labels their names were Latinized: "Antonius & Hieronymus Fr. Amati Cremonen. Andreae fil. F. 1608." Their beautiful instruments resembled their father's models, and were later perfected. From the first the workmanship is exquisite, the outline graceful; the sound holes are smaller than Andrea's, the back usually of one piece. The varnish is dark brown in their earlier years, later a beautiful orange. Of the two brothers, whose instruments can hardly be analyzed as the work of one more than of the other, Hieronymus is now generally conceded to be the greater artist: he somewhat evened the curvature of the top of his father's model, improving the tone. Hieronymus' first wife, Lucrezia Cornelis, had three daughters. After her death he married Laura Lazzarini in 1584: she gave him seven daughters and two sons, Roberto and Nicolò, of whom Nicolò became the most celebrated Amati. According to documents found in the archives of Cremona, Hieronymus died on November 2, 1630, "having reached the sixty-ninth year." Antonius survived his brother, though the date of his death is not known; it must have been soon after 1630.

The Brothers Amati remain beloved of connoisseurs for the sweet, dulcet tone of their elegant instruments. They are perfect for chamber music, provided the instruments of the other players don't have an overpowering sound. Many celebrated makers, among them Stradivari and Pietro (Guarneri) of Mantua, admired the soprano timbre of the violins made by the Brothers Amati.

The greatest Amati was Nicolò, born in Cremona on December 3, 1596; he spent all his life there, dying aged eighty-eight on April 12, 1684. His wife, Lucrezia Paleari, survived him until 1703; they had three daughters and five sons of whom one, Hieronymus (Girolamo) II, became a violin-maker; it is ironic that Nicolò Amati, who educated a whole generation of important makers and did more than any other man to perpetuate the glory of Cremona, was personally succeeded by only one son.

Nicolò Amati was acknowledged the greatest living maker. And for a long time his instruments followed exactly the model of his father's. Only about 1660—he was then past sixty, and the world's most famous *liutaio*—he designed and developed his own model, the "grand pattern" Amati.

The finest of these instruments have a serene beauty that puts them among the greatest violins ever made. In appearance they have a rather high arching, but the curvature of the top blends gracefully into the oblique chamfer of the edges. No maker, not even Stradivari, cut finer f-holes or more elegant scrolls. The wood has a refined beauty: the top is of fine pine, with upright narrow grain; the back is of carefully selected maple, with beautifully rolling "waves." The varnish has its own fire, golden yellow or golden red, soft and translucent.

Their sound equals their beauty: clear and silvery on the higher strings, mellow and dark on the lower ones, always sweet and soft. Nicolò Amati realized that this model must have the exquisite Amati sound, and he refined the design until there was no audible break between the strings. (In Vienna, these violins were later called "Mozart fiddles," an apt description for they are ideally suited to the classical repertory. H. W. Ernst, the brilliant nineteenth-century virtuoso from Moravia, played for many years on a "grand pattern" Amati.) They respond easily and have considerable carrying power. For somebody who loves the violin for its beauty, its exquisite workmanship, its elegance, and its sound this is the perfect violin—though not for a performer who wants to be the loudest and fastest. A "grand pattern" Amati is less expensive today than a fine Stradivari or an important Guarneri del Gesù, but Nicolò Amati's instruments (he also made violas, cellos, and double basses) continue to go up in price because they are so beautiful.

Nicolò's grandfather, Andrea, had helped to evolve and create the modern violin; Nicolò, an unsurpassed teacher of the art of violin-making, kept that art alive for generations. He was proud of his family's achievements: his labels read "Nicolaus Amatus Cremonen. Hieronymi Fil. ac Antonij Nepos Fecit 16. ." Practically all Italian makers after him were directly or indirectly influenced by him. It is a hypothetical question whether Stradivari would have become the greatest violin-maker of all had he not studied with Nicolò Amati.

After an arduous search the Hill brothers discovered an early Stradi-vari violin with the original label: "Antonius Stradiuarius Cremonen-sis Alumnus Nicolai Amati, Faciebat Anno 1666." The next year a label in another Stradivari violin reads: "Antonius Stradiuarius Cre-monensis Faciebat Anno 1667," with no mention of his teacher. Stradi-vari probably became an apprentice in Nicolò Amati's workshop around 1658 when he was fourteen, perhaps before. At that time boys went to work early. By 1660 Stradivari may have been able to make a violin himself and perhaps to print his own labels, but none exist. Most experts believe that young Stradivari remained with Nicolò Amati even after he began to make and sell his own violins. By 1666, the date of Antonio's first known violin, Nicolò was seventy and prob-ably permitted his gifted pupils and assistants to help him. "Careful observation, carried on during many years, has convinced us that very few of the later-dated instruments of Nicolò Amati, i.e. after 1665–1670, are the work of an old man," the Hills write. Detective work always fascinates violin sleuths. Though it isn't always possible to say exactly whose hands cooperated in the finishing of a late Nicolò Amati violin, the experts believe they recognized in certain instru-ments "the unmistakable handiwork" (Hill) of Andrea Guarneri, of Giovanni Battista Rogeri, and of Franceso Ruggieri.

And what about the other, most famous assistant, Stradivari? George Hart, the nineteenth-century English dealer-expert, mentions "certain

[Amati] instruments that have been recognized by intelligent connoisseurs as wholly the work of Stradivari." The Hills were not convinced. "If such instruments existed, where are they? We have certainly not met with them." Hart wrote that after Nicolò Amati's death his tools, models, and patterns passed into the possession of Stradivari, not into the hands of his son Girolamo II. Again the Hills and other experts remain doubtful, though the Hills say, "It is unquestionable that the later specimens of Nicolò Amati . . . were either made by his son alone or by his son and Stradivari."

These mysteries may never be completely solved. It makes sense though that Nicolò Amati, as an old man, had assistants, and that they had a hand in making his late violins. He was then the most celebrated violin-maker on earth. When kings, princes, cardinals, or wealthy amateurs wanted the best violin that money could buy, they went to Nicolò Amati. They certainly would not have ordered from his relatively unknown assistants. Nicolò Amati got the highest prices; the arrangement worked well. If he paid his assistants generously, there was still enough left for everybody.

More important than whether one or another assistant helped to make Nicolò Amati's late violins is the artistic philosophy that the revered old master taught his pupils. Of that fact there can be no doubt. Stradivari's whole work proves that he continued Nicolò Amati's belief in beauty, his uncompromising artistic conscience, his striving for perfection. One can easily imagine Stradivari himself, getting old and remembering more sharply the images of his early life, reminiscing about his mentor.

Eventually Stradivari's genius surpassed Nicolò Amati's, and the violins made by Guarneri del Gesù today are more expensive than Nicolò Amati's because of their sonorous tone and relative scarcity. But history cannot be rewritten: no single man did more than Nicolò Amati to perpetuate the glory of Cremona.

Hieronymus (Girolamo) II Amati was the third son of Nicolò—the only one who continued the family tradition. He was born in Cremona on February 26, 1649. In 1678, he married Angela Carrettoni; they had two girls and one boy, whom they called Nicolò, after the celebrated grandfather. (Nicolò later became a monk in Bologna, and an amateur fiddle-maker; René Vannes calls his violins "worthy of interest." On his labels he called himself "D. Nicolaus Amati," with no reference to the celebrated members of his family.)

Hieronymus II is now regarded a very good maker. It was his misfortune to be overshadowed by Stradivari, who was five years older. A beautiful violin which he made in 1686 is in the Hottinger Collection, now at Wurlitzer's, in New York; it is called "The Pearl" because it has a pearl star in each side of the scroll. It belonged to the instrument collection of King Charles IV of Spain, and was said to be the king's favorite violin. It is graceful and elegant, unquestionably in the great Amati tradition. He continued the "grand pattern" model; the varnish is brown-red. On his labels he called himself "Hieronymus Amati Figlio di Nicolo Amati Cremona 17 . ." He probably inherited his father's considerable fortune, for he made few instruments after his father's death; or perhaps he was discouraged by the competition of his celebrated neighbor, Stradivari. He died in Cremona, on February 21, 1740, three years after Stradivari's death and four before the death of Del Gesù.

❧Ne Plus Ultra: *Stradivari*

That plain, white-aproned man who stood at work
Patient and accurate, full fourscore years;
Cherished his sight and touch by temperance;
And, since keen sense is love of perfectness,
Made perfect Violins, the needed paths
For inspiration and high mastery.
      —*George Eliot* (1819–1880)

No one knows when and exactly where Antonio Stradivari was born. Almost nothing is known about his childhood. His grave no longer exists. "These questions, we fear, can never be answered," the Hills wrote after years of thorough research. It doesn't matter. Mozart's grave is unknown, but his music will survive all but the apocalypse of mankind. Stradivari's instruments assure his immortality.

The Stradivari family—variously spelled Stradivarto, Stradilvertis, Stradivertus, Stradaverta—lived in and around Cremona since the twelfth century. There is a record in the city archives, dated December 7, 1176, about one Lanfranco de Stradilvertis, *"iudex constitutus a consulibus iustitiae Cremonae."* Various records also mention Johannis Stradivertus, *"sindicus Cremonae"* in 1220; Giuliano, *notarius;* Tebaldino, Isacco, Pietro, Balzarino, and Gasparino, all in the fourteenth century. Professor Renzo Bacchetta, today the great Stradivari authority in Cremona, believes that the family came to Italy with the Goths, and that the name means "leader" in the Gothic language. E. J. Payne assumes that the name derives from "Stradiere," a customs officer posted on the *strada* (road). Professor Astegiano, who catalogued the rolls of the ancient community of Cremona, derives the name "Stradaverta" from *"strada aperta,"* open road. The Hills quote Signor Mandelli, a former mayor of Cremona, who found a record, dated August 30, 1622, of the marriage of Alessandro Stradivari to Anna Moroni at the parish of San Prospero (Alessandro was born on January 15, 1602). Three birth certificates were later registered in that parish: Giuseppe Giulio Cesare, in March, 1623; Carlo Felice, in September, 1626; Giovanni Battista, in October, 1628.

No record mentions the birth of Antonio Stradivari. The first official document concerning him is the certificate, dated July 4, 1667, of his marriage to Francesca Feraboschi, also spelled Ferabosca, the widow of Giovanni Giacomo Capra. On June 3, 1680, according to an existing deed, Antonio Stradivari, "of the late Alessandro," bought a house from the Cremonese family of Picenardi for 7,000 imperial lire. The house was No. 2, Piazza San Domenico; today a modern building stands on the site, now known as No. 1, Piazza Roma. Stradivari lived and worked in his home until he died.

Historians have tried hard, and unsuccessfully, to clear up the mystery of the birth of the greatest violin-maker. We know the exact birth dates of his father and of his sons, but not his—one more charming irony in the history of the violin.

During the seventeenth century Cremona underwent several disasters: there were military campaigns in Lombardy, a terrible famine in 1628 and 1629, and the plague in 1630. Hieronymus Amati, his wife, and two of their daughters died that year. (In Brescia, Paolo Maggini died of the plague in 1632.) Two-thirds of the population of Cremona was wiped out; the town had "the appearance of a wilderness." A parish priest in San Vincenzo reported that "Many citizens have left Cremona to live quietly in other towns . . . rich people have by this time (1630) been redued to such a state of poverty, caused partly by the billeting of soldiers in their houses, and partly by the heavy taxes imposed, that, were it not for the shame of it, they would go begging." François Joseph Fétis, the French nineteenth-century writer and authority on Stradivari, concludes that many archives in Cremona "were stolen, concealed or even destroyed." The Hills assume that Antonio Stradivari may have been born not in Cremona but in a nearby town or village where his parents went to escape hardship, persecution, and disease. Yet a search of parish registers in the vicinity turned up no clue.

We have already mentioned the label in an early Stradivari violin, reading ". . . Alumnus Nicolai Amati, Faciebat Anno 1666"; it is the oldest documentary proof of his existence, preceding his marriage record by one year. How then do we think we know when he was born? Again, his labels are helpful. In his last years Stradivari was justifiably proud of being able to make fine instruments at such an old age, and about half a dozen times he added his age to the date on the label. Among these are a violin dated 1732, "de anni 89" ("at age eighty-nine"); a violin dated 1735, "d'anni 91"; a cello dated 1736, "d'anni 92"; a violin dated 1737 (the last year of Stradivari's life), with the notation "d'anni 93," the notation probably added by Stradivari's son, Omobono. The old man was perhaps no longer able to write. All these labels were seen by the Hills, who wrote in *Antonio Stradivari* in 1902, "We may therefore conclude that . . . the matter [of the year of his birth] may be finally placed beyond controversy."

Yet the controversy continues. In 1950 Renzo Bacchetta published the *Carteggio* (Diary) of Count Cozio di Salabue (1755–1840), the Piedmontese nobleman who lived in Casale Monferrato. He had inherited from his father a Nicoló Amati violin, dated 1668; he fell in love with violins and became the greatest collector in violin history. After acquiring many of the greatest instruments, Count Cozio in 1775 bought from Stradivari's youngest son, Paolo, a magnificent collection of Antonio Stradivari's memorabilia—letters, designs, tools, perhaps even a formula for making varnish. Paolo, a textile merchant, was not interested in violins. Cozio then began to write his *Carteggio,* which contains invaluable material about the Cremonese and other masters, exact measurements of famous instruments that he owned or saw elsewhere, information about other owners of important instruments. Gradually the collector became also a dealer and a shrewd businessman.

Cozio admits in his *Carteggio* that he made several alterations on the labels of Stradivari, and added notations to the dates of some labels with his own hand (". . . *e manuscritto sotto di mio carattere come el 31 il datta biglietto pure de . . . d'anni 92.*" "Written below in my handwriting is age 92, the same as in the inscription on ———'s violin, also of the 1731 period.") According to René Vannes, Antonio Stradivari is listed in the *"Stati anima"* (census) of the Cremona archives as twenty-nine and thirty-three years old respectively. Bacchetta believes that Stradivari was born in 1648; he proved this thesis brilliantly in an essay, "Stradivari Was *Not* Born in 1644." Vannes, in his *Dictionnaire Universel des Luthiers,* believes that Stradivari may have been born early in 1649 and that at his death in 1737 (this date is recorded) he was eighty-eight or eighty-nine, and not ninety-three. Thus the matter remains confused. It seems more important to remember that during the last years of his life Stradivari made some magnificent instruments which two hundred years later were the concert violins of celebrated violinists. Kreisler owned the "Lord Amherst" of 1734 and a violin dated 1733, on which Heifetz later performed. Heifetz also owned a Stradivari, made in 1734. Menuhin still performs on the "Prince Khevenhüller," made in 1733. Efrem Zimbalist played the "Lamoureux," made in 1735. What difference does it make whether Stradivari was in his late eighties or early nineties when he made these magnificent violins?

After his marriage in 1667 Stradivari lived in Casa del Pescatore, in the parish of his bride, Francesca Ferabosca Capra, who was four years younger than he. Her father was a noted mathematician. Her first marriage had ended with her husband's suicide. Stradivari seems to have been happy with her; they had two girls and three boys. Two of the sons—Francesco, born in 1671, and Omobono, born in 1679—later learned their father's art and became his only assistants.

The house in Piazza San Domenico which Stradivari bought in 1680 and where he worked all his life was sold in 1777 by Antonio, his grandson, to Giovanni Ancina. It remained unchanged until 1888, when it was bought by the owner of the adjoining "caffé con bigliardo" to enlarge his establishment; he modernized the façade, for no one in Cremona thought to preserve the house where the city's most celebrated inhabitant had lived and worked for over fifty years. During the Mussolini regime Piazza Roma, as it was now called, was modernized and Stradivari's house disappeared altogether. Again no one raised his voice.

Stradivari's house had three floors. The workshop occupied the ground floor; passers-by might see Stradivari there, surrounded by his apprentices, working at his bench. Many people came to see him there, friends and colleagues and customers who wanted to commission or buy an instrument. On the roof was a flat terrace (*seccadour*) where Stradivari hung up his freshly varnished instruments for slow drying. During the warm season he worked there for its light and fresh air. When the house was rebuilt in 1888 workmen found blocks of wood, shavings, and other valuable relics—everything was carelessly thrown away.

Almost nothing is known about Antonio Stradivari's private life and personal habits. After the death of his teacher, Nicolò Amati, in 1684, Stradivari was the most famous violin-maker in Cremona. Twenty years later, after he made a famous violin, the "Betts," in 1704, at the age of sixty, he was admired all over Europe. More important, he was acknowledged as first by his own peers, the prominent violin-makers of Cremona. But almost nothing was written about him, no attention was paid to the absolute ruler of the violin world. There were a few exceptions: in 1720, Don Desiderio Arisi, a monk in Cremona, wrote that "Stradivari's fame is unequaled as a maker of instruments of the finest qualities." Perhaps Stradivari was not personally very interesting. He lived a quiet, busy life; there were no scandals, no crimes. Much more is known about Guarneri del Gesù, for that erratic genius was always involved in some trouble.

There are only two letters written by Stradivari (both are reprinted in facsimile in the Hills' book). The great genius of the violin seems to have had a sketchy education; if he began his training at Nicolò Amati's workshop at age twelve or fourteen, which was usual in Cremona, he hadn't spent much time in school. In his letters, Stradivari makes many mistakes in spelling, omits the article, uses the wrong vowel, "*solo*" for "*sole*," "*mane*" for "*mani*"; he also uses the Cremonese dialect, "*vallio*" for "*valgo*," "*prumisso*" for "*promesso*," "*tedare*" for "*tediare*." The style is unsophisticated and humble. In one letter, Stradivari asks for one *filippo* (a Lombardian silver coin now worth perhaps five dollars) for repairing and varnishing a cracked violin. He writes that the work ". . . is worth more but for the pleasure of serving you I am satisfied with this sum." The other letter ends, ". . . I will now finish, not wishing to weary you further, kissing your hands and making obeisance—Your Excellency's most humble and devoted servant, Antonio Stradivari." At that time Stradivari was perhaps seventy years old, wealthy and famous; he must have been aware of his standing in the town. In 1729 he was looking for a burial place, and purchased a tomb from the heirs of Francesco Villani, member of an old, noble Cremonese family. It was located in the Chapel of the Blessed Virgin of the Rosary, in the Church of San Domenico. Instead of ordering a new tombstone Stradivari had the inscriptions around the sides and the coat of arms in the center effaced, and his own name and inscriptions substituted. This tombstone is the only relic of him that still exists. The traces of the earlier inscriptions are faintly visible. It suggests that Stradivari liked to be prepared for everything ahead of time, even death, and that he didn't like to throw money around, even for a new tombstone. He seemed sure of himself.

Some historians assume that Stradivari may have been Nicolò Amati's godchild, but there is no proof of this. The guild rules in Cremona were strict about accepting an apprentice: master and apprentice appeared before a notary, and a contract was drawn up. Among violinmakers the standards of professional ethics were high; it is unlikely that a man of Nicolò Amati's standing would benefit unfairly from the work of his apprentices and assistants, nor would the younger men dare take advantage of their master's reputation. Although Stradivari could have got more money by selling his early violins under the name of "Nicolò Amati," this was out of the question. A violin-maker's apprenticeship lasted six years but he was expected to make a violin himself after three years. The earliest known Stradivari violin is dated 1666: Antonio was then twenty-two, assuming that he was born in 1644 (or eighteen, if he was born four years later); in any case, he was probably already a young assistant, not an apprentice.

Some experts have wondered exactly when Stradivari's originality began to assert itself—when it would be correct to call a late Amati "an early Stradivari." They claim to detect evidence of Stradivari's hand in some late Amati violins. But a fine violin must be considered in its entirety if it is a work of art, and work of art embodies the spirit of its maker. If a late Amati breathes the spirit of Nicolò Amati—which a good expert will feel instinctively—then it must be classified as a work by Amati even if younger hands helped complete it.

The earliest violins attributed to Stradivari show the influence of the "small pattern" model of Nicolò Amati: they are now called "Amatisé" Stradivaris. They were not copies of Nicolò Amati's violins, for Stradivari's artistic originality was already pronounced at an early age. His Amatisé violins have much of his own early genius: they are bolder, more adventurous, perhaps more masculine than the lovely, somewhat "feminine" small pattern violins made by Nicolò Amati. In tone, however, they were very similar. "The tone of the violins Stradivari made previous to 1684 (the year Nicolò Amati died) cannot be distinguished from that of the average medium-sized Amati," the Hills admit; "There is the same bright soprano, woody quality of perfect purity, the freedom of response which is so helpful to the average player, and the sufficiency of volume for all purposes other than that of the rendering of solos with a large accompanying orchestra in a great hall."

Stradivari was wholly familiar, of course, with both the small and the grand pattern Amati model. He followed the smaller model because there were customers for it. Players were then less interested in sonority and carrying power than in easy response and sweet tone; there were no large orchestras, no large halls. Even professional players in the 1680s were happy with a Nicolò Amati violin or an Amatisé Stradivari.

Stradivari's Amatisé violins were often covered with a golden yellow varnish similar to the varnish used by Nicoló Amati. But Stradivari could not afford imported wood, and used wood from Lombardy. He often cut his maple on the slab, as his teacher had taught him. But his personality became more pronounced as time went on; the scroll, often expressive, is cut deeply into the wood; he already placed his signature on his early violins. And he seems to have had his own customers. Obviously Stradivari's name was becoming known among the *cognoscenti*. In 1682 Stradivari got an order from Michele Monzi, a banker from Venice, for two violins, a viola, a small and a large cello: these instruments were to be presented to King James II of England. The instruments, beautifully ornamented, were sold for 100 ducats; unfortunately they have since disappeared. Stradivari also received an order from Cardinal Vincent Orsini, archbishop of Benevento, for two violins and a cello. In 1686 the cardinal granted Stradivari an appointment (a copy of the document is reproduced in the Hills' book; the original seems lost). The cardinal considers "the faithful service and kindly affection" which Stradivari has shown, desires "to rank him among our familiar friends," and exhorts all and everyone "that they show him the same favor, esteem, and due honor." This friendship continued when Cardinal Orsini became Pope Benedict XIII.

Stradivari also made a beautiful quartet of instruments for the court orchestra of King Amadeus II of Sardinia. He made (and personally delivered) a cello for the duke of Modena, and was honored by the duke in the presence of the court. According to Fétis, Stradivari at that time made not only violins, violas, and cellos, but also viols, with six and seven strings; quintons, with flat backs; and lutes, guitars, and other instruments. But the more accurate Hills mention only two violas da gamba, later converted into cellos; a tenor viol (which Vuillaume converted into a viola, substituting his own arched back for Stradivari's flat one); two small viols; two guitars; two *pochettes;* and a harp, one of three attributed to Stradivari.

But Stradivari already broke the rules and created surprises. In 1679, when still in his Amatisé period, he made a famous inlaid violin, the "Hellier." It is named for Sir Edward Hellier of Womborne, Staffordhire, who went to Cremona in 1734, three years before Stradivari's death, and personally bought the violin—one of the few instruments that can be traced directly to the master's workshop. (Sir Edward paid the equivalent of about three hundred dollars; it remained in his family until 1875.) The "Hellier" is a beautifully ornamented violin, with fine inlaid work. But it is especially interesting for its large proportions. Its length is $14\frac{1}{8}$ inches, and the bouts are $8\frac{3}{8}$ and $6\frac{13}{16}$ inches wide (lower and upper). Even during his "golden" epoch Stradivari never made larger instruments. The "Hellier" violin expresses a prophetic genius in its symmetry, beautifully cut f-holes, and scroll. Though the "Hellier" is not yet a perfect specimen, being somewhat heavy and incomplete, Stradivari was already ahead of himself.

He continued to make Amatisé violins until 1690, but the models were already changing as he experimented. The scrolls vary from one instrument to the next. Some of the violins he made between 1686 and 1690 remain "unsurpassable . . . in point of sharpness, accuracy, and beauty of finish" (Hill). In 1690, he made the "Tuscan," a very famous violin; the Medici grand duke Cosimo III commissioned Stradivari that year to build a set of instruments. Only the "Tuscan" violin, the "Medici" viola, and a fine violoncello, also attributed by the Hills to 1690, still exist; they already show his genius.

Incidentally, I will not call a Stradivari violin a "Strad": it implies an intimacy which is justified neither by history nor familiarity. An Amati is not called an "Am," nor is a Guarneri a "Guar." So I stick to the good old Cremonese name of Stradivari. It has a beautiful musical sound that almost conveys the image of the great violins which Antonio Stradivari created. The least we can do for the genius of violin-making is to spell his name right.

During the fifteenth, sixteenth, and seventeenth centuries the famous viol-makers took pride in their inlaid and ornamented instruments. Gentlemen amateurs were expected to have "a chest of viols." Princes ordered ornamented viols—ivory, tortoiseshell, silver, pearls, and precious stones were used. The custom went out of fashion with the emergence of the violin. The early violin-makers justly considered their violins to be beautiful in themselves, without special ornamentation. (Only secondary parts—fingerboards, tailpieces, bridges, and pegs—were occasionally ornamented.) But a prominent maker sometimes received a special order from a prominent customer. Such a customer was King Charles IX of France, for whose court Andrea Amati made a set of twenty-four instruments, each bearing the king's coat of arms. Ninety years later, Nicoló Amati made a beautifully decorated violin for the French court of Louis XIV. Once in a while he made a violin with double purfling, with inlaid corners and small stones. Perhaps the great violin-makers wanted to prove that they could do what the early viol-makers had done.

Stradivari met such challenges in customary style. His ornamented instruments are the finest. Only ten are known to exist—eight violins, a viola, a cello. The earliest inlaid violin was an Amatisé model made in 1677, which Stradivari proudly showed to his teacher Nicolò Amati. The last was in 1722, the inlaid "Rode" Stradivari (named after the

French virtuoso Jacques Pierre Joseph Rode). Two years earlier, Stradivari's "intimate friend," Don Desiderio Arisi, had written

> . . . he has made many [instruments] of extraordinary beauty which are richly ornamented with small figures, flowers, fruit, arabesques, and graceful interlaying of fanciful ornaments, all in perfect drawing, which he sometimes paints in black, or inlays with ebony and ivory, all of which is executed with the greatest skill, rendering them worthy of the exalted personages to whom they are intended to be presented.

Among these exalted personages was King Philip V of Spain, for whom Stradivari made three beautifully ornamented violins in 1709. But the best known is the "Greffuhle," named after a former owner, Vicomte de Greffuhle; the inlaid viola, made in 1696, is illustrated in color in the Hills' book. A glance explains its beauty better than a thousand words. The ornamental purfling, the beautifully painted sides, and the head demonstrate the artistic perfection of Stradivari. He made all designs himself—some drawings still exist—and personally carried out the inlays and ornamentations. Arnaldo Baruzzi in *La Casa Nuziale: The Home of Antonio Stradivari, 1667–1680* claims that Stradivari made relatively few instruments after his marriage in 1667 because he earned more money as a skilled carver and inlayer, and made violins only as a sideline!

Around 1690 Stradivari began to experiment with a model now known as the "long" Stradivari. (The French expression *allongé*, "lengthened," is more accurate.) A "long pattern" violin made in 1690 has a length of 14⁵⁄16 inches, ⁵⁄16ths of an inch longer than the great 14-inch violins he made in his best previous years. Many experts believe that he was inspired by Giovanni Paolo Maggini's sonorous, large instruments, made in Brescia; these have a fascinating dark timbre and a powerful tone. The typical "allongé" Stradivari was one-sixteenth of an inch longer than the so-called "small pattern" Maggini (14¼ inches). Stradivari's sense of symmetry and feeling for harmony is evident in the new pattern. He did not merely lengthen the body of the violin, but he changed the whole outline of the design in artistic relation to the new length. He made the bouts longer, less curved; the sound holes are a little wider than on his earlier instruments; sometimes the scroll is imperceptibly longer; the elegant purfling conveys a graceful impression. One of the finest "allongé" violins is the "Harrison," made in 1693, which belonged to the Henry Hottinger Collection. A somewhat unusual model, it is beautiful with a symmetry of its own. Stradivari's genius is very apparent when one plays one of the "long pattern" instruments. The tone is quite different from the Amatisé instruments. It responds less easily than the violins he made in the style of Nicolò Amati, but there is a new, soothing, dark timbre, and great carrying power. Stradivari proved to himself that he could do what the Brescians had done, and he did it more beautifully.

Many connoisseurs today love the allongé violins, but apparently there weren't enough when he made them. Around 1698 he stopped, and reverted to the ideas of Nicolò Amati. But now he became interested in the "grand pattern" violins which Nicolò Amati had made in the 1660s. Most were 14 inches long with a width of 8¼ inches, harmonious and beautifully finished. No wonder that Stradivari, now a mature artist, was deeply impressed by the enormous challenge to improve the almost perfect Amati model—and around 1700 he achieved it. He used beautiful wood and, often, a soft, orange-red varnish. Many experts call the early eighteenth century the beginning of Stradivari's "golden period." "That which I have termed the Golden Period commences about 1700," George Hart writes somewhat pompously. The Hills accepted the statement "yet not without considerable reservation." They had too much understanding for the greatness of Stradivari, sensing correctly that the master never stopped looking for wider horizons. To catalogue arbitrarily the changing creations of a genius is to misunderstand them; obviously Stradivari made some of his greatest instruments when he was in full command of his physical powers and deeply understood the intricate psychology, the soul, of the violin. But he made some great instruments when he was relatively young, and he made others toward the end of his life.

For it is not the beauty or the sound of his best instruments that has made Stradivari the greatest violin-maker the world has known. The beauty, elegance, and finish of some of Nicolò Amati's violins have never been surpassed, not even by Antonio Stradivari, and many modern artists claim that the sensuous, exciting sound of certain masterpieces made by Guarneri del Gesù is unique. What makes the supremacy of Antonio Stradivari is his artistic restlessness, his unceasing striving for perfection, and the enormous range of his creation. A quiet man, he led a rather unspectacular life as his works went through an almost incredible evolution, from his earliest Amatisé violins to the mellow, mature works of his last years. An achievement that some would set beside those of Titian, who created masterpieces until his death at eighty-eight, or Michelangelo, who was an old man when he designed the dome of St. Peter's. I also think of Joseph Haydn, who invented the string quartet in his early twenties and wrote his last masterpieces, full of wisdom and beauty, in his late seventies—or of Verdi, who was seventy-nine when he created the unfathomable miracle of love and humor, his finest work, *Falstaff.*

After 1700 Stradivari's designs are entirely his own. He was now certain about the thicknesses of the wood, and he had learned the secret of creating instruments that had everything—an easy response, carrying power, and velvety smoothness. An artist who plays a *pianissimo* or *morendo* on one of these great violins will be heard in all corners of any concert hall blessed with good acoustics—Vienna's Musikverein, New York's Carnegie Hall, Boston's Symphony Hall, Philadelphia's Academy of Music, Amsterdam's Concertgebouw—and he will also be clearly heard against the powerful *fortissimo* accompaniment of a modern symphony orchestra. These violins have both beauty of appearance and beauty of sound. Yet, incredibly, Stradivari created them when the violin music he knew was still far from exploiting the violin's possibilities. Sitting in his workroom in a sleepy provincial Italian town, Stradivari, with prophetic genius, created instruments that would fulfill increased tonal requirements almost three centuries later.

In 1704 Stradivari made one of his most famous violins, the "Betts." The original owner is unknown, rare in the case of an outstanding instrument. The "Betts" is often compared to the finest violins made by the Brothers Amati, but it surpasses theirs in design and finish. The purfling, rather close to the outer edges, has been admired and studied by generations of violin-makers. The f-holes are often reproduced in violin books because they seem perfect.

The known history of the "Betts" begins in 1820 when Arthur Betts, an English violinist who had studied with Viotti, happened into the violin store of his brother John Edward ("Old John"). Viotti had owned several great violins, including a famous violin made by Stradivari in 1709, now known as the "Viotti"; he realized the importance of a Stradivari for performers and helped his pupils get fine violins, possibly on a commission basis. Arthur Betts had seen Viotti's violins and occasionally helped his brother, possibly also on a commission basis, to get a beautiful Italian instrument by way of Paris. John Betts was a dealer of repute; on his business cards it said that he ". . . makes in the neatest manner violins after the patterns of Antonius Stradivari, Hieronymus Amati, Jacobus Stainer, and Tyrols."

On that day in 1820 "a stranger of unprepossessing appearance" came into the store and offered Arthur a violin for twenty-one shillings, according to the Hills. According to George Hart, "Arthur bought the magnificent Stradivari which bears his name for twenty shillings"; in any case Arthur Betts made the bargain of the century— the violin is certainly worth more than $100,000 today. It is one of the five Stradivari instruments that Mrs. Gertrude Clark Whittall purchased to be kept "in perpetuity" at the Library of Congress in Washington, D.C.

Arthur Betts may not have known immediately that he's purchased a Stradivari but he was doubtless aware that it was a beautiful instrument. When his brother died he and his nephew Charles Vernon took over the store. By then both knew the value of his Stradivari; when the nephew demanded that their partnership include the instrument Betts refused, and the partnership was dissolved. In 1852 the "Betts" was sold after Arthur's death to John Bone, a retired judge and amateur player; he sold it nine years later to J. B. Vuillaume, and the names of its subsequent owners are known. Eventually, the violin was bought by the Hills, then by R. D. Waddell, a well-known collector in Glasgow, and then by the Wurlitzer firm. Mrs. Whittall bought the "Betts" in 1937.

Before 1709 Stradivari made mostly a 14-inch model; later, he occasionally made violins with a length of 14⅛ inches. He continued to experiment, making violins varying in width and in depth of sides. He never stopped working for long, and he loved what he was doing. He had found his greatness, and knew he had no competitors. Later, he must have respected the art of Giuseppe Guarneri del Gesù, but Del Gesù's development was not steady and unbroken.

During the ten years between 1710 and 1720 Stradivari made some of his greatest violins, when he was nearly seventy. Among the famous violins of that decade are the "Dancla" of 1710, on which Nathan Milstein has enchanted audiences for years; the "Parke" of 1711, named for W. T. Parke, an obscure English oboist, though it was for years the solo violin of Fritz Kreisler; the "Boissier" of 1713 on which Pablo Sarasate performed during his last years; the magnificent "Batta" cello of 1714, long the instrument of Gregor Piatigorsky; the "Dolphin" of 1714, made famous by Jascha Heifetz; and the "Alard" of 1715, for which Henry Ford offered $150,000 without success.

"It would be incorrect to single out any of these violins as standing supreme in merit," the Hills write. "We cannot too strongly emphasize that amid all the finest Stradivaris still existing there is not one which can with justice claim absolute superiority over all others." Not even the "Messiah," made in 1716, which the Hills considered the absolutely superior Stradivari when they donated it to the Ashmolean Museum, at Oxford University, where it is kept as a national treasure.

The "Messiah" is called the "perfect" Stradivari because it was never exposed to the rigors of climate or the use of ordinary men. Stradivari himself considered it something special; he never sold it, though he must have had many offers. Perhaps he liked to have it around to enjoy it and to use as a demonstration model for pupils and other violin-makers. His sons Antonio and Paolo later inherited it, with the rest of the estate. Paolo, who was a textile merchant, sold it in 1775 to Count Cozio di Salabue; Count Cozio sold it to Luigi Tarisio, also a superior collector and dealer; after Tarisio's death the "Messiah" was acquired by Vuillaume, then inherited by his son-in-law, the French violinist Delphin Alard. Later it was sold to the Hills, passed through other hands, reverted to the Hills, and is now forever in Oxford.

In 1716 Stradivari made two other celebrated violins, the "Cessole" and the "Medici"; the latter somewhat resembles the "Messiah," and Charles Reade wrote about its varnish, "When a red Stradivari is made of soft, velvety wood, and the varnish is just half worn off the back in a rough triangular form, that produces a certain beauty of light and shade which, in my opinion, is the *ne plus ultra*."

In 1724 Stradivari was eighty (if we accept 1644 as the year of his birth). His work showed no serious sign of old age—only an expert will note that the sound holes are cut less precisely or that the purfling is less elegant than that of ten or twenty years before. Sometimes the wood isn't as beautiful as in his earlier violins, but in some years not even Stradivari could get the wood he wanted. He needed assistance, and certainly had helpers in his workshop: according to Vuillaume, Fétis, and Hart, Stradivari had at least a dozen assistants who later became celebrated makers. Fétis mentions Guarneri del Gesù, Lorenzo Guadagnini, Carlo Bergonzi, Francesco Gobetti, and Alessandro Gagliano; Hart mentions also Domenico Montagnana and Tommaso Balestrieri; all writers mention Stradivari's sons.

Today it seems agreed that of this entire list only the two sons, Francesco and Omobono, helped their father. Even Carlo Bergonzi has now been eliminated; he was long believed to have been Stradivari's favorite pupil. No one still claims that Guarneri del Gesù ever worked with Stradivari. Del Gesù studied with his father, "Joseph filius Andreae."

In 1730 Stradivari was in his eighties, but he went on working. (The year before he had bought his grave and ordered the tombstone inscribed.) Even nonexperts can now notice small irregularities. The purfling is not perfectly made, nor are the sound holes. The varnish is still beautiful but not applied as carefully as before. But most of these instruments have a very beautiful tone; they prove that Stradivari had learned the relationship between the exact measurements of a model and its tone. Perhaps his hands were trembling, but his instinct was unfailing. While putting together the parts of a new violin and measuring its length, width of bouts, and height of sides, he could hear in his inner ear how the finished violin would sound. This is conjecture, to be sure, but confirmed by the tonal excellence of his very late instruments. Rarely, for example, is the height of the sides the same at top and bottom: the upper height is often a sixteenth of an inch less than the lower height. He also sensed how the composition and application of the varnish would affect the tone. But he was an artist, and perhaps also a scientist; he was a magician only in what he created with his mind and hands.

The artist expresses his ideas in materials. When Stradivari didn't get the finest wood, he had to work with the next best. He had long realized that the tone of an instrument was more important than its appearance. In the late 1720s and early 1730s, Del Gesù was more careful in his workmanship, perhaps somehow trying to equal Stradivari. Del Gesù's finest-sounding violins were made after the death of Stradivari in 1737. They are also often rather carelessly made. After 1730, Stradivari often made violins that were bolder, more robust in outline, less graceful and finished than his earlier instruments. These late violins have a powerful, incisive tone, closer to the Del Gesù sound than to the Amati sound. By that time Stradivari knew the fascinating violins made by Guarneri del Gesù, with their almost "Brescian" sonority. The old master knew that some of Del Gesù's violins were sloppily made. But there exists no proof that he was aware of Guarneri's discovery of sonority. Still, one can believe that old Stradivari heard the sound of the future in the violins of Del Gesù. And there was no reason why he, Stradivari, a mere octogenarian, shouldn't produce the sound of the future too.

Stradivari's universality remains unique among the greatest makers. None of them had traveled so far, from the sweet beauty of the Amatisé violins to the darker sound of the *allongé* instruments, then to the perfect beauty of Stradivari's masterpieces and the passionate power of his late violins. Even Nicolò Amati's most ardent admirers cannot claim that his beautiful instruments are ideal for the soloist performing, with a large orchestra, the violin concertos of Brahms, Bruch, or Alban Berg. For such tasks a fine Guarneri del Gesù is preferable. But the fanatical partisans of Del Gesù cannot claim that his instruments are ideal for the purity and fineness of chamber music. For that purpose a quartet of Amati instruments is the perfect choice.

It is only Antonio Stradivari's violins, violas, and cellos that seem to suit every musical purpose. They are effective in the largest halls, holding their own with no difficulty against a large orchestra; Oistrakh, Milstein, and Menuhin all play the great concertos on Stradivaris. And the sound of the late Budapest String Quartet performing on the Stradivari instruments of the Gertrude Clark Whittall Foundation at the Library of Congress remains unforgettable to all who once heard it. The sound was perfect, whether they played classical, romantic, impressionist, or modern chamber works.

In the past three centuries popular taste in sound (as in everything else) has changed. What was once considered sweet and mellow may now be called weak and precious; sound now admired as big and sonorous might have once struck its hearers as coarse and exaggerated. People have been shocked by the mystical art of El Greco, or the physicality of Rubens and Fragonard, but the universality and power and charm of Leonardo da Vinci, Pieter Brueghel, and Rembrandt seem to survive oscillations of taste and therefore of price. For the past hundred and fifty years Stradivari prices have been highest on the international violin market; if a late Del Gesù, made after Stradivari's death, surpasses the highest price ever paid for a Stradivari it will not be for aesthetic or tonal reasons, but owing to the iron law of supply and demand.

Experts as well as ordinary violin-lovers who have the chance to hear several prominent violinists perform on the same Stradivari—in a noted dealer's showroom, for instance—are always amazed by the miraculous capacity of a great Stradivari violin for adapting itself to the personality of the player. Great violins don't change their tonal character, but a great Stradivari is extremely flexible. It almost seems to merge with the player's style. They form such a happy unity that it isn't always possible to keep separate the player and the violin sound; in every case they belong together. The sound has its own beauty, woodiness, brilliance, depth, power, and magic, and always the player's timbre, charm, and personality as well. If there were such a thing as "ideal" violin sound, this is it.

Stradivari's first wife, Francesca, died in 1698 and was buried on May 25. A bill for the funeral expenses is one of the few preserved documents signed by Stradivari. He was already a man of wealth and standing, and he gave his wife what Californians would call "a first-class funeral." The bill lists fees to a hundred and fifty religious and assorted orphans, beggars, and torchbearers, and sums for bell-ringings at three churches, including the cathedral. This interesting document is quoted in full in the Hills' book.

Sixteen months later Stradivari married again. Signora Antonia Maria Zambelli was twenty years younger than he, and very pretty. It was again a good marriage; he'd had five children with his first wife, and Antonia gave him five more, one daughter and four sons. There were probably few dull moments in the house, with its two sets of children, apprentices, friends, and important customers from all over Europe who came to admire his instruments or place orders. Still, we know so little about his life, not even how he looked. The often-published pictures are always the same and are not authentic portraits. In Fétis' quotation of Giovanni Battista Polledro, the well-known violinist, is our only hint: "He was tall and thin in appearance, invariably to be seen in his working costume which he rarely changed, as he was always at work." But Polledro was born forty-four years after Stradivari died, and was merely repeating what he had heard.

Signora Antonia died in 1737 at the age of seventy-three, and was buried on March 4 in the family grave in the Chapel of the Rosary, in the Church of San Domenico. Stradivari survived her until December and was buried on December 19. The record, made from the register of San Matteo, calls him "a widower, aged about ninety-five years," and this was confirmed by the register of San Domenico. But even if Stradivari was born in 1644, he would have been only ninety-three. Other members of his family were buried subsequently in the family grave. The last was his son Giuseppe Antonio, who died in 1781.

For one hundred and thirty-two years Stradivari's remains were at rest in the Church of San Domenico. In 1869, the church was pulled down in the absence of money for urgent repairs and restoration. Alfonso Mandelli, an eyewitness, was later quoted by the Hills:

> When the work was in full swing, the masons cared not which part was to be attacked; the pickaxe, incessantly in use, had already rained down its blows upon the Chapel of the Rosary. . . . I was present on a certain day when several distinguished people were assembled around the tomb of Stradivari . . . and I recall, just as if I heard them now, the following words being pronounced by one of these gentlemen: "There is such a confusion of bones, without any special mark whatever, that it seems useless indeed to make any further search." On the same occasion, I heard repeated, several times, the name of Stradivari; but I was young and ignorant of the significance of the name, and did not then grasp the importance of the search which these gentlemen were disposed to undertake. During the following days I saw men with baskets clear that tomb of all human bones found within it. . . . I learnt afterwards that the men themselves interred the bones outside the city. . . .

Later Mandelli wrote, "The matter of the desecration of this grave was perhaps too lightly decided on. In fact, the reverence now felt for everything appertaining to Stradivari had then penetrated but little in Cremona."

That reverence seemed to have penetrated no further by 1948, when I came to Cremona for the first time. Like other pilgrims, I came to Cremona hoping to find something that would evoke the city's glorious past, the memory of its great violin-makers. I found nothing at all. The houses where they had lived had disappeared. No streets were named after them. There was not even a great Cremonese violin left in the city where they had been created. No one I talked to knew the great names, or if he did know he was not pleased to be asked my questions. It was as though the Amatis, the Stradivaris, the Guarneris had been the town's black sheep. I know now that the community had a sense of guilt for the lack of reverence, which had lasted for generations. According to a travel folder, Cremona was noteworthy "chiefly for its gastronomic specialties, such as butter and cheeses, mustards and sausages, marmalade and *torrone*," candy made of nuts, fruits, honey, and sugar.

The visit was no loss, though, because I met Mario Stradivari, the sixth-generation descendant of Antonio. Mario Stradivari was a famous criminal lawyer and an imposing man, tall and big, who might have been part of a Renaissance sculpture with his furrowed face, large, aquiline nose, and high forehead. He walked with long, swaying steps, had a booming bass-baritone voice, and he moved and spoke with magnificent grandeur. He told me that he might have inherited from his great-great-great-great-grandfather "the big nose, the high-domed forehead, the curved mouth, the long fingers"—then immediately ridiculed the idea. His father, Libero, also a famous lawyer, had been a follower of Garibaldi and a friend of Puccini (Libero left his son a signed photograph of Verdi, but nothing from their famous ancestor!).

Mario Stradivari, a man of great wit and irony, told me that back in 1937 there had been in Cremona an exposition of Stradivari violins to commemorate the two-hundredth anniversary of Antonio's death. Some forty violins were shown. Mario hadn't been officially invited, nor had he ever seen a genuine Stradivari. He went to look at the violins. They seemed beautiful, and he wanted to take one into his hands to have a good look at it, but an attendant "came staring at me down his nose, and said the public was not permitted to touch the instruments—would I please leave, or he would have to call the police."

At Mario Stradivari's house I met Renzo Bacchetta, Cremona's outstanding expert on Stradivari, who informed me that this didn't make him popular with the townspeople. They cared little about Stradivari and violins; they cared only that the price of cheese should stay up. If Stradivari had invented a new kind of cheese, they would have built him a monument. As it was, no monument had been raised to Antonio Stradivari.

Late that night the three of us went to Piazza Roma, the modern square in the center of town where Piazza San Domenico had been. On one side was a small park, exactly in the former place of the Church of San Domenico. On the other side was the sumptuous marble façade of a palacelike office building, with the big glass windows of Cremona's most elegant café on the street floor. High above one window was a marble panel reading *"Qui sorgera la casa dove Antonio Stradivari recando a mirabile perfezione il liuto levava alla sua Cremona nome imperituro di artifice somo,"* "Here stood the house where Antonio Stradivari brought the violin to admirable perfection and left to his Cremona an imperishable name as master of his craft."

Bacchetta told me that Stradivari's house had been torn down by the Mussolini government in 1928, because the site was needed for the office building. Mussolini was said to like violins and Bacchetta had tried to stop the authorities, but failed. He remembered well the old building; it had a tailor's shop and a poolroom with billiard tables on the ground floor, exactly where Antonio Stradivari had had his workshop.

We walked across the square into the small park with benches, play areas for children, and gravel paths. At a half-hidden spot near the far side, behind two benches, Mario Stradivari showed me a block of stone three feet high that looked as though left there by mistake. On the lower part, near where the stone touched the ground, I read the name,

STRADIVARI. Bacchetta, overcome with grief, told me what he called "the saddest story in the history of Cremona"; it tallied with Mandelli's version of the destruction of the old Church of San Domenico. Bacchetta intimated that a Milanese wrecker had paid the city of Cremona 42,000 lire for the right to demolish the church and cart off the materials, which he later sold to his profit. No one had done anything to assure the reburial of the bones of Antonio Stradivari and his family. Said Bacchetta, "Maybe the workers took them to the local cemetery and threw them into a common grave. I hope so, though no such grave is known. Or maybe they just walked to the bank of the Po, only a few minutes away, and threw the bones into the river."

After centuries of neglect the city of Cremona has at last put up a small monument on the location of Stradivari's grave in the Church of San Domenico. Via Stradivari now leads off Piazza Roma where once Stradivari's house stood. And most important, there is now a Stradivari violin at the Municipal Museum, where the tombstone and other relics are also exhibited. The violin was made in 1715, and is now called "Il Cremonese"; it was formerly known as one of the instruments owned by Joseph Joachim, who had at least eight Stradivaris.

In *How Many Strads?* Ernest N. Doring calls the two violin-making sons of Stradivari "perhaps the greatest enigma in the story of the old Italian violin-makers." Of the two men—Francesco was born in 1671 and died in 1743, Omobono was born in 1679 and died in 1741—Francesco is now considered the more important artist.

When the sons took over their father's workshop after his death, it surely contained a number of violins that had not been completed; it is also assumed that there were several instruments which the old man had put aside because he was not satisfied with them (he no longer burned such instruments, as he did earlier). Did the sons sell these instruments under their own names? George Hart answers, "Many of the later works of Antonius Stradiuarius have been erroneously attributed to his sons," but he does not supply convincing proof. In 1890 the catalogue of Lyon and Healy in Chicago listed Francesco Stradivari's "Le Besque," with an Antonio Stradivari label dated 1734: "The violins of Francesco Stradivari are among the most artistic of any that came out of Cremona. Although not such a genius as his father . . . nevertheless a great artist in the highest sense . . . Francesco aimed to produce in his violins a beautiful quality of tone which with sufficient volume would combine the best features of the work of Antonius Stradivarius and Carlo Bergonzi. . . ." On the other hand Arthur W. Dykes wrote in *The Strad* of August, 1929: "Francesco Stradivari remains a shadow, as no violin by him is known, so far as I am aware, but the instruments by Omobono which exist prove the latter maker to have been an artist of great ability and . . . one more fully inoculated with the manner of Antonio than any other master in Italy." René Vannes disagrees. "Omobono has produced little. He seems to have done mostly repairs and trading violins." But Doring's book shows three violins made by Omobono Stradivari, all dated 1740 and all doubtlessly authentic works. One, which belonged to Eric Sorantin, much resembles Antonio Stradivari's late violins: the f-holes, the arching, the purfling, the beautiful wood, the red-brown varnish. It certainly doesn't look like the work of a master who "seems to have done mostly repairs."

To be the son of a genius is not an easy role. For a long time the experts argued whether the sons alone had made any violins. The Hills wrote in 1902: "Not a single authentic example of Francesco's work has been hitherto identified by us." Yet the Hottinger Collection contains a beautiful, authentic violin by Francesco; the Wurlitzer catalogue calls it "the finest example of Francesco, in a perfect state of preservation." It was made in 1742, and is called the "Salabue," because it was one of the instruments Count Cozio di Salabue purchased in 1775 from Francesco's surviving brother, Paolo. It is a beautiful violin with a magnificent tone and easy response—I have played on it—and the favorite of Mrs. Lee Wurlitzer Roth, who has refused several offers for it.

Francesco died at seventy-two on November 5, 1743, and with him the Stradivari dynasty came to an end. Today the violins attributed to Antonio's sons are justly called Stradivaris—they are Stradivari violins in every respect. I wish there were more of them.

Paolo, Antonio Stradivari's youngest son (born in 1708), installed his textile store on the ground floor of the house in Piazza San Domenico, where his father's workshop had been for over fifty years, but by 1746 Paolo moved the store to a better location near the Duomo. Antonio's old pupil Carlo Bergonzi occupied Stradivari's house, but he died the following year; the Bergonzi family kept the house until 1758. There came other tenants until the house was finally sold in 1777 by Antonio Stradivari, the son of Paolo and grandson of the great maker.

The exact number of instruments made by Stradivari is another mystery, and there has been wild guessing among the experts for the past two hundred years. It is not known how much time Stradivari needed to make an instrument. Don Desiderio Arisi mentions the visit to Cremona in 1715 by Jean-Baptiste Volumier, then director of the court music of the king of Poland; Volumier came to pick up the twelve violins King Augustus had ordered, and he stayed three months. Some historians deduce that Stradivari made the instruments during that time, one violin per week. Count Lütgendorff, long considered the leading Stradivari expert in Germany, wrote about "Stradivari's unbelievable productivity": "Even if he completed only one violin each week, that gives us three thousand violins through the sixty-year period of his working life." This statement seems unbelievable.

There are few facts. Count Cozio's correspondence tells us that Stradivari possessed at his death ninety-one violins, several violas, two cellos, and an inlaid set of instruments. Cozio does not mention any catalogue kept by Stradivari; a conscientious man might be expected to keep records of his production, but Stradivari was either too busy to bother with paper work or, as his few documents show, had trouble writing and making records. Years of thorough research led the Hills to a lifetime total of 1116 instruments, basing their deductions on all the instruments they had seen or knew about. The available evidence also convinced them that Stradivari's output varied considerably. Relatively few early instruments exist, from the years 1660 to 1684 when he worked for, and later with, Nicolò Amati. After Amati's death in 1684, the number of Stradivari instruments with their original labels increases, and it keeps up well until about 1725, when he was perhaps eighty-one. During the last twelve years of his life his productivity decreased, but it seems miraculous that three violins of great tonal beauty were made in 1737, the last year of his life, and made, to a considerable extent, by his hand.

Stradivari made mostly violins, and perhaps one cello for every ten or twelve violins; it took about twice as long to make a cello. He also made a relatively small number of violas; they are very valuable. No double bass made by Stradivari is known.

There are no instruments with Stradivari's label from the years 1673, 1674, 1675, 1676, and 1678: either he was working for Nicolò Amati, or, as some Italian historians assume, he also worked partly as a carver and inlayer. Even after 1700, his output is sometimes bewilderingly inconsistent. From 1705 we have only five violins, for example, and four from 1706. These were hard years for Cremona; in 1706 the Austrians occupied the fortress of Cremona, the castle of Santa Croce, and turned it into a major Lombardy stronghold. The fortifications cost over eleven million francs, much of the money exacted from the citizens of Cremona. All citizens had to billet soldiers in their houses, and Stradivari probably was no exception. It was not a good time for the making of fine violins.

But 1709, contrarily, remains Stradivari's vintage year: twenty-one violins and one cello! And during the three great years of 1715, 1716 (the "Messiah"), and 1717 he made thirteen, fifteen, and thirteen violins respectively, and three cellos. (These instruments were actually seen by the Hills; Stradivari probably made more. Doring's tabulation lists many as "uncertain.") From the year 1725 we have now only five violins and two cellos, but 1727 was a banner year with sixteen violins and one viola. In 1734, when he was presumably ninety, the Hills attribute to him five violins, and Doring seven. In 1902 the Hills had factually accounted for 540 violins, 12 violas, and 50 cellos, in all 602 instruments; these figures were never claimed to be exact or complete. And if it is frustrating not to know how many instruments Stradivari made, it is worse not even to know how many exist today. "In the case of the violins," the Hills wrote, "we unhesitatingly express our belief that we have only succeeded in recording three-fourths of them, as we have traces, more or less clear, of quite one hundred more."

Certain instruments, known to exist, have been traced for centuries with no success. In 1690 Stradivari made a set of five instruments for the Tuscan court. They were later borrowed by players and collectors who became so enthusiastic about them that they failed to return them: where are they now? Of the pair of violins, only one later turned up in Florence, now the much-admired "Tuscan" Stradivari. A quintet of inlaid Stradivari instruments, and various instruments by the Amatis, Jacob Stainer, and Guarneri del Gesù, were purchased by Charles IV, king of Spain. They were last seen in 1790 at the Royal Palace in Madrid; the year after came the French Revolution, then the French occupation of Spain and bad times for fine violins. In this instance, only four remain. Palaces, churches, and monasteries were ransacked and destroyed in many cities and countries. The Napoleonic wars turned the continent of Europe into a battlefield, and countless fine instruments were undoubtedly plundered and destroyed.

The situation improved after 1815, when the Congress of Vienna brought peace and relative stability. But there were other disasters and catastrophes. In 1808, when Covent Garden burned, a Stradivari violin owned by W. Ware, the orchestra leader, was lost in the flames. The wars of 1866 and 1871, and World Wars I and II, probably destroyed many fine instruments. It is not yet known what became of the instruments in Russia since the Revolution.

Hardly a week passes when a violin-dealer does not have someone step into the store and offer to sell a "genuine" Stradivari. And whenever a newspaper comes out with a story about the discovery of an allegedly old violin in an attic, well-known dealers are invariably deluged with telegrams and long-distance calls from people who think they own a master instrument. Such optimism is understandable, based on circumstances somewhat like the following: an old violin has been cluttering up the attic or a closet for some time. The owners have wanted to give it away, but found no one to take it; when they read of the discovery they open their violin case, finding inside a dusty fiddle bearing the label "Antonius Stradiuarius Cremonensis Faciebat Anno . . ." Now they recall their parents saying that Grandpa brought a violin from the old country in the 1850s. They are convinced that they have a treasure (fifty thousand dollars—that's what it said in the paper). Alas, their violin is probably worth about forty dollars, at the most.

All dealers are eager to find a genuine old Italian fiddle, but they know that their chances are infinitesimal. Many precious instruments have disappeared in the wars, catastrophes, revolutions, upheavals, fires, and accidents of the past two hundred years. Consequently, the experts are convinced that the history of almost all important instruments is now known, even though their whereabouts cannot always be traced, and that almost all instruments known to be missing are now destroyed. The career of most violins can be followed back for fifty to a hundred and fifty years. The entire history of some outstanding instruments is known, from the time they left the maker's workshop.

The experts agree that a few masterpieces may still be hidden, but not in the attic of a North American house. Certain violins mentioned in letters, diaries, and old journals have disappeared; they might be in Italy, France, England, or Spain in the possession of wealthy or aristocratic families who are aware of what they own but choose to say nothing about it. A major unknown quantity is the Soviet Union, where the former aristocrats owned many fine instruments. During the Russian Revolution many of these fine instruments that did not disappear were transferred into the vaults of the state. The state lends them to eminent (and "reliable") artists; David Oistrakh, for example, played for years probably the finest Stradivari in the Soviet Union. In the past years prominent artists have invested hard-currency earnings in fine instruments, with permission of the Soviet authorities.

Perhaps half a dozen Stradivari violins and a number of other fine Italian instruments—violins, violas, cellos—are now in the Soviet Union, we don't know exactly how many; some so-called authentic instruments might turn out to be otherwise and some genuine ones may still be unidentified. The saddest story is that of Italy, where most of the fine instruments originated and where very few now are. "If a Cremonese wants to look at our great heritage he must go to New York, Hollywood, Switzerland, or Germany," Renzo Bacchetta once said. The chief culprit was an Italian, the expert dealer Luigi Tarisio; during the first half of the nineteenth century he took perhaps more than a thousand violins from Italy to Paris and London.

Ever since my articles about rare old violins in *The New Yorker* in 1953, I've had letters telling about the "treasures" found among American family heirlooms, and asking me where to take them. It seems useless to explain that American households have undergone too many upheavals to make such a discovery probable; I suggest that they take the instrument to the nearest reputable dealer or send him photographs of it. But owners of "old" violins are incorrigible optimists. They will make a long journey to a dealer and try to persuade them-

selves and him that their forty-year-old violin has been in the family
for over two centuries. They accuse the dealer of lying when he tells
them the unpleasant truth; they announce they will to go to another
dealer—who, of course, tells them the same thing. They go home, not
quite convinced; some believe that all dealers are crooks. They put the
violin back up in the attic. In thirty years their children will think
they've found a treasure. It's a vicious circle. No one ever throws a
fiddle away, no matter how bad it is.

Once in a lifetime—if he is lucky—a dealer may discover a previously
unknown masterpiece. At the end of World War II Rembert Wurlitzer, on his first trip to Spain, found a Stradivari, made in 1720, that
was not known to any dealer. He bought the beautifully preserved violin, christened it the "Madrileño," and brought it to New York.

One day in 1911 Emil Herrmann traveled to Posen, at that time in
Germany, to deliver an instrument to a customer. He was told that an
old postal clerk in the town owned several violins, "among them even
a Stradivari." Herrmann was only twenty-three but already a convinced skeptic, as a violin-dealer has to be to stay in business. But a
sense of duty made him go to the clerk's apartment; his skepticism
deepened when the living room looked like a second-rate antique
shop. The postal clerk showed him a dozen factory-made violins, and
Herrmann was about to leave when the clerk brought out a battered
old case and opened it. Herrmann often described the scene, the moment every dealer dreams about: "I couldn't have been more surprised. It was a Stradivari; no doubt about it. An Amatisé instrument,
made in 1684, with a one-piece back and a light-brown varnish. It was
in a bad state of repair, with several cracks, but it was definitely genuine. I offered to buy it, along with some of the other violins. The clerk
didn't want to sell. I paid him several hundred marks for some bad
china and bric-à-brac, in the hope of establishing good will, and said
I'd be back. Two weeks later, I returned with four thousand marks in
gold—nine hundred and fifty dollars in those days. The clerk still
didn't want to sell. We argued all afternoon and well into the evening.
Finally, around ten o'clock, I took out the money and put the whole
four thousand marks, in twenty-mark gold pieces, on the table—four

long rows of fifty coins each. It was a tempting, gleaming sight, and the clerk couldn't resist."

It would be more difficult today. Gold coins are no longer legal tender. The sight of banknotes, inflated paper money, might not have the same effect.

In his book *How Many Strads?*, published in 1945, Ernest N. Doring quotes from a letter from Alfred Ebsworth Hill:

> . . . You ask me to help you trace Stradivaris that found their way to the States. This is asking for much for it has amazed me to note how easily your countrymen part with their instruments and how quickly they pass from one end of the States to the other! Consequently, I am no longer well informed as to the whereabouts of these instruments . . .

Fridolin and Emil Hamma, the noted dealers in Stuttgart, agreed. "Among the many transactions which have taken place in recent years, you can no longer keep track. One believes a certain Stradivari to be found in the possession of a German family, only to hear that it has already long been in America!"

The majority of the great instruments has now shifted to the United States. The dollar may no longer be what it was, but America is still the land of the rich. There are more collectors in the United States than in any other country, and some now own magnificent quartets of great instruments. The former Hottinger Collection, now sold to Rembert Wurlitzer, Inc., was the most important of its kind. The Wurlitzer vaults at 16 West 61st Street today contain more treasures than those of any other dealer. America is where the violin action is. In the golden days of Hollywood, the 1940s, more Stradivaris and other great instruments were played by musicians in the orchestras of the major movie studios than in any other city of comparable size.

The concertmasters and leading string players in the larger American orchestras own some great violins. Rafael Druian, the concertmaster of the New York Philharmonic, owns the "Nightingale" Stradivari, made in 1717. Back in 1960 Isaac Stern played the Beethoven Concerto with the New York Philharmonic under Leonard Bernstein, at Carnegie Hall; during the first movement the E string on Stern's Guarneri del Gesù broke, but he exchanged his Guarneri for the concertmaster's

Stradivari so adroitly that he missed only one measure.

Granted that no one will ever know how many instruments were made by Stradivari, Lütgendorff's ridiculous estimate of 3000 is obviously high. The estimates of the Hills (a grand total of 1116) and of William Henley (1400) are closer to the truth. Of these, Doring estimated in 1945 that 509 Stradivari instruments had survived. Herbert Goodkind, in his latest estimate in *Iconography of Antonio Stradivarius,* lists 630 violins, 15 violas, and 60 cellos, but does not claim that all the instruments listed are fully authenticated. Dario d'Attili, of Rembert Wurlitzer, Inc., believes that about 550 Stradivari instruments still exist.

The bitter truth is that roughly half of all the instruments that Antonio Stradivari made are lost forever.

The Challengers: The Guarneri Family

Today the name Guarneri comes closest to Stradivari. Some great violinists prefer a Guarneri del Gesù to a Stradivari, at least for the performance of certain works. But the five violin-making members of the Guarneri family were hardly known outside of Cremona during their lifetime, except for a small circle of cognoscenti. During the last ten years the instruments made by members of the Guarneri clan have gone up in value on the international violin exchange, more than those of most other makers. The Amatis and Jacob Stainer have gone down. Stradivari is still on top but his primacy is not unchallenged.

Andrea Guarneri, the founder of the dynasty, was probably born in Cremona in 1626, some hundred and twenty years after the birth of Andrea Amati, the founder of the Cremonese school. Compared to the Amatis, the Guarneris are Johnnies-come-lately. "The five Guarneris proved themselves to be well versed in their art," write the Hills in *The Violin Makers of the Guarneri Family,* the standard work on the subject, "yet not one of them showed that perfection of fitness for his

calling which was made manifest in the more varied and skilled productions of their predecessors, the members of the Amati family." So
much for their perfection of fitness; on today's market a fine Guarneri
del Gesù would easily get four times the price of a fine Nicolò Amati.

The Guarneris were a noble family which has been traced back to
1209 in Cremona. The name was also spelled Guarnieri, Guarnero,
Guarniero, Guerneri, and the Latinized form Guarnerius, which they
always used on their labels. Andrea Guarneri's exact birthdate is unknown, but a census return in 1641 of the household of Nicolò Amati
includes Andrea Guarneri, aged fifteen. This would make 1626 the
year of his birth. He was the son of Bartolomeo Guarneri, profession
unknown.

Andrea Guarneri may have become an apprentice at Nicolò Amati's
workshop by 1636, when he was only ten. Nicolò Amati was then forty
and already famous, though some people may have admired more his
uncle Antonius, who was still alive, the last survivor of the Brothers
Amati. At the courts of Europe and in the monasteries and academies
where people played string music, "Amati" meant supreme quality. Nicolò had more orders than he could fill; he needed help. He seems to
have selected gifted boys, and must have been a great teacher or we
wouldn't have so many fine instruments made "sotto la disciplina,"
and under the influence, of Nicolò Amati.

The first of these gifted apprentices was Francesco Ruggieri, six
years older than Andrea Guarneri; one of the last was Antonio Stradivari, perhaps eighteen years younger than Andrea Guarneri. (I must
use "perhaps," or "probably," or "possibly" so often because to make
flat statements would be irresponsible; others have done so, and later
turned out to be wrong.) The first known violin made by Andrea
Guarneri has a label dated 1638. Some experts believe they can recognize Andrea Guarneri's hand in certain violins of Nicolò Amati made
in the 1640s. This is not impossible, but problematical; even if some
details show the hand of the young man, the conception and the finishing touches must have been the teacher's. Nicolò Amati, a conscientious artist, would never have permitted to be sold under his name an
instrument for which he didn't feel responsible.

Andrea Guarneri was a witness at Nicolò Amati's wedding in 1645,
and we know that when he married Anna Maria Orcelli in 1652 he

was still living in Amati's house. He moved out two years later and set up his own working place in his father-in-law's house; Casa Orcelli was later known as Casa Guarneri. In 1655 his first son was born, Pietro Giovanni, later the famous "Pietro of Mantua."

The few of Andrea Guarneri's violins that survive betray no particular originality. Andrea was an able craftsman, not a true creator. He never made much money and couldn't afford expensive wood; he often used local maple for his violin backs. He made only a few violas and cellos; his whole output, mostly violins, was perhaps not more than two hundred and fifty instruments. But even at that, he was the most productive member of the whole Guarneri family. His oil varnishes are always good, sometimes beautiful. His favorite color was chestnut-brown, but occasionally he used brown-red and yellow-amber shades, perhaps under the influence of Nicolò Amati. Sometimes his varnish dried too quickly and hardened; when he had to deliver an instrument quickly he may have used dryers. Andrea Guarneri's best instruments are his violas. More robust than Amati violas, they are beautifully proportioned, modeled, and varnished, and their tone has a beautiful dark timbre; few better violas were made in Cremona. He also made a few fine cellos.

Andrea Guarneri and his wife had seven children in all; of their three boys two continued their father's profession: Pietro Giovanni, the oldest, and Giuseppe Giovanni Battista, the third. Pietro began working in his father's shop in 1670. In 1677 he married; soon afterward he moved to Mantua. Giuseppe, now generally known as "Joseph Guarnerius, filius Andreae," started working with his father after 1676, also as a teenager. Andrea had other apprentices, but Joseph became his main assistant.

In 1687 (he was only sixty-one) Andrea Guarneri had his will drawn up, and arranged for his burial place in the Chapel of the Rosary, in the Church of San Domenico (where Stradivari was later buried). He was upset that his oldest son, Pietro, had gone to Mantua, and made other wills in 1692 and 1694 stipulating that Pietro should inherit only his legal share of the estate. The father came close to disinheriting Pietro.

Andrea died on December 7, 1698, at the age of seventy-two. His business was taken care of by his youngest son, Joseph, then only thirty-two. A few months earlier, in August of that year, Joseph had had a son who was to become the greatest Guarneri of all—Giuseppe del Gesù.

Andrea's heir, "Joseph filius Andreae" (to distinguish him from Joseph's son Giuseppe, Joseph del Gesù), was a good violin-maker. It is ironical that he remains immortal mainly as the father of Giuseppe del Gesù. The *filius* continued Andrea's work, mostly following the Amati models but adding details of his own, and some of his instruments seem influenced by his very gifted brother Pietro of Mantua. The brothers were friendly, though Joseph had inherited much more from his father than Pietro had. Some experts also notice Stradivari's influence in the violins of Joseph filius Andreae—not surprising, perhaps, since they were neighbors in the San Domenico district. Around 1700 the great violin-makers were a closely knit group, visiting each other and talking about their instruments and their problems. There was admiration and also jealousy. People have since wondered why Stradivari's influence was not stronger than it appears: fortunately great violin-makers are individualists, and his contemporaries followed their own ideas.

Joseph had taste and skill and ambition, but his violins never got high prices because he couldn't afford choice wood and other rare materials. He used native maple, the violin backs often cut on the slab, and when he ran out of good wood he would use other pieces. Sometimes he had to use poplar and lime wood; the backs, sides, and scrolls of some of his violins do not match. He knew that he would always be overshadowed by his neighbor Stradivari in No. 2 Piazza San Domenico, and after 1715 Joseph turned to making a different type of violin —somewhat longer (up to 14⅛ inches) and bolder in design, with elongated bouts and heavier f-holes. He used variously colored varnishes—brown with red or orange, sometimes a deep red. Many of his violins remain unlabeled, which has caused confusion among the experts: some believed that Carlo Bergonzi had a hand in making them; others attributed them outright to Carlo Bergonzi, who had his early training in the workshop of Joseph filius Andreae. Consequently, certain elements of Bergonzi's models—dimensions, curves, the placing of the f-holes, the purfling—reveal a noticeable affinity with the Guarneri pattern. Bergonzi's choice of wood and method of varnishing are closer to Joseph filius Andreae and Guarneri del Gesù than to Stradivari.

Joseph produced few instruments after 1720. His last-known was a cello in 1731. He was only sixty-five, an age when many celebrated makers were at their best. It is assumed (though never proved) that his home was not a happy one, and that he had lost interest in his work. He died in 1740, and soon afterward Casa Guarneri was sold. According to the deed his estate was "loaded with debts." He was not buried next to his wife, Barbara Franchi, who had died two years earlier and was interred in her family's grave in San Domenico. Some historians have speculated that he may have left home and died elsewhere. It was Joseph's lifelong tragedy to be always overshadowed by greater makers —his brother, Peter of Mantua; his neighbor, Stradivari; and later his son, Giuseppe del Gesù.

Pietro Giovanni Guarneri, born February 18, 1655, is now known as "Pietro of Mantua" to distinguish him from his nephew, "Pietro of Venice." For a long time the two were believed to be cousins, but the Hills established the true relationship. Pietro of Mantua is not the most famous Guarneri—this distinction goes to his other nephew, Giuseppe del Gesù—but he may be the most interesting one. He is now being "discovered" as a very original creator and great artist. In the past hundred years his violins have risen steadily in price. For long-range "investors" (a terrible species of violin collectors) "Peter of Mantua" is now a very hot number. Late in November, 1969, a Peter of Mantua, dated 1715, "set a new record for a violin other than a Stradivari or del Gesù" at an auction at Sotheby's in London.

There are two reasons for this: the excellence of his work, and the small number of his surviving instruments. He made perhaps fifty violins. The Hills, who had seen nearly all important violins Pietro had made, wrote, "If we judge him purely from his craftsmanship point of view, we should say that he surpassed all the others of his family, not excepting Giuseppe del Gesù." In craftsmanship he approaches Nicolò Amati, whom he admired, and it is no wonder that his violins were often mistaken for Amatis at first sight. He is original in his design and exact in his finish, and his varnish is often of unsurpassed quality.

It is now widely believed that Pietro might have become a most important violin-maker had he stayed in Cremona, devoted himself full-time to making violins instead of playing them—and if he had worked closer to Stradivari. But apparently this was exactly what he did not want to do. So he left Cremona, and though all his instruments follow the large models of Nicolò Amati they also show his originality, one might even say courage, particularly after 1700.

Pietro is the only famous maker who divided his life between making fiddles and professional performance. Naturally all makers could play their instruments, otherwise they couldn't have understood them so well. But Pietro of Mantua was for many years primarily interested in playing the violin, and must have been a very able violinist.

He lived in his father's household until about 1679, and had married Caterina Sassagni two years before. He had learned his trade in his father's workshop, and experts again claim they can recognize his hand in some of his father's violins, made between 1670 and 1680. Their claim of joint production in this case is on safer ground than usual, for Pietro's originality gives him away, especially his f-holes, purfling, and deep fluting.

In 1685 "Pietro Guarnieri of Cremona, Maker of Musical Instruments, and of Violins in particular" presented a petition to the chamberlain of the duke of Mantua, "to be appointed successor to Francesco Scalfoni, viol-player, with all the stipends and privileges enjoyed by him." His official appointment is dated May, 1690; the mills of musical bureaucracy in Mantua were grinding slowly. The appointment mentions "the virtuoso's talents of Pietro Guarneri and taking into account his upright conduct and great skill in playing the violin, we are pleased to . . . promote him to be Our Master of the Violins with all the honors, benefits, privileges & prerogatives attached to the position."

Why would a famous Cremonese violin-maker leave home and go to Mantua to play the fiddle? Certainly it was for professional and personal reasons. A man of great individuality—this is apparent from his instruments—Pietro may have disliked the small-town atmosphere, gossip, and professional jealousies around Piazza San Domenico in Cremona. He went to Mantua, then the most important musical center in Italy. Mantua had an "Academy" for the study of poetry and music, founded in 1568 by Duke Guglielmo Gonzaga, who was a composer. In 1590 Claudio Monteverdi from Cremona had gone to Mantua, joined the court orchestra as a viol-player, and risen to the position of maestro di cappella. Duke Vincenzo Gonzaga (reigned 1587–1612) loved music and opera, and spent much money on them.

The Gonzagas knew what they were doing; as their small duchy had no great political or geographical importance the dukes wanted to make Mantua important in the realm of music, and they succeeded admirably. (Other minicountries, such as Andorra, Monaco, or Liechtenstein, have become famous for smuggling, gambling, or philately—the Gonzagas had more style.) Mantua's finest hour came at Carnival in 1607 when Claudio Monteverdi's first opera, *Orfeo,* was produced, the first public opera premiere in history. The libretto was by Alessandro Striggio, state secretary of Mantua and the son of a noted madrigalist.

Monteverdi is a genius and a giant, the "Aeschylus of music" (Paul Henry Lang). He created his personal style of opera; he can be said to have invented opera, and in his use of the orchestra to express the psychological mood on the stage a straight line leads from Monteverdi to Wagner's *Musikdrama.* Monteverdi was seventy-five when he wrote his masterpiece, *L'Incoronazione di Poppea,* an achievement comparable to another masterpiece, *Falstaff,* written by Giuseppe Verdi at the age of seventy-nine. Verdi lived in Sant' Agata near Parma, a short drive from Mantua and Cremona. The landscape of Lombardy seems to suit the musical genius.

About a hundred years after Claudio Monteverdi had gone from Cremona to Mantua to play in the court orchestra, Pietro Guarneri did exactly the same. His father, hurt and angry, left most of his possessions to his younger son, Joseph filius Andreae, but after their father's death Joseph signed a deed compensating his older brother Pietro with the amount of 600 lire. Pietro seemed to enjoy playing at the court, and made fine instruments in his spare time. As a practicing viol- and violin-player Pietro was especially interested in beautiful tone. He knew the easy response and sweet timbre of the Jacob Stainer violins that were in Mantua; he may have played one himself. Stainer's violins surpassed the earlier viols in many respects. They had subtle shades of expression, and sounded more human; their tone was often compared with a soprano voice. Pietro did not adapt the design of Stainer's highly arched instruments, for he instinctively preferred the "grand pattern" Amatis; but some added details show Stainer's influence. After 1700, when he was widely recognized—in Mantua and Cremona at least—he often used foreign maple and beautiful pine. He made and applied a fine varnish, either orange, red, or golden-brown.

Pietro's first wife died, and in 1694 he married Lucia Guidi Borani. They had six children. Pietro died in Mantua on March 26, 1720, at seventy-six. He was buried in the Church of the fathers of San Francesco di Paola "with the usual ceremonies." Fifteen finished violins and some other instruments and bows were found in his workshop at his death.

Pietro left no pupils. His sons were not interested in his profession, and one, Alessandro, entered the monastery of San Francesco di Paola. Except for Nicolò Amati, most famous violin-makers were not eager to accept apprentices from elsewhere. Perhaps a feeling lingered that the art had secrets which should remain in a family. There was no real "school" of violin-making in Mantua, but several good makers lived and worked there after Pietro Guarneri, and all were inspired by him. Antonio Zanotti from Ceretto, near Lodi, worked in Mantua after 1725; his pupil Camillo Camilli was born in Mantua after 1704 and died there in 1754. Camilli made beautiful violins with fine sound, and though he was for long said to be a pupil of Stradivari, it seems certain now that he was under the influence of Pietro Guarneri, perhaps trained by him. Tommaso Balestrieri (c. 1740–1790) was probably born in Mantua though he calls himself "Cremonensis" on his labels. His work shows the influence of both Stradivari and Pietro Guarneri. He made large instruments somewhat like the Guadagninis, using a reddish-yellow varnish, and a few fine cellos. The tone of his instruments improves with the years, and his prices are increasing.

The greatest Guarneri, Bartolomeo Giuseppe del Gesù, is the most fascinating member of the family, and the most mysterious of all the great Cremonese masters. His life and his work are surrounded by legends which no research has elucidated. He remains known, and revered, as Joseph Guarnerius del Gesù—he did not Latinize his Biblical name into "Joseph"—because he marked his labels with the monogram IHS, the Greek abbreviation for Jesus. Above the monogram is the sign of the Cross. (IHS may also stand for "Iesum Habemus Socium," which would be connected with a popular trend in Italy that was influenced by the Jesuit movement.) For a long time he was usually described as the cousin of "Pietro of Venice." It is now established beyond doubt that both were the sons of Joseph filius Andreae. Del Gesù's uncle, Pietro of Mantua, was his godfather.

Del Gesù was born on August 21, 1698—a few months before the death of his grandfather Andrea. He regularly appears in census returns as the son of Giuseppe filius Andreae and of Barbara Franchi. He started working with his father. "Repeated examinations of various instruments, the work of respectively Giuseppe filius Andreae and Giuseppe del Gesù, have long convinced us of the working intimacy which existed between the two men," the Hills conclude, and dispose of the legend that Del Gesù was an apprentice in Stradivari's workshop.

In 1723, at twenty-five, Del Gesù left his father's house. The earliest violin known to have been made by him is dated 1726. It already had his label "Joseph Guarnerius Fecit Cremonę" with a cedilla under the final "e," and his monogram IHS; he used this label all his life. We don't know what he had been doing between 1723 and 1726. Why didn't his early labels mention that he was the son of the famous Joseph filius Andreae? Again we draw a blank. Apparently he was like other members of the family, proud, strong, and independent, the spirit that shows later in many of his famous violins. By the 1731 census his name is registered in Casa di San Bernardo, in Cremona.

Fétis quotes Carlo Bergonzi II (1780–1838), grandson of Stradivari's great pupil Carlo Bergonzi (in his biography, *Antonius Stradivarius*), as saying that Guarneri del Gesù led an irregular life, was "lazy and negligent, and addicted to drink and other pleasures of the world." His wife, who was from Tyrol, had not found happiness with him; she might be Catterina Roda, whose name is mentioned on the same census return of 1731, at Casa di San Bernardo. Fétis is not always a reliable source, but that del Gesù led an irregular life is proved by his violins.

The most reliable guide to the lives of the great violin-makers is the evidence of their works. The violins of Nicolò Amati and Antonio Stradivari reflect artistic discipline and solid character: responsible, hardworking, enormously gifted men always searching for improvement; obtaining the best materials, applying inspiration and knowledge, careful in making their masterpieces. Probably conservative in their habits. Regular working hours. Self-discipline and genius.

The works of Guarneri del Gesù reveal much genius and little self-discipline. His enormous gifts are seen all over his violins, but the workmanship is often erratic. That he was not a pupil of Stradivari is now certain; neither his models, his execution, nor his working habits correspond with Stradivari's standards. Could his inspiration have come from masters of the Brescian school? Gasparo da Salò and Paolo Maggini made violins that were bold in design though not always beautiful, and very powerful so far as their tone is concerned. There is much boldness in the outlines of many Del Gesù instruments and often a certain carelessness about them, as though he were saying, "I can afford not to be careful, wait until you hear them." Tonally, they are almost always extraordinary; tone was what he cared about, not style or beauty. Among the great makers he was the great nonconformist, constantly experimenting. "Del Gesù offers a problem as his works show a great variation in style, workmanship, and finish," writes Doring. This doesn't do justice to Del Gesù. What matters more is that he was a genius who tried to combine in a violin the dulcet, mellow sound of the Amatis and Stradivari with the dark sonority of the Brescians—a beautiful, sensuous tone that would be balanced on all strings. He succeeded so well that some of his violins may become more valuable than Stradivari's most beautiful specimens.

The best-known and silliest legend about Del Gesù concerns some violins sloppily made toward the end of his short life. Count Cozio di Salabue started the rumor that Guarneri del Gesù killed a man in a fight, perhaps another violin-maker. (Cozio took a dim view of Del Gesù's work: "A third-rank maker whose name is listed here mainly because of the illustrious family name he bears.") It does seem probable that Del Gesù got involved in brawls when one reads his character out of his violins, and the story was snapped up by romantic-minded biographers. Fétis, a man of vivid imagination, writes about the jailer's beautiful daughter falling in love with the dashing Giuseppe. She managed to get wood, tools, and varnish to him in his prison cell, and there he made magnificent, rough, irregularly shaped violins called "prison fiddles," or "prison Josephs." For almost two hundred years this story has been told and retold. Other great men, including Paganini, have similar legends about a prison episode. If the prison story about Del Gesù is true, then why did he make such bad instruments in his cell, where he had time to concentrate on his work? Today no serious expert believes the story. The *"violons de la prison"* were often found to be fake specimens labeled "Guarneri del Gesù"; they showed many eccentricities of the maker's work, but none of his genius.

Yet he did often show a certain disregard for careful work, finish, and execution even earlier in his life. Authentic Del Gesù violins may have something wrong: the f-holes, the edges, the purfling, the scroll. After long and intimate observation one senses that it was not merely Del Gesù's shaking hand: in 1740 he was only forty-two years old, a young man by the standards of the Cremonese makers. Was he seriously sick, or deeply disturbed? There are also marvelous violins of the same time such as the "David" of 1742 on which Jascha Heifetz plays gloriously, or the "Leduc" of about 1743, the concert violin of Henryk Szeryng. Listening to their sonority, depth, and volume of tone, you wonder: could anything be wrong with a man while he made such instruments?

In 1742 Giuseppe del Gesù made the violin that became his most famous, for it remained Nicolò Paganini's favorite instrument. Paganini called it his "Cannon," for its powerful tone. The label it contains is authentic, but the date may have been changed. It is fascinating to see the violin that was played for many years by the man who was the greatest fiddler of all times—great not for his incredible technique but because he invented new possibilities in violin-playing, abruptly advancing the art by a century. As he got fame, he could get almost any violin he wanted, and he had quite a few great instruments made by Stradivari and Guarneri del Gesù. But he always returned to the "Cannon."

For sheer beauty it cannot compare with the finest violins made by Nicolò Amati or Stradivari. It is a well-balanced instrument, virile but not very large, one-sixteenth of an inch under fourteen inches long. The lower and upper bouts are $8\frac{3}{16}$ and $6\frac{5}{8}$ inches wide, the sides at bottom and top are $1\frac{5}{16}$ and $1\frac{3}{16}$. The f-holes are tall, elegant, manly.

The edges are fluted, the purfling quite accurate (by Del Gesù's standards). The varnish is not spectacular, rather soft reddish-brown, and much of it is left even on the back, where it usually wears off. The pine of the top is fine, with rather wide grain, but the maple of the two-piece back is not spectacular. The curves of the upper bouts are rather sloped, but that made no problem for Paganini's large hands and long fingers; the scroll is powerfully cut. There is a lengthwise rut parallel to the E string, alongside the fingerboard; it may have been caused by the bow lying against it in the case, or by Paganini's right thumb, practicing his bravura *pizzicato* passages.

A malaise seems to run through the Guarneri family. It is noticeable when Pietro, in a sharp break with tradition, left his father's house in Cremona and went to play the fiddle in Mantua. It continues when Joseph filius Andreae spent his last years in a void, perhaps away from Cremona, and was not buried in the family grave. The malaise still affects the generation of Guarneri del Gesù, for his brother Pietro also left Cremona and went to work in Venice. The Guarneris were an immensely gifted but restless family.

Giuseppe del Gesù's early violins, those between 1726 and 1730, are well made but not spectacular. The influence of his father can be recognized, and a faint suggestion of Stradivari and Bergonzi. "These violins are not the work of a consummate craftsman whom we should rank with the foremost of the Amati, or Stradivari," the Hills say. These early instruments already possess a certain boldness and originality—many experts call them "virile." Such facile generalizations can be misleading: Nicolò Amati remains remembered for his "feminine" violins, and Del Gesù for his "virile" ones. Some violins made by Antonius and Hieronymus Amati seem to me charming and graceful rather than "feminine."

In his earlier instruments Giuseppe del Gesù didn't use choice wood. He couldn't afford to; his clients were not rich. Dukes and cardinals patronized Stradivari, the doyen of Cremona's violin-makers.

About 1730 begins the short happy period in the life of Guarneri del Gesù. His work shows more order and method than at any other time, and some of his finest violins were made early in the decade. The quality of the wood is getting better, and the varnish is often in beautiful lighter colors, orange or reddish-orange. It is widely believed that Del Gesù's violins are "larger" than Stradivari's; this is because they often sound more powerful and harder to play. Actually Del Gesù usually made rather smaller violins than Stradivaris. The length is less than 14 inches, often 13⅞ inches and sometimes even shorter. His models are flat. The f-holes are elongated, and have a very characteristic feature: Nicolò Amati and Stradivari always carefully determined the position of the f-holes, but Del Gesù seems to have taken a long look, decided on the position of the top and bottom holes, and begun cutting. The f-holes are never alike, and they reflect the strong personality of the artist. The same sense of freedom determined his scrolls; these are never pedantically accurate, often irregular, but always charming. One can almost sense his mood as he made them. It is almost impossible to define correctly the style of his violins. He may give a hint of Amati, of Stradivari, or of the Brescians, but always he remains himself.

In 1735, his best, most prolific year, Del Gesù made sixteen violins, possibly more. After 1735 ". . . the master lets himself go, and it is this very 'abandon,' at times bordering on the audacious, which calls for our admiration" (Hill). Some details may be very strange, but the basic construction is always correct. Del Gesù had all the right instincts, but because he had no patience he could make inaccurate details. He worked fast; after 1740 he seems to have worked even faster. He might have had a premonition of death, for he died in October, 1744, and was buried on the seventeenth in the Church of San Prospero. He was only forty-six, but in these years he had made violins that have been played by the greatest artists and fascinated millions of people with their wonderful, sonorous tone.

Giuseppe del Gesù and his wife had no children. He surely had helpers in his workshop, but we don't know who they were, and he certainly wasn't interested in teaching. He sold his instruments quickly, and for relatively low prices. He must have believed in his works, but did he think they would one day provide the sound of the future? In this connection, a typical Beethoven story tells about the violinist Felice Alessandro Radicati, who went to Vienna in 1818 and at Beethoven's request worked out the fingering for the three Rasumovsky quartets, Opus 59. When Radicati asked the composer, "Surely you don't consider these works to be music?" Beethoven loftily replied, "Oh, they are not for you, but for a later age." Del Gesù may also have known that his violins were for a later age.

Giuseppe del Gesù was "discovered" fifty years after his death, when some violinists became interested in his violins. In tone they were different from a Stainer, an Amati, a Stradivari, and they were less expensive. Nicolas Lupot in Paris, the most famous French luthier of his era, who copied mostly Stradivari models, made in 1806 a fine copy of a Guarneri del Gesù, reproducing the original label (and adding an inscription saying that this copy was made for a certain customer). But Del Gesù's real renaissance was brought about by one man—Paganini. Suddenly every prominent violinist became interested in a Del Gesù violin. The demand soon outran the supply. It was a great time for skilled fakers, and a Del Gesù is easier to imitate than a Stradivari. A Del Gesù fake could be called "eccentric," its shortcomings explained away as "typically Del Gesù." Another "prison fiddle," maybe.

Such fakes are known today, for the demand still outruns the very limited supply. In 1931 the Hills listed only one hundred and forty-seven Del Gesù violins known to them, suggesting there might be thirty or forty more. Guarneri del Gesù probably made less than two hundred and fifty violins—perhaps about two hundred. (By comparison Stradivari, who lived almost twice as long, made perhaps twelve hundred.) No viola, no cello made by Del Gesù are known to exist.

After the great violinists had discovered the magic of Del Gesù, they never changed their mind. Among prominent owners of a Del Gesù since Paganini have been Kreisler, Huberman, Kubelik, Ysaÿe, Vieux-temps, Ole Bull, Alard, Heifetz, Stern, and Szeryng. Among famous Del Gesù violins are the "Kreisler," dated 1733 but perhaps made earlier; the "Devil" ("le violon du Diable"), 1734; "The King," 1735; the Ysaÿe, 1740; the "Alard," 1742; the "David" that will be known as the "Heifetz," 1742; Paganini's "Cannon," probably 1742; the "Leduc," 1743.

Giuseppe Guarneri del Gesù died in October 1744, almost exactly one hundred years after Antonio Stradivari was born. The blessed century gave us the greatest masterpieces. Violins were made after 1744, but never greater ones.

Wine needs time to mature, to reach its full taste and bouquet, and some of the greatest red wines need the most time of all. Violins, too, need time to mature and acquire their full sonority and mellow beauty of tone. No wonder, for wines and wood are both living matter.

Fortunately there are no vintage charts for violins. But it is known by experience that violins with a sweet, softer tone—Jacob Stainers, the small-pattern Amatis, the Amatisé Stradivaris—attain their full power in less time than the large-model works by Stradivari after 1700, and by Guarneri del Gesù, Bergonzi, and Montagnana. Probably no Cremonese violin reached its acoustical potential before it was twenty years old. Stradivari's masterpieces made between 1715 and 1737 needed perhaps sixty years for their full vigor and capacity, and even more for some by Guarneri del Gesù. "Time" for a violin means both age and use. A new violin, made of aged wood, is not mature; the test of the best new violins will come in fifty years. No one can tell now how they will sound.

Guarneri del Gesù's violins were never used by leading violinists during his lifetime. Nicolò Amati and Antonio Stradivari surely had the satisfaction of hearing their instruments played by fine artists, and lived long enough to know how their earlier instruments sounded. Del Gesù never knew that. When he died his early violins were only twenty years old, and probably they didn't respond easily and sounded somewhat hard. Among the first virtuosos to perform on a Guarneri del Gesù was Gaetano Pugnani from Turin (1731–1798), a pupil of Somis and Tartini, and the teacher of Viotti, Bruno, and Polledro— an important link in the history of violin-playing. (He was also a gifted composer, but the well-known *Praeludium and Allegro,* long attributed to him, was composed by Fritz Kreisler.) Pugnani played on a Del Gesù that was probably made in 1734, then perhaps forty years old and not yet in prime condition. The Cremonese violinist, P. Spagnoletti (1761–1834), who became a founding member of the London Philharmonic Society and conducted that orchestra during Paganini's appearances there, also performed on a Del Gesù violin. On January 26, 1770, Mozart wrote to his sister from Milan, "At Cremona, the orchestra is good, and the first violin is named Spagnoletta." He must have meant the father or uncle of Spagnoletti, who was then only nine years old; Mozart's friend and string quartet partner, the composer Karl Ditters von Dittersdorf, mentions Spagnoletti in his autobiography as "a famous violinist from Cremona." The great French virtuoso Pierre Rode (1774–1830) played often on a Guarneri del Gesù made in 1734; he also owned the famous ornamented "Rode" Stradivari, of 1722. The German violinist and composer, Ludwig Spohr, a contemporary of Paganini (both were born in 1784), loved the Guarneri del Gesù which an admirer gave him as a nineteenth-birthday present. It disappeared (for the whole story, see pp. 167–168) in 1805 in Göttingen, when Spohr was on his way to Paris, and he was heartbroken about the loss of his "splendid Guarnerius."

Paganini too was given his beloved Guarneri del Gesù when he was only fifteen, in 1799. The violin was fifty-seven years old, just attaining its maturity. Paganini played on it for forty-one years.

Paganini's contemporaries were ecstatic about the sound of his Guarneri. Fétis writes that "the poetry of the great violinist's playing consisted principally in its brilliancy." Abbé Antoine Sibire wrote in *La Chélonomie, ou le Parfait Luthier* (1806) about the "brilliancy" of a Del Gesù violin: "The E is sparkling, the A is equal in its brilliancy, and the D, likewise brilliant, possesses a certain roundness but the G is dry as an almond. . . . For some time, Guarneri del Gesù's violins have been in favor. One perceives there are some musicians who place them above the Stradivari itself, so much does the extraordinary brilliance of the first three strings impose upon their ears. It is a great pity that this unhappy G string exhausts itself for the ungrateful others." Paganini had no problem with the G string of his Del Gesù; his wizardry with G-string playing was part of his fame. Had the abbé (who died in 1826) heard Paganini perform the *Prayer from Rossini's "Moses,"* a theme and variations on the G string, he might have changed his mind. Ignaz Moscheles, the famous pianist, heard Paganini in London in 1831 and writes, "the long-drawn, soul-searching tone . . . always his own and unique," one of our best descriptions of Paganini's tone. The Hills summed it up, "The tone of the Del Gesù violin impresses us as one of intense brilliancy, allied to concentrated power. Verging towards the metallic quality on the E and G strings, the A and D possess that 'full body' which supplies so desirable an adjunct to the tone of the middle strings."

The argument about which is preferable, the tone of a Guarneri del Gesù or a Stradivari, will never be settled. Fétis called the Guarneri tone "stronger than Stradivari," an opinion still shared by many people. Comparative tests have proved that the strength of tone depends on the player. After the experiment of recording fifteen famous violins from Cremona, among them six Stradivaris and five by Guarneri del Gesù, Ruggiero Ricci wrote,

> A Stradivari generally requires a more gentle and coaxing approach than does a Guarneri. With a Strad the note change is often more fluid. The sound of the Guarneri, on the other hand, has more core and often permits greater intensity in playing. One can dig with the bow and sob or break on the note as Italian tenors do. . . .

Ricci also admits, "Personally, I am in the Guarneri camp," which reduces his value as a witness. It is probably a fact that the full sonority of a great Guarneri can be brought out only by a strong left hand and incisive bowing. Arnold Gingrich, a thoughtful amateur fiddler (who admits being in the Stradivari camp), wrote,

> Generalizations are probably as unreliable in this field as in any other but in general it does seem to work out that the fiddlers fall into two broad categories—those who have a natural affinity for the Strad and those who love the Guarneri. The division is about as accurate, say, as the division of mankind into introverts and extroverts, with the former preferring the Strad and latter the Guarneri.

One could go on and on. Most wine-lovers prefer either Bordeaux or Burgundy; could it be that wine-loving violin-lovers in the Stradivari camp have an affinity for the elegant, refined, velvety wines of Bordeaux, while the Guarneri fans instinctively prefer the full-bodied, fruity, heavier wines of Burgundy? In my case it works out: I am in the Stradivari-Bordeaux camp. I perceive the Guarneri tone as the glorification of the dark, sonorous, penetrating sound of the Brescians, while Stradivari seems the culmination of the sweet, beautiful, velvety Amati tone. Each of us hears his own ideal sound in his "inner" ear, and it involves instinct, emotion, and tonal psychology more than intellect or reasoning. A Guarneri del Gesù is often sought by great soloists who must rely on the sonority of an instrument against the power of the modern orchestra. But amateurs and collectors, who love the violin for its sound and also for its beauty, often instinctively prefer a Stradivari. We violin-lovers are lucky to have such a choice.

Giuseppe del Gesù's older brother, Pietro, generally called "Pietro of Venice" to distinguish him from his uncle "Pietro of Mantua," was born in Cremona on April 14, 1695. He worked first with his father, Joseph filius Andreae, and stayed in his shop until 1718. The following year he is not mentioned in his father's census return. During the next years, almost nothing is known about him. The labels in his instruments say he was in Venice after 1725. Where was he between ages twenty-three and thirty?

Pietro may have left home for various reasons; we know that life wasn't happy in the Guarneri house; and there is the mystery of the last ten years of his father's whereabouts. In 1720 his uncle Pietro died in Mantua. Some have speculated that the nephew went to Mantua to close up the workshop and perhaps to complete some remaining half-finished instruments. Of the violins which young Pietro made in Cremona, or which bear original labels dated 1720 and 1721, only a handful survive. They are somewhat enigmatic, influenced by Stradivari rather than the Guarneris. Some features—sound holes and scroll— show considerable originality. Perhaps the influence of Stradivari explains Pietro's departure from Cremona: like other makers, he may have felt that a young man had no chance there as long as old Stradivari was alive.

Venice was a sensible choice. It was an important musical center, much larger than Mantua, and about 1720 there were at least a dozen theaters performing opera, as well as orchestras, conservatories, and musical groups. Monteverdi had left Mantua to become maestro di cappella at the Church of San Marco in 1613. In 1637, the first commercially run opera house in history was opened in Venice, in the parish of San Cassiano; it was not subsidized by a prince or cardinal for the happy few, and anyone could go who bought a ticket. Its first manager was Claudio Monteverdi. The composer from Cremona surely knew about the astonishing development of instrument-making in his hometown. He was an accomplished violist, and used violins in the orchestra scores of his operas. His dramatic genius and musical gifts made Venice a city of opera fans.

The musicians who came to Venice from everywhere needed the makers of musical instruments—lutes, guitars, viols, and finally violins. By the time Pietro arrived in Venice, the Venetian school of violin-making was second only to Cremona. If Pietro left Cremona because of the competition, it may have been a shock to discover that in Venice too the competition was considerable. Domenico Montagnana, Santo Seraphin, Francesco Gobetti, Carlo Tononi, and Matteo Gofriller, all were busy, and together formed the Venetian school.

Pietro may have worked for Santo Seraphin and Carlo Tononi; their influence can be seen in some of his violins, and the severe Venetian guild laws required him to work for some time with a master or dealer accredited in that city. This may explain why he was more influenced by the Venetian school than by the early training he'd received in his father's shop in Cremona. And he was still in his twenties, an age when one is subject to various influences.

The first instrument he made in Venice was a cello, in 1725. It shows him under the wing of Stradivari, although the varnish, red and soft and rather heavy, points toward Montagnana. During the next years he still worked along the lines of Stradivari, but his finish, varnish, and general workmanship were already close to the Venetian masters. He rarely uses beautifully patterned wood; perhaps the finest wood was cornered by the most successful Venetian makers, Montagnana and Santo Seraphin, and Pietro had to take what was left. But occasionally he was lucky. One of his most beautiful violins, made after 1735, has a beautifully figured one-piece back; the varnish is applied with great skill; and the sound holes are very characteristic. It was the favorite instrument of Henri Wieniawski, the eminent Polish artist, during his last seven years, and later the concert instrument of the Hungarian violinist Jenö Hubay. Pietro made several more cellos; nearly all Venetian makers excelled in the production of cellos for the local orchestra musicians. Many Venetian composers wrote solo pieces for the cello.

After 1740 Pietro Guarneri made mostly violins. The outlines often recall Amati, Stradivari, or Santo Seraphin, but many details show the influence of Pietro of Mantua (some have actually been attributed to the celebrated uncle). Experts recognize a Guarneri family resemblance in the scrolls. One masterpiece made in 1743, called the "Baron

Knoop" because it was in the collection of that English enthusiast, later came to the Hämmerle Collection in Austria, and finally to the Hottinger Collection in New York; the violin has a one-piece back of beautifully patterned maple, and the varnish, a deep golden brown, is applied with loving care.

Oddly, Pietro of Venice, who seems influenced by several masters, shows no trace in his work of his celebrated brother, Del Gesù—another psychological enigma that will probably never be explained. Perhaps Pietro was not on friendly terms with his brother; all the Guarneris were difficult, and Del Gesù was certainly especially so.

Pietro married Angiola Maria Ferari in Venice in 1728; they had five sons and five daughters, but none of the sons followed the father's profession. When Pietro died in Venice, on April 19, 1762, the Guarneri dynasty came to an end. (Del Gesù had died eighteen years before.) The great days of the Cremonese school ended with Carlo Bergonzi in 1747, and now the great days of Venice were over. The rich in Italy were less rich, and fewer fine violins were in demand. Less expensive instruments continued to be made in Milan and Naples, and the great Italians came to be well imitated by able makers in France, England, Germany, and the Netherlands. "Petrus Guarnerius filius Joseph," as he called himself on his labels, was the last master of a great era.

No More Secrets—
Wood and Varnish

The violin is made of wood. It weighs between nine and ten ounces. For centuries, violin-makers and experts have argued about the wood which the great masters selected, and about the influence of the wood on the tone quality of their instruments. Theories were developed about "magical" properties of certain "resonant" woods. It was claimed that the Amatis, Stradivari, and the Guarneris could just look at a piece of wood and know exactly how it would sound. The old masters were credited with mysterious knowledge of acoustics that guided them to select "miraculous" material. Some modern makers who have not yet produced instruments with the tonal excellence of the Cremonese have claimed it's partly the wood; they say they can't get the wood which the Cremonese used "because it no longer exists."

The argument was started by F. J. Fétis, the famous nineteenth-century musicologist. His father had been an able amateur fiddler. Fétis became fascinated by the violin and an authority on the subject, after writing a book on Stradivari. Nowadays he sometimes sounds pompous and prejudiced. In 1865 he wrote,

Maple and deal are the constituent elements of the violin: which woods present infinite varieties, by reason of the different countries which produce them, and the climate under which their growth is developed. The maple used by the old Italian makers came from Croatia, Dalmatia, and even from Turkey. It was sent to Venice. The deal [pine] employed by the Cremonese makers was selected from the southern side of the mountains of southern Switzerland and the Tyrol. Stradivarius generally chose those parts of it in which the fibers were small, straight, slightly separated, and always placed perpendicularly to the plane of the violin.

Nothing is incidental in the violin, that marvel of mathematics and physics, chemistry and acoustics. The smallest part has its purpose, and the principles of design, size, and form have been tried and tested for centuries. Wood is no dead matter. Its cells are alive. Its qualities change. Naturally, the great makers knew the importance of the proper selection of the right wood. They aged their wood, storing it in light, moderately damp rooms. The oxygen in the air affects the tannic acid in the wood, and this process may take from ten to twenty years. It cannot be speeded up artificially by modern techniques. But some people's excuse that certain varieties of wood are no longer available can no longer be accepted. Their prominent spokesman was George Hart, the London dealer and expert, who wrote in 1887,

> There can be no doubt whatever that the Cremonese and Brescian artists were exceedingly careful in their choice of material, and their discrimination in this particular matter does not appear to have been exercized so much from a regard for the beauty as for the acoustic properties of the wood . . . The old masters seem to have preferred to retain a piece of wood of known acoustic properties rather than to work in a better preserved portion at the probable expense of tone.

A statement introduced by "there can be no doubt" may easily become gospel. But in 1902 it was refuted by the brothers Hill, who wrote in their book on Stradivari that they "failed to perceive his [*George Hart's*] remarkable discrimination," and went on: "These Brescian and Cremonese masters were purely and simply working artisans, guided by practical experience and the circumstances of the moment. When well remunerated, either in money or patronage, they did their best, and used the finest material then obtainable, and vice versa. . . ." Specifically, they pointed out, "that he [Stradivari] possessed any special knowledge other than that of an intelligent craftsman . . . we are constrained to deny." (There goes another bit of *mystique.*) "We unhesitatingly assert that modern violin-makers have a choice of material equal in every respect to that which existed at the time of Stradivari, and of infinitely greater variety." It can be concluded that great violins do not result from any materials—wood and varnish—but from the genius who made them. The best makers, including J. B. Vuillaume, have always admitted this.

The early Brescians used pine for the tops, and poplar, lime, pear, or cedar for the backs, sides, and heads of their instruments. Andrea Amati and Paolo Maggini used maple for their backs; this is harder wood than those previously used. Maple remains sturdy even when cut thinner; it would produce a brighter, stronger tone in the instrument and its wavelike patterns and figures could be very beautiful. Most of the maple came from local forests in Lombardy, and there were large pine woods near Brescia. The first Amatis—Andrea and his sons, Antonius and Hieronymus—used local maple with a rather small-figured curl. Only when Nicolò Amati became prosperous and got higher prices for his instruments did he begin to buy foreign maple with its beautiful broader markings; much of it came from Venice, where hard maple was used for the interiors and the oars of gondolas. Imported wood was more expensive than the local varieties, and pieces with strikingly handsome patterns commanded extra prices. For the backs the wood was cut either on the quarter (following the grain) or on the slab (across the grain). Some of the most beautiful Stradivari violins have backs cut on the quarter, in one piece or in two. The Guarneris couldn't afford very expensive wood. Joseph filius Andreae often used poplar, lime, and even beechwood for his backs. Giuseppe del Gesù used poplar, willow, beech, or maple for his backs, but rarely pieces of exceptional beauty. In Venice Montagnana and Santo Seraphin, who got good prices and probably had excellent wood suppliers, sometimes worked with very beautiful maple. In short, a violin-maker got the sort of wood he was able to pay for.

That nonsense about "magical" wood was created by people who considered the great makers "magicians." Actually the violin-makers were excellent craftsmen and practical artisans; some became great artists also. They knew about wood and selected the qualities they could afford, but they had no supernatural powers of divining sound in pinewood. Stradivari's late instruments may have magnificent sound, but he often used less beautiful wood than in his earlier "golden" period, when his superb fine-grained pine and maple made stunning pictorial patterns.

A violin depends on three components: construction, wood, and varnish. The Cremonese violin-makers rarely used wood less than ten years old. Vuillaume sometimes used wood from old torn-down buildings for his copies of Cremonese instruments, but this does not prove the superiority of old wood. True, bad wood will not make a fine violin. But if the construction is faultless, good wood—not exceptional—will suffice. A modern maker who will pay the price can get fine, sonorous pine and handsome maple; the trees are still growing. Only the genius of the Cremonese makers seems to be missing.

No component of the violin is more mysterious than the varnish. The importance of the varnish is unquestioned; a well-constructed violin, made of good wood, can be tonally ruined by a bad varnish. But much of what has been written about the "secret" of old Cremonese varnish is nonsense. "Today most people who are interested in the making of violins know that the 'secret' only conceals ignorance," writes Konrad Leonhardt in 1969 in his scientific book, *Geigenbau und Klangfarbe* (Violin-Making and Tone Color). Professor Leonhardt is the director of the School for Violin-making in Mittenwald, Bavaria (pp. 149–151). "Somehow the profession of the violin-maker has become the expression of an enigma." Seventy years ago the Hills wrote in their Stradivari biography about "the ever-ready pens and fluent tongues of the many self-constituted authorities." Dario d'Attili says, "The composition of the Cremonese varnish is a 'secret' only to those who cannot reproduce it. The varnish formula has been rediscovered nearly every week for the past hundred and fifty years. The discoverers of the 'secret' are members of the largest club in the violin world." The search for Stradivari's "secret formula" for varnish has been as ardent as for the elixir of eternal youth—and as unsuccessful. Concerning varnish, legend must be strictly separated from fact, and exact science from wishful thinking.

In older days most experts believed that varnish was used a) to preserve the wood, b) to give the instrument a beautiful appearance. They were right, but not completely right; recently a connection between varnish and the tone color of string instruments has been definitely established. Twin instruments by the same maker, one varnished and the other unvarnished, were tested behind a curtain; experts discovered no difference in tone quality. But after a few years the "white" violin lost its tone, the varnished one preserved it. Complicated electronic tests have established the influence of oil varnish and alcohol varnish on the tone of an instrument, and also the influence of such secondary parts as fingerboard and chinrest.

Some earlier experts underrated the importance of varnish. They believed that tone depended mainly on the construction of an instrument, and on the quality of the wood. They rightly pointed out that a strong curvature accounts for a sweet, softer tone, while a flat construction results in a harsh, stronger tone. Naturally a badly constructed violin will not sound well even if made of the finest wood and coated with exquisite varnish.

But the varnish will give a well-made violin its distinctive timbre. The oboelike tone quality of a Stradivari is quite different from the French-horn-like sound of a Guarneri del Gesù. Some soloists now use both a Stradivari and a Guarneri for performances. (Henryk Szeryng plays Mozart on his Stradivari of 1732, and Brahms on his "Leduc" Del Gesù of 1743. But not every soloist is able to switch from one instrument to the other.)

Unfortunately the original varnish disappears in time, usually worn off on the right-hand side of the back, where the left hand rests, and on the top, where the chinrest often leaves a mark. But varnish is so important for a violin that even what remains of it after three hundred years helps preserve its particular tone color.

J. B. Vuillaume made copies of violins by Stradivari and Guarneri del Gesù that look exactly like the originals but don't sound like them. In fact, Vuillaume's copies both have a distinctive timbre which is the tone of neither the Stradivari nor the Guarneri, but the Vuillaume tone. The same goes for Vuillaume's Amati copies. And no wonder; while Vuillaume copied the Cremonese instruments so exactly that only genuine experts can distinguish the copy from the original, he did not have the exact method of Cremonese varnishing. It is a method, not a "secret." Vuillaume used his own varnish for all his copies; as a result all Vuillaume violins sound somewhat alike. The formidable French maker caused sleepless nights for collectors and students, experts and violinists, all wondering whether their "Cremonese" violin may have been made by Vuillaume. But he unwittingly helped to prove the influence of the varnish on violin tone.

Once the principle of varnish is understood, it can be confirmed by experiments. Carlo Bergonzi often followed Stradivari's design for his violins, but Bergonzi's violins sound more like Guarneri's because Bergonzi's varnish resembles Guarneri's. Guadagnini constructed his best violins along the lines of Stradivari, but they don't sound like Stradivari; they have the Guadagnini sound, because he had his own method of varnishing.

David Laurie, the English oil man who became a noted violin expert, writes amusingly about the varnish of Vuillaume, "the finest modern maker": every Thursday Vuillaume had open house for his admirers, many of them amateur violin-makers, at his Paris residence, a château in the rue des Ternes (actually he received his guests in a glass-paneled greenhouse). Vuillaume was wearing a working blouse and varnishing a fiddle; a pot of varnish stood before him, and at the other end of the bench stood bottles filled with varnish, for sale. They went like hot cakes, and Vuillaume happily put the money away. After the guests had gone, Laurie (having been asked to stay) accompanied Vuillaume to his real workroom at the château. There Vuillaume ("of medium height and meager in body, like Stradivarius; he was all muscle, which made him capable of undergoing the greatest fatigue in his favorite occupation") quickly removed the new varnish he'd just put on the fiddle. He was amused about Laurie's astonishment, explaining that it would be foolish to give away his own varnish. He said he was selling a decent varnish to these amateur luthiers, but his real varnish was something else again. He never gave Laurie the exact recipe, though they became friends. The varnish, in Laurie's description,

> . . . was more like a paint . . . very delicate and easily peeled, when exposed even to a mild heat. I have seen it curl up like brown paper when

near a fire. Now and then Vuillaume had a superior quality which was only used on special instruments and this was generally, although not invariably, magnificent in its suppleness, purity and color . . . very like that on some of the best of the beautiful Peter Guarnerius instruments.

The composition of Cremonese varnish is no secret: in principle it consisted of gums soluble in oil, with coloring ingredients added. The principle is known to all violin-makers, professional or amateur (of whom there are said to be two thousand in Sweden alone; no one knows how many there are in the United States; at Wurlitzer's, in New York, they sell quantities of varnishing ingredients). But the question is: exactly how much of each ingredient, and what to do with them? It's like the blending of a famous brand of Champagne; the great houses in Reims and Épernay make a distinctive blend year after year, each quite different from the competitors' products. This is done by blending a number of slightly different wines (all grown in the Champagne district) until the special bouquet is achieved by experts with extraordinary palates. They do it year after year; though the various wines are never quite the same, they manage somehow to mix a blend that has the "taste of the firm"—because they know how. Unfortunately in the case of the old Italian varnish, no one knows any longer the exact blend and the exact method.

In a small town like Cremona in 1700, few professional secrets could be kept. The aristocrats of the violin-makers' guild around Piazza San Domenico knew the ingredients of the varnish and how to apply it. But, as in the case of the Champagne-blenders, each house had its semi-secret ways of doing things—the supposedly best proportion of the ingredients, whether to mix them hot, lukewarm, or cold, and how to apply the varnish. It was no accident that some masters who were never in Cremona—Jacob Stainer from the Austrian Tyrol, David Tecchler from Augsburg—also used a fine varnish. The Brescia masters knew about varnish long before Stradivari was born. Perhaps their knowledge came from the early sixteenth-century lute-makers who, in turn, may have learned from artists of the Renaissance. In Cremona, Andrea Amati made a fine, translucent varnish and applied it beautifully to his violins made around the middle of the sixteenth century. Four generations of Amatis have since given yellow hues to the shade now known as "Amati yellow." When Stradivari broke away from the influence of his teacher Nicolò Amati, he began using reddish tints, perhaps to make his instruments look different.

Modern science fails paradoxically to provide conclusive analysis of old Italian varnish. Bits of Stradivari's varnish have been analyzed chemically and studied under the microscope with no success, since the ingredients had long been oxidized. Charles Reade wrote about the "lost art" of Stradivari's varnishing,

> . . . I found in the chippiest varnish of Stradivarius, viz., his dark red varnish, the key to all the varnish of Cremona, red or yellow . . . Look at this dark red varnish, and use your eyes. What do you see? A red varnish, which chips readily off what people call the bare wood. But . . . it is not bare wood. Bare wood turns a dirty brown with age; this is a rich and lovely yellow . . . It is not bare wood, but highly varnished wood. The varnish is evidently oil, and contains a gum. Allowing for the tendency for oil to run into the wood, I should say four coats of oil varnish. And they call this bare wood . . .

Reade believed that Stradivari, after using an oil varnish for the groundwork, and filling the pores of the wood, had then used a coloring matter in a solution of alcohol; this would indicate that Stradivari's varnish—part oil, part alcohol—was not homogeneous. Today this theory is discarded because Stradivari's varnish is absolutely homogeneous though sometimes chippy; highly colored varnishes are usually more chippy than the lighter-colored ones. Some of the chippiness is due to the lack of adhesion to the ground or filler varnish, but doubtless Stradivari used a pure oil varnish. George Hart wrote:

> A violin varnished with a fine oil varnish takes time to mature, and will not bear forcing in any way. At first the instrument is somewhat muffled, as the pores of the wood have become impregnated with oil. This makes the instrument heavy both in weight and sound, but, as time rolls on, the oil dries, leaving the wood mellowed and wrapped in an elastic covering which yields to the tone of the instrument, and imparts to it much of its own softness.

The coloring matter also influenced the tone; the old masters knew that certain coloring matters affected it more than others, and never used acid to stain the wood because it too would hurt the instrument's tone. They understood that a string instrument must look beautiful as well as sound beautiful. Prominent dealers have always agreed that it is easier to sell a violin that both looks well and sounds well, than one whose fine tone is not matched by its appearance. The old masters may occasionally have sacrificed a little tone for beauty; this was often an economic problem, not merely an aesthetic dilemma. Guarneri del Gesù, who cared more about the tone of his violins than about money, aimed for beauty of sound rather than appearance. He never got the prices paid to Nicolò Amati or Stradivari, whose instruments are almost always beautiful.

Stradivari's varnish is never heavy, always soft and transparent. No one knows how he achieved the broken-up effect on the back of many of his violins, where the varnish seems to play and dance as one moves the violin. Perhaps the passage of time has helped to do this. Stradivari, who understood the secret of a violin's beauty, would be pleased to see his fine violins today. They look more charming and mysterious than when he made them. Time, the great helper, cannot be speeded up artificially.

It is a fact that violin-makers cannot obtain the resins and dyestuffs used by the old masters. Stradivari's supplies came from Venice, where originally Marco Polo had brought from the Orient certain substances such as "dragon's blood," a dark red, gummy substance derived from the fruit of the Malayan palm tree. Such substances are now available only in synthetic form, and many other raw materials are refined and "purified" before they are sold. But perhaps it is not so much the ingredients that have changed. It's the method.

The great Cremonese makers were patient. As they were men of artistic perception, they knew that the freshly varnished instruments must be exposed gradually to subdued light. They didn't violate the laws of nature by hanging their violins to dry in plain sunshine. (The makers of fine wines, too, know that the natural process of fermentation, and later of maturing young wine in the cask, must not be hurried, otherwise the wine might revolt.) In one of the two hand-written letters known to exist, Stradivari writes, "I beg you will forgive the delay concerning the violin, caused by the varnishing of the large cracks so that the sun may not re-open them." Oil varnish takes much more time to dry than alcohol varnish, even in the sunny climate of Cremona.

After the death of Stradivari in 1737 and of Guarneri del Gesù and

Carlo Bergonzi a few years later, the violinists' outlook in Cremona and elsewhere in Italy began to change. There were many customers for new violins and they didn't want to wait. Rich princes of the Church and noblemen ordered instruments. The demand surpassed the supply, and violin-makers began to work faster. They wanted the money, and some may have underestimated the importance of slowly drying their varnish. Around 1770, only a little over thirty years after the death of Stradivari, the last violins were varnished in Milan in the Cremonese manner; J. B. Guadagnini in Turin, perhaps specifically exhorted by Count Cozio, still varnished his violins with loving care and put them up for slow drying in the 1780s. But by 1800 the method was no longer practiced. The gums dissolved so much more readily in alcohol, and an alcohol varnish would dry fast. The decline of the mixture concurred with the decline in the technique of applying the varnish. Varnish that is applied too thickly mutes the tone of an instrument. Hard, alcoholic varnish gives it a harder tone. The difficulty is to find the right medium and apply the varnish in such a way that the instrument will have a better tone in thirty or fifty years. A violin must vibrate. The composition and application of the varnish have their influence on the degree of vibration. The Cremonese masters must have sensed—with the instinct of great creators—exactly how time would influence their varnish and, through the varnish, the tone of the instrument. Here again we approach the borderline between science and metaphysics. Nicolas Lupot, who made very good copies of some Stradivari violins, applied heavily his rather soft varnish. His violins may look like Stradivaris but today they have a somewhat muted tone.

Every detail of Stradivari's greatest violins is executed with near perfection, but it is the varnish which is most admired. He probably first applied a foundation varnish of golden yellow. After it dried, he covered it with a layer of red varnish. Did he foresee that two hundred years later this mixture would result in the "flaming" reddish-brown nuances which we admire today? No one can tell. But, as Charles Reade said, use your eyes. Stradivari's varnish seems alive with an inner fire, and one never tires of looking at it. As one turns the instrument in the light, there are always new, exciting changes in its radiance. Looking at the back of a beautiful Stradivari is like looking out at the ever-changing sea.

When the Hills published their famous biography of Stradivari in 1902, they were convinced that his formula for varnish was still in existence. They had met Giacomo Stradivari (1822–1901), Antonio's great-great-grandson, who told them that he had seen the legendary formula:

> I was a boy when my father died, and a few years later it was decided that our family should remove to another house. As a consequence, all our belongings were turned over. In the course of looking through old books, my eye was arrested by this Bible, and, opening it, I read the writing inside the cover. I had heard repeated mention made of the skill of my famous ancestor, and of the fame of the varnish he had used. Here, then, was the prescription for the same. I grasped the importance of my discovery, and determined to take possession of the book without mentioning the matter even to my mother. But how to hide this bulky volume I knew not; so forthwith I resolved, firstly to make a faithful copy of the prescription—it was dated 1704—and then to destroy the book, which I did.

This sounds like another romantic legend, but the Hills spoke to Giacomo Stradivari on several occasions and said they had "no reason to doubt the sincerity of his statements." He admitted to them that "he perceived the foolishness of his act of destroying the only absolute proof of the veracity of his story. But as he truly remarked, 'Young people cannot possess the wisdom of their elders.' "

There the matter rests, for Giacomo Stradivari never confided the secret to anyone else. He wrote to Alfonso Mandelli, a former mayor of Cremona and an authority on Stradivari, that he had never showed the formula of the varnish to anybody ("You may consider it an eccentricity on my part"). Back in 1848, a penniless refugee from the Habsburg police in Turin because he'd been a follower of Garibaldi, refused a Frenchman's offer of fifty Napoleons for the formula ("And bear in mind that at that time fifty Napoleons would have been as so many brothers to me, yet still I had the courage to resist the temptation"). He also refused offers from Vuillaume and Count Castelbarco (and perhaps from the Hills).

Does the formula still exist, and where is it? In 1948, when I met Mario Stradivari in Cremona, he told me that he owned no instrument nor any relic from his immortal ancestor. He admitted that he knew nothing about the secret formula of the varnish. He made this statement late at night, after he and I and the noted Stradivari scholar Renzo Bacchetta had had a lot of local wine, and I am sure he told me the truth.

Dario d'Attili says, "I've made varnish all my life. I would dream about varnish and wake up. I kept paper and pencil at my bedside. I would get up and try what I'd just dreamed, but now, thirty years later, I am wiser and sadder. I don't know what is right, but I know what is wrong. The more I learned, the more frustrated I became. I would grade my varnish from 1 to 10, depending on visual appeal, texture, wear, chip, elasticity, and so on. I usually wound up between 5 and 7½, never higher. I give the Amatis and Stradivari 10 points, but not one later maker. The last true classical varnish is found on some instruments made after 1800 in the school of Venice. Perhaps they had learned the secret from Pietro Guarneri, Montagnana, Santo Seraphin.

"Perhaps one of the big problems is that while a painter is concerned with opacity—he puts colors on the canvas, he thinks of color, not of the canvas—the violin-maker is concerned only with transparency. He thinks of the wood underneath. He uses only such colors as will mix with certain ingredients and can be applied and are inoffensive to vibrations. Perhaps that is the reason why violins are colored from yellow to brown to red. Even Stradivari couldn't control the exact shades.

"After a lifetime of experimenting, I haven't the slightest idea what went into a Cremonese varnish, and exactly how it was made."

The books on violin-making contain many recipes for varnish. There is nothing secret about it: for the oil varnish, which is elastic and doesn't evaporate as quickly as alcohol varnish, turpentine and lavender are often given as ingredients. Linseed oil is added for firmness. Usually, the violin is first stained with wood vinegar, potash, or other extracts, and takes on a brownish color. Then several foundations of a mixture of white shellac and soft resin are applied, to which pumice and oil may be added. For reddish color, "dragon's blood" from India or South America, gum-lac, or santalic acid is used; for brown color, cashew or aloe oil; for a yellow, gamboge or turmeric. Several layers of this coat are applied, very thinly. After the instrument is dry a tinting varnish is applied, which is then polished or ground; its ingredients are orange shellac mixed with turpentine, mastic, or sandarine. Some new violins have a very fine varnish, and it will be interesting to hear how they sound in fifty or a hundred years.

Some modern violin-makers try to return to the methods of the Cremonese makers. They work under similar conditions in a dry, warm climate; they mix their varnish from the best ingredients they can obtain, apply it with great care, and permit their instruments to dry slowly, exposing them gradually to light and giving them plenty of time as the old masters did. It would be absurd to compare their violins with the Cremonese instruments which are two hundred and fifty years old and have been played for many, many years. Use and time have given them the beauty, warmth, and sonorous tone we love today. Let's not forget that a great Italian violin is the result of its maker's art and of the flow of time, and there's no substitute for time.

⚕Other Italian Makers

The "golden age" of Cremona lasted less than two hundred years: Andrea Amati's earliest surviving violins were made around 1550; Stradivari died in 1737; Hieronymus II, the last of the Amatis, in 1740; Giuseppe Guarneri del Gesù in 1744.

The golden age of Cremona ranks with the Periclean epoch of Athens, the High Renaissance in Florence, and the era of Classicism in musical Vienna—all of them glorious, brief climaxes in Western civilization.

Fine violins were still made. In Cremona Lorenzo Storioni, Joannes Rotta, and the younger Carlo Bergonzi, grandson of the great Bergonzi, continued the tradition. The last Cremonese maker, Enrico Ceruti, died on October 23, 1883. But for some reason no violin made after the late 1740s surpassed the heritage of Nicolò Amati, Antonio Stradivari, and Guarneri del Gesù, though there were gifted masters who made very good and occasionally great instruments.

Francesco Ruggieri (his name is also written Ruger, Rugier,

Rudger, Ruggier, Rugeri, Ruggeri, Ruggerius) was one of Nicolò Amati's best pupils. He called himself on his labels "Rugier detto il Per." His first instruments are dated 1650. He lived in Cremona at No. 7, Contrada del Coltellai, and perhaps he was born there. His birth date is not known; he died in Cremona around 1720. After leaving the workshop of Nicolò Amati he still followed the "grand pattern" model of his teacher, but gradually he evolved his own style with wider lower bouts and somewhat higher arching. His sound holes are shorter than Amati's. His choice of wood is mostly good, and the finish very fine; he carved beautiful scrolls. His varnish is brilliant, often orange-yellow like most of the Amatis', and sometimes there are exciting reddish highlights. Ruggieri's violins have a rich, mellow sonority. Ludwig Spohr advised his pupils to try to get a Francesco Ruggieri violin if they couldn't afford an Amati, Stradivari, or Guarneri, and that is still good advice today. Ruggieri's cellos, however, are now very expensive. His two sons Giacinto and Vincenzo continued the profession, making instruments on their father's model. Vincenzo also made good cellos and violas. In Vienna Prince Lichnowsky gave Beethoven a viola made in 1690 by Vincenzo Ruggieri, now preserved in Bonn in the house where Beethoven was born.

Carlo Bergonzi is considered one of the important violin-makers in Cremona, ranked closest to the great triumvirate by many experts. He was born in Cremona in 1683 and died there in 1747, three years after the death of Guarneri del Gesù. He lived near the homes of the Amatis, Stradivari, and Del Gesù. For a long time it was accepted as fact that he was Stradivari's favorite pupil—his only pupil except his sons, Francesco and Omobono. As recently as 1951 René Vannes calls Bergonzi "the most distinguished pupil of Stradivari." In 1902 the Hills ventured the opinion that the two sons "and possibly Carlo Bergonzi" worked with Stradivari. ("Possibly—and that seems to us the only hypothesis—Stradivari permitted them to rough out the work, and went all over it after them, thus removing all traces of their cooperation.") But in 1932, in their standard work on the Guarneri family, the Hills had second thoughts on Bergonzi:

> The accepted dictum that Bergonzi was a pupil of Stradivari—a dictum to which we ourselves subscribed at the period of our "Life of Stradivari,"

has never been supported by evidence. And the more we have been given the opportunity to reconsider the point, the less we are disposed to allow it to continue unopposed. . . . Nor are we today in a position to offer any positive evidence connecting Bergonzi with Giuseppe Guarneri del Gesù. Yet, when in searching for proof of affinity of workmanship, we do find there exists much to connect the three men. The assumed relationship with Guarneri rests on conjecture only; and as . . . in the case of Guarneri del Gesù, statements were light-heartedly made, accepted and repeated.

This proves again that the greatest experts on the violin, of whom there are few, rarely agree on anything and never on everything. And only the best have the courage to admit that they might have been mistaken; eventually, the Hills reached the conclusion that Bergonzi was probably closer to Del Gesù than to Stradivari. This vindicates the judgment of the earlier English expert, George Hart, who wrote in 1875,

The work of Carlo Bergonzi is now pretty well understood; in England, particularly, we have some splendid specimens. I need only ask the unbiased connoisseur if he can reconcile one of these instruments with those of Stradivari at the period named. I have no hesitation in saying that there is not one feature in common.

Yet the opinion persists that Bergonzi was "Stradivari's favorite pupil." The two makers were competitors, and perhaps friends. When Paolo Stradivari, the master's youngest son and heir, moved from the house to a better location in 1746, he offered it to Bergonzi. This was a businesslike arrangement; after he died the following year, his family kept the house until 1758.

Carlo Bergonzi made relatively few instruments, perhaps less than one hundred, and only violins. (It is now established that he made no violas or cellos.) Owing to their rarity Bergonzi's violins are expensive, but "only in his best efforts does he rank in sound and value with the middle range of Stradivari's and del Gesu's violins" (Dario d'Attili). On his labels ("Anno 1741 Carlo Bergonzi fece in Cremona") there is no mention of his being a pupil of Stradivari, which would even then have increased the price of his instruments. His finest violins are masterpieces, made of the finest wood, beautifully designed, gracefully finished, and elegant. The varnish, often thick but always transparent, has sometimes a cloudlike pattern, and the colors vary from reddish-brown to amber. Luigi Tarisio, the amazing dealer who saw almost all great Cremonese instruments, loved a 1733 Bergonzi violin so much that he never sold it.

After Bergonzi's death his son Michelangelo took over the workshop but didn't live up to his father's greatness. He made violins, double basses, guitars, and mandolins. His son, Carlo Bergonzi II (1780–1838), made some good violins.

The last eighteenth-century maker in Cremona was Lorenzo Storioni, 1751–1801. He used fine wood, and followed the Guarneri model, but his yellow-orange or red varnish doesn't match the beauty of the earlier Cremonese. Perhaps he didn't take the time for oil varnish and used the fast-drying spirit varnish of other makers. The sound holes are unusual, but the tone of his violins is very good, especially those made between 1775 and 1795. (Henri Vieuxtemps performed on a Storioni.) He also made a few beautiful cellos and double basses, and his violas are very expensive today.

No city comes close to Cremona as *the* great violin town, but several great masters worked in Venice, that rich and cultured city whose people loved beauty and beautiful things. Santo Seraphin (Serafin, Seraphino) was born in nearby Udine in 1668 or later. He came to Venice in 1709, and died there about 1748. His labels say ("Sanctus Seraphinus Nicolai Amati Cremonensis Alumnus Faciebat Udine . . .") he was a pupil of Nicolò Amati: later he used the label "Sanctus Seraphin Utinensis Fecit Venetijs . . .", with no mention of his teacher. His work shows the influence of Jacob Stainer—the outline, curvature of the top, the shape of the waist Cs, even the f-holes. His varnish is yellow-brown or a beautiful red, and his careful execution is compared to Nicolò Amati and Stradivari. His violins have a mellow, even tone; he also made beautiful cellos and a few double basses. Not many of his instruments survive, and their price is very high. His nephew, Santo Giorgio Seraphin, also worked in Venice.

The second great Venetian master was Domenico Montagnana. He was born in 1690—one doesn't know where—and may also have worked in Cremona, perhaps with Nicolò Amati. He came to Venice around 1721 and signed his labels "Dominicus Montagnana Sub Signum Cremonae Venetus. . . ." He seems to have admired Stainer, and

Stradivari during his Amatisé epoch; later he followed Stradivari's larger models. He used superb wood and was a great artist. His scrolls are famous for their bold "masculine" beauty. His varnish is admirable, thick and transparent, often deep ruby-red. His instruments have power and sonority; he remains "The Mighty Venetian." His cellos are among the finest in existence, second only to Stradivari's. The number of his violins is not known, but he was probably more prolific than Carlo Bergonzi, who made less than one hundred. René Vannes mentions ten violas made by Montagnana, but other experts do not know any violas made by him today. A magnificent violin made in 1749, named after Baron von Steinheil, a Russian aristocrat, was in the Hottinger Collection.

The third Venetian master, Matteo Gofriller (also spelled Goffriler, Goffriller, Gafriler), may one day be considered the first. "Gofriller's star will ascend when this greatest of all Venetian makers will be recognized as the equal to his Cremonese contemporaries," says Dario d'Attili. Being Tyrolean, he was a "foreigner" in Venice, where he worked and died in 1742. He did not appear on the list of well-known Venetian makers for over a hundred years after his death, but he is now generally admired. The curvature of his violins, the sound holes, and especially their sweet tone suggest Jacob Stainer, but he was also inspired by Stradivari—not a bad mixture. His early labels mention his Cremonese influence ("Mattio Gofrilleri in Venetia Al' Insegna di Cremona . . ."), but later he says only "Matteo Goffriller fecit Venetijis anno . . ." His violins are now much in demand. The wood is beautiful, the workmanship exquisite, the varnish often a transparent reddish-yellow, sometimes a charming cerise, and the tone is noble and sonorous. He is getting more expensive all the time, especially his cellos, that for long time were believed to be by Carlo Bergonzi (quite an accolade, considering that Bergonzi was then known as "Stradivari's best pupil"). The famous "Baillot" Stradivari, made in 1732, is now authenticated as a work of Matteo Gofriller. He was assisted by his brother Francesco, who made some instruments on his own.

Francesco Gobetti, who worked in Venice from 1690 until 1732, follows the models of Amati, Stradivari, and Ruggieri. For some time he was believed to be a pupil of Stradivari, but no longer. He made fine instruments, and his red varnish, that has become pale in the past two hundred and fifty years, is very attractive. Not in the same league was Carlo Antonio Tononi, who started working in Venice around 1721. The Tononi family came from Bologna; later some of them went to Rome. Carlo Antonio followed the school of Amati, using medium wood but always a fine varnish, reddish or orange. He flattened his violins; they had a strong tone and were popular in Italy. He died in 1768, probably in Venice.

Giovanni Battista Rogeri, born in Bologna around 1650, must not be confused with the Ruggieri family from Cremona. Six years younger than Stradivari, he was probably a fellow apprentice in the workshop of Nicolò Amati; later he went to Brescia (his son, pupil, and associate, Pietro Giacomo, was born there in 1680). Rogeri followed the small Stradivari model and Amati's golden varnish. Later he also made "large-pattern" violins, using beautiful wood and working with attention to detail; he had learned his lesson well at Nicolò Amati's workshop. His label reads, "Io: Bapt. Rogerius Bon: Nicolai Amati de Cremona alumnus Brixiae fecit Anno Domini . . ." It tells the whole story ("Bon is short for "Bononiensis," the Bolognese). The Rogeris also made small-design, beautifully executed cellos. Father and son both died about 1730, in Brescia.

Another pupil of Nicolò Amati was Goffredo Cappa, born in Saluzzo, near Cremona, in 1644 (the same year as Stradivari). He copied the Amati style so well that many Cappa violins were sold as Amatis, though Count Cozio already noted in his *Carteggio* that Cappa never used Nicolò Amati's very fine wood and that his workmanship wasn't as exquisite. But his violins, violas, and cellos were much admired for their beauty, fine varnish, and sweet tone. Viotti and Pugnani played on Cappa violins. George Hart writes that Goffredo worked in Turin, but he confused him with his brother Gioncchino.

The large and important Guadagnini dynasty began with Lorenzo, born in 1685 in either Piacenza or Cremona, and died in 1760. (The last violin-making member of the family, Francesco Guadagnini, who died in Turin in 1948, printed on his labels, "Founded in 1690.") On his labels Lorenzo Guadagnini called himself a pupil of Stradivari, "Lavrentius Guadagnini Pater, alumnus Antoni Straduari, fecit Placentie Anno 1743." Charles Reade pointed out that in Piacenza it was easy to call oneself a pupil of Stradivari—it would have been more difficult in Cremona. Lorenzo's violins, close to the Amati-Stradivari school, are made of fine wood with a reddish-gold varnish, and their powerful tone makes them popular among orchestra musicians; their prices are presently going up.

Lorenzo's son, Joannes Baptista (J.B.) Guadagnini (thought by many earlier experts to be Lorenzo's brother), is the most famous Guadagnini. He was born in Cremona in 1711. On some labels he calls himself "Alumnus Antoni Stradivari," on others "filius Laurentii Guadagnini" with no reference to Stradivari. He was the most restless among the great Italian makers. Doring estimates that J.B. made thirty-one violins and seven cellos in Piacenza, then moved to Milan in 1749 where he made over sixty violins, some violas, and cellos during the next ten years. After a trip to see what was happening in Cremona since the deaths of Stradivari and Guarneri del Gesù, he established himself as official court maker of the duke of Parma, who gave him a pension. But J.B. moved on again, and around 1771 he made more instruments for Count Cozio di Salabue in Turin. There he died, at the age of seventy-five, on September 18, 1786.

J. B. Guadagnini's violins are well made of fine wood, beautifully varnished—sparkling yellow or brown-red—and famous for their powerful, sonorous tone. They are expensive and still rising in price because their sonority makes them valuable in today's concert halls. J.B. often follows fine Stradivari models, but his own personality is quite apparent: he was no imitator.

Other members of the Guadagnini family made instruments, but none reached J.B.'s prestige and fame. His son, Giuseppe I ("The Soldier"), born in Cremona around 1736, inherited the father's restlessness. He worked in Parma, Milan (perhaps to be closer to his father who was then in Turin), and about 1790 in Pavia; he died there around 1805. Tracing the travels of the Guadagninis through their labels is an exciting job for experts, always provided that the labels are genuine.

The Milanese school of violin-making begins with Paolo Grancino, probably born there in 1640; his father, Andrea, may have been a lute-maker. Milan, then as now, was an important commercial center, though not as rich and cultured as Venice or Florence. (A century and a half earlier Duke Ludovico Sforza had brought musicians, artists, and instrument-makers from all over Italy to his court, including Leonardo da Vinci.) Paolo Grancino went to nearby Cremona and was trained by Nicolò Amati. Around 1665 he returned to settle in Milan, where he died in 1692. He first followed his teacher's models but gradually developed his own, somewhat different in outline. He couldn't afford expensive wood; the backs and sides of his violins are often made from inexpensive poplar. He was not one of Amati's best pupils for his work is somewhat irregular: he made good, less good, and sometimes indifferent violins. His second son, and pupil, Giovanni Battista (1670–1735), surpassed his father and is now considered the best maker of the family. He worked in Ferrara and Milan, used fine wood, built a less arched model, applied a good varnish, yellow, orange, or a warm, soft brown. There are other members of the Grancino family, confusingly named Giovanni Battista II and Giovanni Battista III. All followed the tradition of Nicolò Amati and Paolo Grancino.

The Testore family of violin-makers is also prominent in Milan. The best of these was Carlo Giuseppe Testore, born in 1660 in Novara. He was a pupil of Giovanni Battista Grancino and Goffredo Cappa. Carlo Giuseppe came to Milan around 1687 and set up shop in Contrada Larga, "Al Segno dell'Aquila" ("under the sign of the eagle"). He died probably in 1737 (the same year as Stradivari). On the backs of his violins is branded the family sign, the double-headed eagle. He used good wood, but his varnish, yellow-brown or red-brown, is often chippy, rarely distinguished. His instruments have a penetrating tone, rarely sweet and mellow. He was a fast worker. (The Hills call the Grancino and Testore family "the Milanese cheapjacks.") Carlo Giuseppe had two sons, Carlo Antonio (1688–1766) and Paolo Antonio (1690–1760); Carlo Antonio's son, Giovanni, was the last maker in the family, and put the whole family history on his labels: "Carlo Antonio e Giovanni Padre, e Figlio / Testori, il qual Carlo e Figlio Maggiore / del fu Carlo Giuseppe Testore obitanti / in Contrada Large al segno dell'Aquila / Milano, 1764." The Testore makers were good second-class producers. They used the designs of Nicolò

Amati, Stradivari, and Del Gesù, and never developed a personal style of their own.

Carlo Fernando Landolfi was the last maker of the Milanese school. He was born in Milan around 1714, and in 1734 opened his workshop "Al Segno della Sirena." He copied Guarneri del Gesù and was once believed to be Del Gesù's pupil, but this is extremely doubtful. (In his eccentric manners he certainly imitated Del Gesù.) He was a great experimenter, always trying out something new. But occasionally he would make a beautiful violin or a fine cello, using a translucent red varnish that seems almost "Cremonese." His instruments have a rich, sonorous tone. They are especially valued in England, where eccentrics have always been understood.

The school of Naples is represented by the large and productive Gagliano family. The oldest and best of them was Alessandro Gagliano, born in Naples around 1660. He is another so-called pupil and assistant of Stradivari, but the Hills "very much doubted" Fétis' statement, made on the authority of Vuillaume. By 1695, Alessandro Gagliano was back in his hometown, and never left it, but it is accepted that he learned his craft in Cremona. His violins have little similarity with either Amatis or Stradivaris. They are large and well built, often made of fine wood with big, wide-open sound holes. The back is mostly of one piece. The varnish, usually a beautiful orange or red, is soft, though not as soft as Cremonese varnish. The violins have a powerful tone. In the Hills' biography of Stradivari, they list the dimensions of the bass bars of various makers: of all makers, Alessandro Gagliano uses the longest original bass bar, in a violin made in 1720; it is 10⅞ inches. (The smallest bar was in a Nicolò Amati of 1650—only 8⅝ inches.) The Hottinger Collection contained a beautiful, impressive Alessandro Gagliano violin, the "Rotondo," made in 1710. It shows what a not-so-great maker could do in a moment of inspiration.

Alessandro's sons, Nicolò and Gennaro, continued his work: Nicolò (1695–1763) made sonorous instruments, often inspired by the Amatisé Stradivari models; Gennaro (1700–1770) made fine violins along the patterns of Stradivari, and a few cellos. Gennaro's instruments have the powerful Gagliano tone. Nicolò had four sons—Ferdinando, Giuseppe, Antonio, Giovanni; they became the third generation of Gagliano violin-makers. Ferdinando (1724–1781) returned to the models of his grandfather, Alessandro. The best of the brothers was Giuseppe (1725–1793), whose instruments have a clear, beautiful tone. Giovanni's three sons—Nicolò II, Antonio II, Raffaele—were the fourth generation, all working in Naples. Raffaele's son, Vincenzo, carried on the family firm in Naples, "Vincenzo Gagliano Figli"; it was best known for manufacturing violin strings.

Rome never claimed to be the violin-making capital in Italy. The best-known maker in Rome was David Tecchler (also known as Techler, Tekler, Teccler, Decler), who was born in Augsburg (not in Salzburg, as often claimed) in 1666; he worked in Rome after 1705, and died there about 1748. He was a gifted master, first following the models of Jacob Stainer and later creating his own design. His wood is always fine and sometimes splendid; his rich varnish is yellow-red, his f-holes are wide, and his scrolls strongly carved and full of character. Tecchler is an interesting maker, and his instruments were famous for their powerful tone. He also made violas, cellos, and double basses, the cellos are today very expensive. He died in Rome around 1748.

Cremona saw the beginning of the violin-making art, with Andrea Amati. It also saw the end. The last dynasty of genuine Cremonese makers were the Ceruti. Giovanni Battista Ceruti was born in Cremona around 1750. He was a pupil of Lorenzo Storioni and later his successor. He was a very productive worker, making violins along the models of Guarneri del Gesù, and his varnish is still Cremonese and beautiful, either yellow or red. His instruments have a powerful tone. He died in Cremona after 1817; two years earlier his son Giuseppe (born in 1785) had taken over the workshop. Giuseppe made small-pattern violins, with a dark-red or yellow-brown varnish. He died in Mantua, in 1860. His son Enrico was born in Cremona in 1808. He was a prolific worker, though his cellos are more valued than his violins. On his labels he Latinized his name, "Enricus Ceruti fecit Cremonae . . ." He was much respected by the prominent violin-makers of Europe. He died in Cremona on October 23, 1883, at Via Borgo Spera No. 14, and on that day the violin history of Cremona came to its conclusion.

Jacob Stainer:
A Lonely Genius

Jacob Stainer remains an enigma among the great violin-makers. For a long time he and the Amatis were rated the greatest masters; still today he remains close to the Amati-Stradivari-Guarneri trinity. What we know of Stainer's life is a bizarre blend of truth and legend, myth and reality. Truth and reality are in his violins: their beauty and especially their tone prove that Jacob Stainer was great—truly one of the greatest—and the only non-Italian to be mentioned in the company of the Cremonese. During the seventeenth and eighteenth centuries many musicians were bewitched by the sweet tone of his instruments: Johann Sebastian Bach left a Stainer violin among his prized possessions. In 1774 George Simon-Löhlein in Leipzig wrote that "Stainer's tone is full and soft like a flute" and that he preferred them to Amatis for solo playing. Many violinists agreed with him. In Paris eleven years later the *Encyclopédie Méthodique* reads: "The violins of the greatest reputation are those of Jacob Stainer . . . who finished every violin by his own hands, and made a prodigious number, as he lived to the advanced age of nearly a hundred years. . . . His violins are very rare and much sought after." In 1800, Count Cozio di Salabue called "Giacomo Steiner of Switzerland" (*sic*) "the best violin-maker of all."

Back to reality. Stainer's violins combine various sounds. The E string and A string have a warm, luscious, flutelike tone. Even the highest notes are never shrill. The D string has often the warm timbre of an oboe. The G string reminds of a masterly, softly played French horn. It was the variety of tonal shades that made Stainer's instruments so highly valued. He was the first non-Italian who understood the secret of the Italian violin tone. Mozart, another non-Italian who understood the secrets of Italian music, loved Stainer's instruments.

Stainer's violins have a very high curvature of the back and especially of the top; one can see through the f-holes of a Stainer when it is held horizontally. This arching explains the sweetness of tone and the lack of carrying power; the wood is thick in the middle but thinner toward the edges. The shape has some of the longish elegance of the Brothers Amati and the earlier Nicolò Amati, but Stainer's characteristic f-holes are different from those of any Cremonese maker. They seem to reflect the difference between the sunny landscape of Cremona and the overcast skies of the Tyrolian mountain village of Absam, where Jacob Stainer was born. The birth date is not certain; many biographers believe it was July 14, 1621, but Professor Walter Senn, whose biography of Stainer is the most thoroughly documented, believes that Stainer was born earlier, about 1617. Andrea Amati, the principal creator of the violin, had then been dead for almost forty years; Hieronymus was still working in Cremona, and sometimes Antonius would lend him a hand; Nicolò Amati was learning his trade; Stradivari was not yet born.

Some historians claim that Jacob Stainer spent some time in Cremona, perhaps working with Nicolò Amati. No proof exists. Senn believes Stainer may have been in Venice around 1635, possibly working with Martin Kaiser; there is no doubt that in the Tyrol Stainer saw Italian violins, perhaps some made by the Amatis. Absam is a short distance from Innsbruck, where Archduke Ferdinand Charles of Habsburg had his court orchestra. There Italian influence was strong—the archduke's wife was Claudia de'Medici. Many court musicians came from Italy, bringing along their Italian instruments, probably many made by the Amatis. Anyway, no Brescian influence is apparent in Jacob Stainer's instruments. He began selling his violins at a young age, perhaps eighteen. His violins were very popular, and no wonder, for he was very conscientious even as a young man, executing all details with care. Like the Amatis he made two models, one small and one large. Stainer's varnish is justly celebrated; it is different from Cremonese varnish but soft and beautiful, applied carefully, and enhancing the beauty of the wood. Sometimes he used two shades of varnish on the same instrument, the top yellow, and the back, mostly of two pieces, deep red; the contrast is striking. Sometimes he used a yellow foundation with several layers of deep red upon it; since he couldn't have known how the Cremonese makers mixed their varnish he must have made his own, and it presents another unexplained mystery. How could a lonely man in a small Tyrolian village understand the top secret of the Cremonese varnish—something that no prominent maker has understood since? In 1644, when Stradivari was born, Jacob Stainer was already famous for his sweet-sounding violins.

Of his life little is known that stands up to critical scrutiny. The people in Absam and the nearby town of Hall worked in the salt mines. In their spare time many were skilled wood carvers. Perhaps young Stainer began working with some of them. But in the 1640s he got restless; Senn has traced his travels to Salzburg (1644), where proof of his work was found in the archives: Stainer repaired some instruments there. In 1645 he shows up in Munich; in 1648 he is in Venice, Bozen (Bolzano), and perhaps in Meran (Merano). After 1649 he seems to have remained in Absam, but an interesting correspondence was found concerning the instruments that Stainer made for Karl Liechtenstein Castelcorno, the prince bishop of Olmütz (Olomouc) in Moravia. Stainer's scrolls were beautifully carved, sometimes with a lion's head instead of the scroll. He was always a great expert on wood, living in a village that was practically surrounded by deep pine forests. For his violins he used the finest resonant pine from his own region, and fine maple from the South Tyrol, just beyond the Brenner Pass.

He sold his instruments to the merchants who came with the "salt caravans" from all over Europe to Hall. He was paid about four florins for his early instruments, a very small sum. In 1648, Archduke Ferdinand Charles became Stainer's official protector, and presumably bought some instruments for his court orchestra. Ten years later, Jacob Stainer was appointed court violin-maker. But after the death of the archduke in 1662 the court orchestra was dismissed by Ferdinand's brother, Archduke Sigismund, and after Sigismund's death Tyrol became part of the Habsburg Empire. Emperor Leopold I was a most musical-minded ruler. He celebrated his marriage in 1666 with Infanta Margareta Teresa of Spain with a two-year musical festival, climaxed by the performance of Marc Antonio Cesti's *Il pomo d'oro,* an enormous opera with sixty-seven scenes, fifty soloists, a cast of a thousand, and a reputed cost to the Emperor of over 300,000 guilders. In 1669 Leopold confirmed Stainer's position as court violin-maker, and also named him court musician; Stainer must have played the violin very well. A maker who plays well on his violin has no trouble selling them, and by that time Stainer got 24 guilders for one instrument.

Still, he had worries; as a young man he had married a girl from Absam, Margarete Holzhammer, and they had eight girls and one son. During the years of struggle he had made several instruments for an Austrian merchant, Salomon Huebmer, who later claimed that Stainer had for some time lived in his house and owed him money "for board, rent, and expenses." Local historians give various versions of the story, and it cannot be checked. Huebmer seems to have sued Stainer, asking for money and a compound interest. Stainer was also in trouble with the powerful Catholic Church when informers accused him of buying heretical Lutheran publications in Hall. Austria and the Habsburgs were militantly Catholic, and Jacob Stainer and a friend, Jacob Mehringer, were sent to prison. There was more trouble to come. Huebmer was still after him, and earlier Stainer (who must have been a rather unworldly artist) had guaranteed a debt of four hundred florins that his father-in-law owed to the Fugger salt works in Hall. Stainer didn't have the money, and his appeal to the Emperor was unsuccessful; the Emperor could not protect a suspected "heretic."

That was too much for poor Stainer; he became deranged and "had to be tied up as a madman." He died in Absam in 1683—the exact day is not known—at the age of sixty-two. This was the year of the Second Turkish Siege, the finest hour in Vienna's long history, and no one paid attention to the death of the great violin-maker in faraway Absam, in Tyrol. Western civilization was saved from the Turks. Stainer was forgotten. His house was sold by auction in 1684, the money was distributed among his creditors, and his wife died in poverty five years later. In 1842 a memorial plaque was fastened to the wall of the church in Absam, stating that Jacob Stainer had died "on the Friday after St. Aegidi, before sunrise." His house was later restored, and has become a tourist attraction.

Jacob Stainer made many instruments during his lifetime. He used handwritten labels, "Jacobus Stainer in Absam prope Oenipontum Fecit . . .", and often made spelling mistakes. Genuine Stainer violins are relatively rare today. Many of his instruments had been commissioned by Austrian monasteries, and after Emperor Joseph II dissolved many monasteries these violins were sold by dealers to collectors in England especially. At the end of the eighteenth century collectors valued a Stainer violin at four times the price of a Stradivari. Spurious "Stainer" violins appeared all over Europe: because he remained influential he was often copied. Even in Italy, the land of the violin, Stainer's instruments were widely admired for their easy response and sweet tone. Stainer's influence reached southward to Udine and Venice, where Santo Seraphin, Gofriller, and Montagnana worked; Pietro Guarneri in Mantua probably knew Stainer's violins, and some of his fellow musicians at the Gonzaga court orchestra probably played them. How strong was Stainer's influence in Cremona remains speculative. Stradivari certainly knew about him but never seems to have experimented by way of Stainer's model. With his prophetic genius Stradivari may have sensed that Stainer's violin tone was not the sound of the future—and Stradivari was right, as we know today. Many fine Stainer violins were ruined when their owners became convinced that "the wood was too thick"; some vandalistic repairers made them thinner! Stainer's violins are still much loved by collectors, but their prices have been going down. In 1969 a Stainer violin was offered at Sotheby's in London for £1350, then about $3300. That is a far cry from the prices paid for Stradivari's violins, and also from the report by William Sandys and Simon Andrew Forster in *The History of the Violin* (1864), that a Stainer violin brought "half the price of Pittsburgh."

Stainer had a younger brother, Marcus, who was born in Absam in 1647 and successfully copied Jacob's grand-pattern models. He worked in Kufstein, Tyrol, and his violins were appreciated for their beautiful varnish. The Florentine virtuoso and composer Francesco Maria Veracini (1685–1750), a celebrated violinist during the first half of the eighteenth century, owned two violins by Marcus Stainer and called them "St. Peter" and "St. Paul"; unfortunately, he lost them during a shipwreck in 1746. Marcus Stainer died probably around 1680, before his older brother. Jacob Stainer had no apprentices, and the Stainer violin model died with him.

Matthias Albani (also Alban or Albanus) was also a Tyrolean maker. His instruments were famous for a long time, though he had none of the genius of Jacob Stainer. Albani was born in Kaltern, the beautiful wine village near Bozen (Bolzano) in the South Tyrol, on March 28, 1621. (Jacob Stainer was probably born less than four months later.) Very likely they were friends, for Albani's early violins have the same model as Stainer's. Later—about 1680, when Stainer had stopped working—Albani developed a different model, somewhat elongated like the violins of the Brothers Amati. His early instruments have Stainer's curvature, and the f-holes are wide open. He too knew about fine wood and he had a beautiful amber varnish, sometimes with shades of brown. Musicians loved Albani's violins for their sweet, dulcet sound, and paid almost as much for them as for a Stainer or Amati. Albani became prosperous and died in 1712 in Bolzano at the age of ninety-one, a rich man. His two sons, Michael and Joseph, continued the father's business. (There is no relation to Paolo Albani, who worked in Palermo, Rome, and possibly Cremona during the second half of the seventeenth century.)

For a hundred and fifty years after his death, Jacob Stainer remained the most copied master in England, Germany, Austria, and Bohemia. He may not have been the most influential; when a local violin-maker had a chance to see a genuine Amati, he switched to the Cremonese models. But only the few makers who worked in the shops of the leading dealers ever saw a genuine violin from Cremona. The others studied a Stainer, if they were lucky; most copied a copy of Stainer.

William Forster (1739–1808) in England followed the Stainer model until 1770, then changed to the Amati model. He opened his store in London in 1759, and soon became famous. After the 1750s another London maker, Richard Duke, also began with Stainer and ended up making Amati copies. A locally admired maker of that time was Peter Wamsley, who made good copies of Stainer violins and also violas and cellos. He employed Joseph Hill, now known as Joseph II (1715–1784), an early member of the famous family; his four sons all became his apprentices and later violin-makers. Another important violin-making family were the Kennedys. Thomas Kennedy (1784–1870) was a prolific maker, best known for his cellos.

The English makers were good craftsmen, and the outline and thicknesses of their copies were accurate, but the arching was often exaggerated—proof that they rarely saw a genuine Stainer. Daniel Parker (c. 1700–1775) went against the Stainer trend, copying instead the long-pattern Stradivari. Benjamin Banks (1727–1795) of Salisbury, one of the best English makers, gave up the Stainer model early and switched to Amati. At the beginning of the nineteenth century John Hart (1805–1874) and William Ebsworth Hill (1817–1895) became makers, repairers, and eminent judges of fine instruments. Their firms became very important for the history of the violin.

In Vienna, Prague, and the cities of Germany the influence of Stainer was also very strong in the eighteenth century. In Vienna, there was Daniel Achatius Stadlmann (1680–1744) and his sons, Johann Joseph and Michael Ignaz; Johann Georg Thir (1738–1761) and other members of that family (also spelled Thirr, Thier, Dirr, Dir); Johann Georg Thir's pupil, Franz Geissenhof (1754–1821), who came to Vienna from Vils, near the Bavarian town of Füssen, where many of the old lute-makers had worked; and Gabriel Lemböck, a good nineteenth-century maker who had come from Budapest. In Prague there were Johannes Ulrich Eberle (1699–1768), also from Vils and famous for his violas and violas d'amore; Johann Georg Helmer (1687–1770) from Füssen, whose instruments were popular for their strong tone and beautiful auburn varnish; and Ferdinand August Homolka (1828–1890), who copied Stradivari so well that he was known as "the Prague Stradivari." In Nuremberg there was Leopold Widhalm

(1722–1776), one of the best German makers of his time, who followed the Stainer model but used a beautiful amber varnish and made violins that had a beautiful tone. In Hamburg there was the celebrated Joachim Tielke (1641–1719), whose best instruments were often compared to those from Italy. His tessellated viols are kept in many museums. There were gifted artisans elsewhere—but only one Jacob Stainer.

There was also a "Russian Stradivari"; Anatol Ivanovich Leman, born in Moscow in 1859, was a chemist, dentist, technician, musician, composer, and amateur violin-maker who wound up making excellent violins (about two hundred of them), violas, cellos, and bows. He experimented with various models, studied the science of varnish, and wrote on everything from violin design to acoustics, in Russian, French, and German. He died in St. Petersburg in 1913.

ᴥ Some Brilliant
French Luthiers

The French did not participate in the creation of the earliest violins
—as some French historians once claimed—but their later contribution to the art of violin-making has been the most important next to
the Italians. (Jacob Stainer was, of course, a glorious exception to
everything.) What the Amati family did for Cremona, the Médard
family did for Nancy; they founded the great French school. Claude
Médard died in Nancy, prior to 1597, and over a dozen members of
his family were *menusier-luthiers* (woodworkers and viol-makers) in
Nancy. Francois Médard III probably spent some time in Cremona,
where he might have worked for Nicolò Amati. Later he went to Paris
and became court luthier for Louis XIV. His violins, dated between
1690 and 1710, follow the small Amati pattern, with one-piece back,
yellow varnish, and the sweet, rather small tone.

The municipal archives of Mirecourt, a small town in the depart-
ment of Vosges on the Madon River, contain the name of Dieudonné
Montfort, who made the first violin there in 1602. Mirecourt is the

hometown of almost all important French families of luthiers: Lupot, Vuillaume, Pique, Chappuy, Chanot, Jacquot, Gand, Bernardel, and others. Among the earliest families were the Trevillot: Charles (1645–1718) made Amatisé instruments with a golden-brown varnish similar to that of the Médards. The best Mirecourt makers later went to Paris, where the musical action was, setting up shop there and employing relatives and friends from Mirecourt as apprentices and assistants. Estimates of the Mirecourt-born makers range from fifty, according to Antoine Vidal, to "almost one thousand," according to Pierre Charles Jaquot. When the guilds in Mirecourt began to divide, and to assign certain jobs to certain families, the varnish-makers made some important contributions. They modified the earlier alcoholic varnish and returned in part to a softer, more flexible oil varnish. (The guild qualifications of the luthiers are dated 1738.)

For a long time Mirecourt remained the center of the French violin industry. (The industrial method developed in Mirecourt must not be confused with the first-rate work of the craftsmen and artists who lived in Paris and elsewhere.) Since the early nineteenth century Mirecourt violins were exported to many countries; they were especially popular in England, the United States, and South America. The more expensive instruments had a nice appearance and a good tone. People liked the shape, the good wood, the elegant varnish, the glossy finish; there was some of the charm of France about them. Mirecourt's most doubtful contribution was the development of *le violon moulé* ("pressed violin"). The backs and tops of such instruments were not cut and finished by hand: machines would cut boards of wood one fifth of an inch thick; other machines cut the outlines and the f-holes; instead of carving the curvature out of the boards, the workers "softened" the wood by applying steam, and "pressed" them between hot plates until they had the required arching. Thus the name "pressed violin." Other machines were used to produce scrolls, ribs, purfling. The instruments were inferior, for the fibers of the wood, which is living matter, were killed by the application of extreme heat, and the pressed violins would never vibrate properly.

The French school of violin-making produced several first-rate masters. Many of them were excellent copyists, working on the models of the great Cremonese and occasionally adding a few touches of their own. But the best—Nicolas Lupot, François-Louis Pique, Jean-Baptiste Vuillaume—had definite originality, imagination, and a French sense of style and elegance. Their beautiful instruments don't have the noble sonority of the greatest Cremonese, however, or the sweet tone of a Stainer. The French products were better visually than acoustically. The main French contribution to the art of the violin remains the development of the bow, climaxed by the immortal François Tourte.

After the Médard dynasty, the Lupot family is very important in the early annals of French lutherie. The first Lupot, Jean, "le jeune fils," was born in Mirecourt around 1652. (Nicolò Amati was then fifty-six; the Cremonese had a head start.) Of Jean Lupot's eight children, Jean-François and François-Laurent became luthiers but little is known of them. François-Laurent had a son, François I, who was born in Plombières (Vosges) in 1725. He studied with his father in Lunéville and later in Nancy. In 1754 he married the daughter of Jean-Baptiste Touly, also a good maker. Ever since this event the French luthiers have intermarried; they form a big, happy family, close to each other and remarkably devoid of family feuds and professional jealousy. In this respect French violin-makers are unique.

In 1758, François Lupot I went to Stuttgart as court instrument maker to the duke of Württemberg; eight years later he left Germany and established himself in Orléans. In 1794 he followed his son Nicolas to Paris and died there in 1804. He was never in Italy; he couldn't have been a pupil of Guarneri del Gesù, as claimed by some French historians (Constant-Pierre and Chouquet, among others). He made good copies of Stradivari violins, was careful in selecting the wood and applying his yellow-brown varnish. Sometimes he made the tops brighter than the backs, which created an interesting contrast.

His son Nicolas became the greatest of the Lupots, and the finest French maker. He has been called *"le Stradivari français."* There have been many local "Stradivaris," but Nicolas Lupot comes closest to deserving the title. Both his father and maternal grandfather were able luthiers: Nicolas seemed predestined to become a gifted maker. Curiously, the greatest French luthier was born in Stuttgart, Germany, on

December 4, 1758, where his father was then working for the Duke, but even the most nationalistic German historians have not claimed Lupot as German. He was as French as the *Vièrge d'Orléans*—the city where he studied with his father and made his first instruments. In 1794 he went to Paris and worked with François-Louis Pique. Four years later he opened his own workshop in rue de Grammont, and in 1806 he moved to larger premises in rue Croix de Petits Champs. In 1815, after Napoleon's downfall, Nicolas was named *luthier de la chapelle royale,* and the following year *fournisseur de l'école royale de musique.* (Antonio Stradivari was never so honored in Cremona.) Nicolas Lupot died in Paris on August 14, 1824. His pupil and son-in-law, Charles-François Gand, who had married Lupot's adopted daughter, became his successor and took over the firm. Gand was from Mirecourt, and so was another Lupot apprentice, Auguste Sebastien-Philippe Bernardel (1798–1870). Bernardel's two sons, Ernest and Gustave, later merged their firm with Eugène Gand to found the firm of Gand & Bernardel, which became very prestigious in Paris. Auguste Sebastien Bernardel made copies of Stradivari, Guarneri, and Guadagnini. His cellos are much esteemed for their tone.

In Paris Nicolas Lupot was often asked to repair important violins from Cremona and he studied them carefully. With unfailing instinct he recognized the genius of Stradivari, and when he began to develop his own model he followed the outlines and principles of that great master. But Lupot had his own ingenuity and personality. His best violins have a harmonious design; the lower bouts are somewhat wider than Stradivari's, the sound holes are well cut, and the purfling is done with French elegance. He worked with care, omitting no detail; Antonio Stradivari would have approved of him. His fine red or red-brown varnish was applied rather thickly, but it is soft and transparent and many experts consider it close to Cremonese varnish. His violins have a sonorous tone, perhaps not very big but always round and pleasant. Ludwig Spohr once exchanged a good J.B. Guadagnini for a new Lupot on which he often performed after his "beloved" Guarneri del Gesù had been stolen. Occasionally Lupot made a beautifully ornamented violin: on the back of one, dated 1817, are painted the figures of Apollo, Orpheus, Terpsichore, and Amor, and a gold-lettered inscription, "*Jeunes coeurs, méfiez-vous du perfide amour, mais livrez-*

vous sans crainte á la douce mélodie" ("Young hearts, do not trust per-
fidious love, but abandon yourself without fear to sweet melody").

François Lupot II, Nicolas' younger and less gifted brother
(1774–1837), called himself on his labels "élève de Antonius Stradivarius"; this asks for some credulity, since Stradivari had died thirty-seven
years before François II was born. But he was a good bow-maker.

François-Louis Pique was born in 1758 (the same year as Nicolas
Lupot) in Roret, near Mirecourt. He studied with Edmond Saunier
and went to Paris in 1777, where he died in 1822. He made beautiful
violins of carefully chosen wood, mostly with one-piece backs. The design is always elegant, and the beautiful varnish, red or red-brown, is
also somewhat thickly applied (like Lupot's), but again soft and fine.
Pique probably sometimes worked for Lupot, who gave him unvarnished instruments for the varnishing job. They thought alike, and
shared an admiration for Stradivari. Pique rarely used printed labels,
marking instead his name and address on the inside of the back, near
the sound post. Some handwritten labels say, "Pique, rue de Grenelle
St. Honoré, au coin de celle des deux écus No 35 à Paris." Perhaps he
worried that a customer might not find him; but he was too good not
to be located.

Next to the Lupot family the Vuillaume dynasty, also from Mirecourt, dominates French violin-making. Its first members are listed in
the early seventeenth century in the birth registers of Nancy and Mirecourt. Most of the information about the Vuillaume family is based on
the research of Albert Jacquot, whose family is related to the Vuillaumes. René Vannes, in his *Dictionnaire Universal des Luthiers,* admits that it is impossible to check some of Jacquot's statements and
believes they contain "certain errors." Not all violin historians have
the courage for such frankness.

One of the earliest members of the Vuillaume family, Antoine, was
known in Mirecourt as a *"facteur de violons,"* somewhat less than a
full-fledged luthier. Vannes mentions almost two dozen Vuillaumes.
The most important was Jean-Baptiste (J.B.), born in Mirecourt on
October 7, 1798 (the year Nicolas Lupot set up his shop in Paris).
Vuillaume studied in his home town and in 1818 went to Paris, where
he first worked with François Chanot.

The Chanots are another celebrated family of luthiers. Georges

Chanot II (1801–1883) made good violins, following the Cremonese models. His older brother Francis (1787–1823), a curious though very French mixture of violin-enthusiast and naval officer, invented the *violon guitare,* with simple slits instead of f-holes, and strings fastened to a glued-on bridge as in a lute. The scroll was turned backward at a slanted angle, which made it easier to fasten the strings to the pegs. Chanot gave one instrument with the initials C.I.D. (Capitaine Ingénieur Deuxième-classe) to Viotti, whose reaction is not known. Auditions were arranged with a violinist playing alternately a Chanot violin (an orthodox one) and a Cremonese instrument; naturally some were convinced they heard the Chanot when the old Italian violin was played, and vice versa. But gradually it dawned upon people that Chanot's instruments couldn't compete with the old violins, and professional violinists stopped playing them in public. After three years Vuillaume gave up his association with Francis Chanot.

In 1828 J. B. Vuillaume opened his store at the rue des Petits Champs; in 1860 he moved to rue Demours and there he died on March 19, 1875. Vuillaume remains revered as the finest copyist of the great Italian instruments, and a fine maker in his own right. His copies of Maggini, Stradivari, and Guarneri del Gesù have been called masterpieces; only great experts can distinguish them from the originals. Vuillaume, in addition to fine instruments of his own, also made very good bows. A thoughtful artist, he experimented with so-called innovations but always returned to the orthodox design of the violin, convinced it was the best. In his late years, when he was famous and rich and somewhat careless, his instruments were not up to his highest standards, but he should be forgiven; others have done worse. No one in his time knew as much about violins, and with the help of the dealer Luigi Tarisio he introduced some of the greatest Cremonese violins to Paris.

Vuillaume had enemies. It was claimed that he sold some of his copies as genuine old violins, but this was never proved. On the contrary, Antoine Vidal and other experts have clearly stated that J. B. Vuillaume was an honest man, and never sold a copy as an original. *But,* he could not prevent an unscrupulous dealer from getting a Vuillaume and selling it as a Stradivari. Such things have always happened. Vuillaume sold his copies for 300 francs, at a time when a fine Cremonese fiddle might bring 10,000 francs. He is said to have made three thousand instruments in his lifetime, and it is not pleasant to think that some "Cremonese" instruments in private collections may be genuine Vuillaumes.

Vuillaume's varnish never attains the texture and softness of Cremonese varnish. He diligently searched for the best wood he could find, cut it in boards one and a half inches thick, and dried it for ten years. He carefully studied the thickness of wood in relation to tone color, and left some valuable papers about various violin problems. In 1929, his copy of the "Messiah" Stradivari was listed by Lyon and Healy in Chicago at $5000.

Vuillaume never copied slavishly. Occasionally he introduced certain characteristics in the style of the old master which (in his opinion) the old violin failed to possess. Such stylistic cosmetics are unacceptable today but they prove Vuillaume's intellectual perspicacity. Some violins which Guarneri del Gesù made between 1725 and 1740, his best period, are somewhat smaller than those made after 1740. Vuillaume had made some excellent Stradivari copies from the "golden period" that were 14 inches long and 6½ by 4½ by 8¼ inches wide, and he "decided" that this would be an ideal size for his copies of Del Gesù's "golden period"; he would have argued that he might even have convinced Del Gesù of this. So he made copies of the Guarneri violins with Guarneri's outlines and f-holes, very different from Stradivari's, but using the measurements of the fine Stradivari models. The scroll would be made less exactly; he was, after all, copying a Guarneri. He thought that some Del Gesù violins didn't have an ideal tonal balance on all strings, and after many experiments he thinned the wood of both top and back on the G string side until he was satisfied. Such experiments could be disposed of as the intellectual pastime of a sophisticated Frenchman, but it is astonishing that some Vuillaume copies of Del Gesù do have a better tonal balance than the originals, though they don't have the authentic Del Gesù sound.

The best-known Vuillaume story concerns Paganini's "Cannon" Guarneri del Gesù that he brought one day to J. B. Vuillaume for repairs; according to one version, Vuillaume showed Paganini "one week later" two identical violins. Perhaps apocryphal, this could be true: Vuillaume was as famous for speed as for skill. He asked Paganini which fiddle was the Del Gesù, and Paganini is said to have pointed to Vuillaume's copy. This could certainly have happened, for Paganini was not an expert; few great violinists are. His gift was to play them more beautifully than anyone else, Vuillaume's was to make perfect-looking violins.

Vuillaume's copy of the Del Gesù later passed to Paganini's favorite pupil, Ernesto Camillo Sivori. After Paganini's death his "Cannon" was placed in the Municipal Palace at Genoa, in accordance with his last will, in its original state—with short neck, low bridge, and strings very close to each other, so useful for playing double stops. Sivori, like Paganini a Genoese, was asked to perform on Paganini's violin in honor of the great violinist, and two city councilors delivered the "Cannon" Guarneri to Sivori's flat on the morning of the concert. But when Sivori left for the evening concert he put his Vuillaume copy into the original Guarneri case. He was used to his copy, with its higher bridge and more space between the strings, and no violinist likes to perform on a violin without practicing on it first. Everybody was delighted with the wonderful sound of the "Guarneri," and Sivori wisely kept his mouth shut. The next morning the councilors picked up the Del Gesù, complimenting Sivori on playing so beautifully on "Paganini's violin." Vuillaume, who had a sense of humor, would have been pleased.

How Inexpensive Fiddles Are Made

Inexpensive violins are necessary, and their production is a legitimate sector of the violin world. It would be not only snobbism, but idiocy, to put superior instruments into the hands of street fiddlers, beer-garden virtuosos, and small boys with penknives, bent on finding out what's inside. I still remember the day when my cousin Raoul, ten years old, invited me to his room, and with a magnificent gesture threw his three-quarter fiddle, with its "Antonius Stradivarius" label inside, from the fourth-floor window into the courtyard, where it landed with a hollowed, thoroughly unmusical sound. There is a healthy, large, and steady market for cheap violins that are strong in body and tone.

And all over the world there are also good-quality violins, often produced and exported by violin-makers who have preserved the tradition of "a good product at a modest price." Such instruments are made with dedication and skill, often handmade reproductions of Stradivari and Guarneri models. They must not be confused with the cheap "factory fiddles" which hardly deserve that name. For a young student, a well-made new violin may be better than grandfather's revered heirloom from the attic with its inadequate bass bar and bad pegs that never stay in tune. "From a physical standpoint, there is no question that a well-made modern string instrument is best for a child" says a catalogue of the Roth String Instruments.

Prior to World War II, Markneukirchen in Germany was turning out over fifty thousand such fiddles a year. "Markneukirchen" had a world-wide reputation; the town was known to have more "mark millionaires" prior to World War I than any other town of comparable size.

Today in West Germany the small town of Bubenreuth, near Erlangen, has become the center of the production of "factory fiddles." After World War II several hundred instrument makers settled there who had formerly worked in Schönbach and Graslitz in Czechoslovakia. It was not the first such exodus. During the disastrous Thirty Years' War many instrument-makers left their homes in Bohemia and settled on the other side of the mountains, founding new industries in Markneukirchen and Klingenthal. Guilds were organized, and for centuries the towns exported good-quality mass-produced instruments. Several violinmakers—Reichel, Schönfelder, Pfretzschmer—became well known for their instruments, bows, and cases.

It's quantity and price that count in Bubenreuth, not quality. Instruments are produced by efficiency experts, almost as cars are built in Detroit. No one goes into the woods to search for resonant pine; instead wholesalers deliver blocks of wood by the carloads. There is little time to "age" the wood. Machines cut up to ten violin backs or tops in a single operation, like the sections of mail-order dresses in a clothing factory. The bass bar is not cut separately and later glued to the inside of the top, but an ingenious machine cuts it and the top out of the same piece of wood. To the inexperienced eye it may look like a bass bar but it will never fulfill the bass bar's acoustic functions—to spread the vibrations of the top. So much for *that*.

The customer, bless him, will never know. He sees the violin only from the outside, and is blissfully ignorant of corner blocks and linings which should be there but aren't, and he doesn't know that the ribs are just glued to the back, as in an ordinary box. (Good violin-makers call such an instrument, disrespectfully but accurately, a *Schachtelgeige,* or "box fiddle.") If one holds such a "violin" between the knees to put in a new string, it may fold like a better cigar box if one isn't careful. Sometimes the fingerboard is made of cheap birch-wood instead of expensive ebony. But the contraption, euphemistically called a "violin," sells well because it is cheap.

The best inexpensive violins were made in Mittenwald; this thousand-year-old Bavarian town, known in the Middle Ages as Media Silva, was located in a thickly wooded valley at the foot of the Karwendel mountains, halfway between Munich and Innsbruck, where Jacob Stainer lived. With its surrounding area, the town has about ten thou-sand inhabitants. Its somnolent squares are surrounded by old, patri-cian houses whose gables and façades are adorned with eighteenth-cen-tury baroque frescoes of apostles, saints, and Madonnas. Before brightly painted shutters hang violin forms, indicating that the owner of the house used to make violins. In front of the baroque church there is a monument of Mathias Klotz, the most important violin-maker in Mittenwald, put up by his grateful fellow citizens. Klotz was no Stradivari, but this monument is more than the people of Cremona have done for their illustrious fellow citizen.

Mathias Klotz was born on June 6, 1656; Stradivari was then about twelve years old. Klotz died on August 16, 1743, at the age of eighty-seven. Both masters enjoyed longevity and fame, but there the similar-ity ends. Klotz was a good maker, not a genius. He left Mittenwald as a young man, learned the rudiments of violin-making in nearby Vils, possibly worked for a while with the great Jacob Stainer, and certainly spent six years in Padua as an apprentice to the well-known maker Giovanni Railich. He may have worked for a while under Nicolò Amati in Cremona, as so many others claim.

Klotz returned from his travels to Mittenwald in 1683 (the year Stai-ner died). The town had prospered for centuries as a stopover on the busy trade route from Augsburg to Venice; Venetian merchants used to store their goods and hold fairs there. The great trading families— the Fuggers, the Welsers, and others—had branch offices in Mitten-wald. But after the Thirty Years' War Mittenwald went into a slump, and by 1683 the depression was very bad.

Mathias Klotz was the town's salvation. He began making good violins, using the fine pine wood from nearby forests and for the backs the maple from nearby Tyrol. He studied Stainer's beautifully varnished violins and followed Stainer's design, but developed his own varnish with the methods he'd learned in Italy. His instruments, far above average though never superlative, were quite popular for their pleasant, sonorous tone and good appearance. Klotz began training apprentices and assistants, which was no problem, since many people in Mittenwald were experienced wood carvers. Mathias Klotz' five sons, and their sons later, continued the trade. Mittenwald had almost forty violin-makers named Klotz. Mathias, the founder, and his son Sebastian (1696–1767) were the best; Sebastian surpassed his father in some ways. His violins had a dark-brown or reddish varnish, soft and fine, resembling the works of Matthias Albani. The work of Sebastian's son Joseph I (1743–1809) was also much esteemed. But the successors to the Klotz family imitated Stainer and Mathias Klotz, and some began faking Stainer's labels. Mittenwald had many good and conscientious violin-makers—but also some shoddy practitioners.

Guilds were organized (as in Mirecourt). Salesmen were trained and peddled the instruments all over Germany; they knew how to play their instruments, and if they couldn't make a sale they could always earn money as entertainers. As the local violin business expanded it began to be dominated by enterprising producers who introduced mass-production methods: some artisans made only bodies, others specialized in scrolls, or chiseled pegs and bridges, or cut finger boards. Specialists assembled the parts, and some did nothing but varnish.

A few diehards clung to the old-fashioned notion that the whole violin should be the work of one man, but they couldn't prevail. Violin-making became a piecework cottage industry. In the early nineteenth century one violin part or another was produced in almost every house in Mittenwald. Some producers were honorable men who turned out reputable products; others were more interested in making money than good instruments. Children innocently busied themselves at stenciling beautiful labels inscribed "Stainer" or "Stradivarius." (The practice is no longer permitted.)

Things went well for the producers, and soon they bought forests and sawmills, hired crews to cut trees, and built warehouses for aging the lumber properly. Until World War I production went up as prices and wages went down. By 1914 some producers were paying as little as sixty cents for a violin body. But life was inexpensive in Mittenwald; people had their own gardens and livestock, they got fuel and building material from the nearby forests, and taxes were low. Everybody was at least getting by, and the producers became rich men.

After the war business boomed again for a time. In 1925, the town's oldest violin firm—Neuner & Hornsteiner—had a hundred and eighty employees on its payroll, and J. A. Baader & Cie. had a hundred and sixty. Then the Depression came. Mittenwald was unable to compete with Graslitz and Schönbach in Czechoslovakia, which had even lower wages and sold fiddles for half a dollar. Even the smartest Mittenwald producer couldn't match that price. Neuner & Hornsteiner went out of business, J. A. Baader & Cie. barely staggered along, and independent craftsmen had to look for other work. By 1938 highly skilled Mittenwald violin-makers were glad to get government jobs putting up barracks for the German Army, and their wives were glad to take in tourists.

On a visit to Mittenwald years ago, I found little of what Mathias Klotz had created. "Mittenwald," an old violin-maker said, "cannot carry on in the old manner when an inexpensive violin was made with care and devotion. The German Cremona, they used to call Mittenwald; it meant that people had a sense of quality, even of beauty. Today the only fellows that have a chance do it in the new manner—talking about cost per unit and overhead, turnover, export figures, and such."

I met a factory owner who worked "in the new manner," a Sudeten-German from Schönbach, who told me with offensive pride, "Sure, none of us are Stradivaris, but we get the work done. Our violins have a good, shiny varnish, you can hear their tone, and they're not expensive. I buy my varnish in five-liter cans from a manufacturer in Regensburg who used to live in Schönbach before World War II. It's good, cheap, and dries quickly. We hang the violins up in rows and varnish them with a spray gun. Yes, time is money, as they say in America. We start to assemble a batch of violins in the morning, and the next day, in the afternoon, we'll have it all done, varnished and crated, and at the railroad station bound for New York. Our two most popular violins are a Strad and a Guarneri. They come in three shades: dark-brown, brownish-red, orange-red. Our best customer is America, then Sweden and Switzerland. Our specialty is a violin glued with lime, for use in tropical countries; it can stand heat and damp-ness that would make an ordinary one fall apart."

I didn't tell him that I could have used such an instrument when I was a fiddler aboard the ships of the Messageries Maritimes, going from Marseille through the Red Sea to Djibouti, India, Indochina, China, and Japan. Air-conditioning wasn't known then, and occasion-ally my violin did fall apart. In desperation I bought one that was held together by nails, and sounded that way too.

I went to visit Mittenwald's Staatliche Fachschule für Geigenbau (State Trade School for Violin-making), which was founded in 1858, then the oldest such school in Germany, and supervised and subsidized since 1910 by the state of Bavaria. In 1958 the hundred-year-old school was enlarged: special workshops, a library, a small concert hall, and an acoustics laboratory with modern research facilities were added. The curriculum is based on the sound idea that a young violin-maker must not only make and repair instruments, but should play them reasona-bly well and know their history and the purpose and possibilities of string instruments. "The curriculum aims to maintain the principles of classic violinmaking in accordance with modern needs," says Konrad Leonhardt, the director since 1958. "We hope our students will retain the enthusiasm that they show during their studies." A man may be-come a passable accountant or lawyer without enthusiasm for his pro-fession, but never an able violin-maker. He must love his work.

The number of students is limited to thirty-five, and it takes three and a half years to pass the general examination for a diploma. The student may spend two more semesters in a master class, and a master's diploma assures him of a job almost immediately; leading violin-mak-ers throughout the world are short of well-trained young assistants. The Mittenwald school is the only one of its kind in the Western world.

After three semesters the student must design and complete a "white" (unvarnished) instrument. Aside from instrument-making there is violin or cello instruction, regular lectures in theory, harmony, and musical history, and later in physics, acoustics, and the science of string instruments. The students are trained in chamber music and orchestra playing. (Once a year, they give a public concert.) During the fourth semester they learn to mix and apply varnish, and the art of finishing. In the fifth semester comes the study of the repair of old instruments; this is important, for the number of able repairers decreases everywhere and some day there may not be enough able repairers to take care of the great string instruments. The last two semesters are devoted to recapitulation and review, and possibly preparation for the master class. Director Leonhardt and his staff of full-time teachers read on problems of artistic design, style, and aesthetics and there is an increasing amount of modern research done in the acoustics laboratory. The early results were published in 1969 in Leonhardt's book *Geigenbau und Klangfarbe* (Violin-Making and Tone Color), with scientific analyses on that subject, on the relation between varnish and tone color, the specific acoustical properties of wood, and the importance of measurements.

The students come from all over the world; more than half of them are foreigners. There is a long waiting list. Despite the gloomy predictions of many dealers and experts, there are still young enthusiasts who want to devote themselves to the beautiful and demanding profession of violin-making.

At the school's woodpile the student is introduced to the mysteries of wood. On four floors of a black silo I saw various stacks of wood: square boards of maple for the backs of violins, large ones for violas and cellos, rectangular blocks for scrolls and pegs; spruce and fir for the tops, lime for the blocks, ebony for the finger boards. The maple is either "cut on the slab," across the grain, or "cut on the quarter," the right way of the grain, when the cutting planes appear as the radius of the trunk's section. The texture of the wood is better visible if the timber is cut on the quarter.

Violin experts sometimes talk about vintages of wood as connoisseurs of wine talk about vintages of a certain *cru;* (1927 was a vintage year in Bosnian maple). One expert would walk through the forests, knocking with a small hammer against the trunks of resonant pine.

(Perhaps that legend of the old violin-makers is true after all.) Only branchless timber is used. The wood is cut into long equal boards in which the annual rings are marked as dark stripes. The best fir comes from high-altitude eastern slopes where the trees grow slowly and don't get too wet in winter; the best time to cut the tree is January and February when the trees are low on sap. Fir must never be cut by an electric saw because that might hurt the fibers; it should be split with an ax. While the wood is aging it must be dusted and inspected periodically; worm-eaten pieces are eliminated.

And that is just the beginning. "The first two years are the most difficult," a student says with feeling. "Learning to make linings and ribs, to cut bellies and backs, to make and attach the bass bar, to cut scrolls, attach necks and fingerboards. The only machine permitted is a circular saw, for the preliminary cutting. Everything else is done by hand. By the time you assemble an instrument, the worst is over. Working with varnish is fun. So is the cutting of bridges, to chisel pegs and make the peg box, to fit in the sound post. It's wonderful to finish one's first violin. Mine wasn't worth fifty marks but I wouldn't have traded it for a Stradivari."

"How Much Is It Worth?"

Yes, Old Violins

Are Big Business

The city of Cremona.

Niccolò Paganini.

A drawing of Paganini by Sir Edwin Henry Landseer.

THEATRE ROYAL,
COVENT GARDEN.

SIGNOR
PAGANINI's
THIRD
CONCERT,
THIS EVENING,
Friday, July 13, 1832,

When he will perform three of his

FAVOURITE PIECES:

PART I.

GRAND SINFONIA — — — — *Mozart.*

AIR, Miss E. ROMER, " Fair Agnes, beauteous flow'r." - - - *Auber.*

SONATA RELIGIOSA, IL MATTUTINO NEL CONVENTO DEL MONTE San. **BERNARDO** e " **Pendule a Sonnerie,**" (or the Matins of the Convent of St. Bernard,) followed by the **Rondo detto del' Campanello, composed and to be performed by Signor PAGANINI.**

RECIT and AIR, Mr. BENNETT, " In native worth," *(Creation)* *Haydn.*

AIR Miss POOLE, " Meet me by moonlitgh." - - - *Wade.*
(Accompanied on the Piano-Forte by Herself.)

FANTASIA,

PART II.

GRAND OVERTURE to OBERON. — — *C. M. von Weber.*

SCENA e CAVATINA. Signora PIETRALIA, " Al suo tramonto." *Pacini.*

Recitativo e Variazione Sopra le Arie seguenti:
" **Deh cari venite,**"
" **Nel cor piu,**"
" **Di certi Giovani conosco l'arte,**"
composed and to be performed on ONE STRING ONLY,
(the Fourth String.)
by SIGNOR PAGANINI.

AIR, Miss E. ROMER, " Bid me discourse." - - - *Bishop.*

AIR, Mr. BENNETT, " The Soldier's tear." - - - *A. Lee.*

Capriccio e Variazione, upon the Neapolitan Canzonetta " Oh! MAMMA CARA," descriptive of a Venetian Carnival, composed and to be performed by
SIGNOR PAGANINI.

Leader of the Band, *(with the kind consent of Capt. Polhill)* **Mr. T. COOKE.**

Conductor, — — — **SIR GEORGE SMART.**

Doors opened at HALF-PAST SEVEN O'CLOCK, the Concert to commence at EIGHT.

Boxes 7s. Pit 3s. 6d. Galleries 2s

Applications for Boxes, Orchestra Seats, and Tickets to be made at the Box-Office, Hart-street.

On Saturday, MOLIERE's celebrated Piece, **TARTUFFE; OU, L'IMPOSTEUR.**
With **LE MANTEAU; OU, LE REVE DU MARI.**
Mlle. MARS will perform in both Pieces.
To conclude with a New Ballet, in One Act, by M. TAGLIONI, to be called, **LA RESSEMBLANCE,**
In which **Mlle. TAGLIONI** will introduce some new Dances.
The celebrated Drama, in Five Acts, **HENRY III. ET SA COUR,** and a new grand Ballet, called **LA SYLPHIDE,** are in active preparation and will shortly be produced.

Printed by W. REYNOLDS, 9. Exeter-street, Strand.

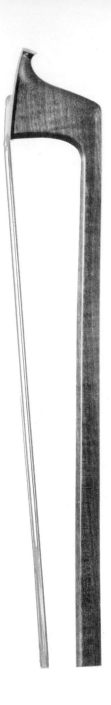

François Tourte, *circa* 1830.

Jacob Stainer, 1659.

Nicolò Amati, 1659.

Antonio Stradivari, 1679.

Joseph Guarneri del Gesù, 1742.

Strange Names and Strange Labels

Violinists use a jargon in order to describe exactly a certain instrument, just as wine people use wine words trying to define the characteristics of a certain wine. Many wine words are clichés, but when used with discrimination they may help to convey the color, bouquet, taste, and aftertaste of a certain wine. Wine experts use about eighty such words, from *acerbe,* acid, balance, and body, to *sève* (sappy), silky, suave, supple, tender, and velvety. Violin-lovers and experts have a more limited, even more cliché-ridden vocabulary. An instrument is in a "good" or "fine" or "remarkably fine" state of preservation, or even in an "exceptionally rare" state of preservation. It is "plentifully covered with varnish." It may have "its original varnish in full glow." The colors and shades of the varnish are described in subtle variations. Superlatives may reach dangerous proportions: "one of the finest existing examples of the master's work," or "unsurpassable plum-red color." Originally the violin words were merely for description and identification, but during the past centuries dealers and collectors have used them for promotion and evaluation. The back is "of handsome maple," or "iridescent," or "with tiger-like stripes." The scroll is "elegant," "graceful," "manly," or "forceful," but few experts could differentiate between a "manly" and a "forceful" scroll.

Certain expressions have a definitive function. Rembert Wurlitzer's certificate of my Stradivari says, "The back is cut on the quarter from one piece of maple with handsome medium narrow flames sloping upwards from treble to bass side. The wood of the sides and scroll matches the back. The top is cut in two pieces from spruce with medium width grain at the center, broader on the flanks. The varnish has a deep red-brown color and has been somewhat retouched on the back." Such a description conveys to the reader a definitive impression. But just as the wine words cannot always convey the subtle sensations of taste because taste is subjective, violin words fail to recreate the magic beauty of a violin, the unfathomable quality of its sound, the way it responds and sings. Everybody uses these violin words because they are the best available substitute, but they are only that. If one wants to really get to know a certain violin one has to see it, hear it, and best of all, play it.

Many famous violins, violas, and cellos have been given names, almost like human beings. Originally such names were used like code words to describe a certain instrument. When the "Messiah" Stradivari was mentioned, everybody who had anything to do with violins knew what it was; no explanation was needed. Later the names preserved the identity of the most important instruments, particularly after many of them had been copied. There might be copies of the "Dolphin" Stradivari, but the "Dolphin" was unique.

Sometimes the story behind a name is as interesting as the story behind the violin itself. Names reflect many emotions—vanity or beauty, greed or greatness. In the early years instruments were named after their prominent owners. This might be justified when the owner was a celebrated artist; a violin once played by Paganini, Viotti, Tivadar Nachez, Leopold Auer, Charles Dancla, Rode, Kreutzer, Spohr, Ferdinand David, Wilhelmj, Vieuxtemps, or Jesus de Monasterio deserves to be called for that artist. The name will also raise the violin's value according to the principle, what was good enough for Vieuxtemps or Viotti ought to be more than good enough for you. Paradoxically, violins are rarely named for contemporary violinists: Jan Kubelik kept until his death his beautiful Stradivari of 1715 known as the "Emperor," even in Prague, where they never liked emperors; now it is the "Kubelik" Stradivari and owned by his son Rafael, the conductor. Heifetz played for many years the "Dolphin" Stradivari of 1714; he no longer owns it and it remains the "Dolphin," though most violinists would rather play on the "Heifetz" Stradivari. Yehudi Menuhin's Stradivari of 1733 is still the "Prince Khevenhüller" (who was he?), though Menuhin has performed on it for many years. Nathan Milstein renamed his "Goldman" Stradivari of 1716 "Marie-Thérèse," after his wife. Isaac Stern plays on the "Alard" Guarneri, of 1737, yet Delphin Alard, the French violinist, never owned that instrument: Vuillaume "baptized" it after Alard, his son-in-law, and sold it to the Vicomte de Panette, a pupil of Alard. (But Alard did own a famous Stradivari of 1715, which is also called after him.)

Almost as much mischief has been done with naming violins as with fancy names for bad wines. France and other nations have laws forbidding unjustified wine names; the violin world urgently needs such laws. In principle names should be restricted to truly important instruments; actually, names are often thought up by dealers eager to enhance the price of an instrument. There is no law against this practice. Violin-owners have become so name-conscious that a violin without a name is like a man without status. Most of Stradivari's violins and many of his violas and cellos have names, and so do a number of violins made by Guarneri del Gesù. Instruments by other celebrated makers are only occasionally baptized. Violin-lovers love the game; they love to read about the pedigree of a famous instrument and the gossip connected with it. An instrument's pedigree is a valuable guarantee against getting a fake Strad. If the owners of a famous violin are known from the moment it left the maker's workshop to the present day, one need not hesitate to write out a check for it in five or six figures. The roster of former and present owners of a great violin is not snobbism, it is proof of the instrument's authenticity.

Many fine violins were named for their early owners or collectors, often men whose names would otherwise be completely unknown. Who would know of Count Cesare del Castelbarco if he hadn't owned five Stradivari violins and a famous cello? Who was Count Eugène de

Cessole, the owner of a famous Stradivari still bearing his name? Fate is often capricious in naming a violin. The "Soil" Stradivari of 1708, a famous specimen, is named for a Monsieur Soil (first name unknown), the Belgian consul in Moscow who owned the violin toward the end of the nineteenth century. The "Soil" had prominent possessors before M. Soil and after him, but his name remains attached to it. Another Stradivari also remains the "Soil," this one of 1714, though it has been Menuhin's for years. A beautiful, reddish-brown Stradivari of 1721 is named after the American violinist Francis Macmillen, from Marietta, Ohio. He bought it from Hart and Son, who had purchased it from the heirs of Anthelme Brillat-Savarin, the immortal epicure. Anyone might rather have the "Brillat-Savarin" Stradivari, but he will have to settle for the "Macmillen." Violins which are noble instruments are often named for aristocratic patrons, among them King Maximilian of Bavaria, the Marquis de Champeaux, the Duke of Edinburgh, and Lord Norton. Some names are deceptive. A small Stradivari of 1734 is named "L'Aiglon" after Napoleon's son the duke of Reichstadt, because it was said to have been given to him, though this was never proved. The duke never learned to play a fiddle; his connection with the violin is as nebulous as that of his father with a certain brandy. Then there is the "Lord Nelson" Stradivari, found in an officer's stateroom on Lord Nelson's flagship after the battle of Trafalgar. Lord Nelson, who had lost his right arm, never played the violin and didn't care for violinists. (Lady Hamilton, his lovely lady friend, hired Paganini once for a musical soirée in Leghorn, and Lord Nelson had to sit quiet and listen. Perhaps it wasn't such a sacrifice.) But the "Lord Nelson" certainly went up in price when a London dealer promoted it as a national symbol.

Shrewd dealers know there is money in a good name. Emil Herrmann christened a Stradivari made in 1727 the "Venus," because of its beautiful varnish and "very fine state of preservation" (cliché). There is the "Titian" Stradivari, the "Vesuvius," the "Apollo," the "Red Diamond," and the "Nightingale" (which sounds that way when played by its present owner, Rafael Druian). When dealers ran out of poetic names, they began to refer to prosaic places and events: the "Irish" Stradivari, the "Scottish University," the "Rochester," the "Berliner," the "Siberian," the "Spanish Court." On December 15, 1895, an article in the London *Violin Times* reads, "The fantastic name of 'Hercules' has just been given to a violin belonging to Eugène Ysaÿe, and it seems necessary to protest against such absurd names . . . The American papers have been quick to take note of this fact and to make fun of it."

The most famous Stradivari has two names. Made in 1716, when the master was seventy-two, it is now generally considered the most perfect of all Stradivaris. Originally it was called the "Salabue," after its first owner, Count Cozio di Salabue, whose name is attached to other famous instruments, and its entire pedigree is known. Count Cozio acquired it together with so much else, from Stradivari's youngest son, Paolo, but Paolo died in 1775 before concluding the transaction to sell the violin. Ever since there has been a superstition attached to this violin; it was taken seriously enough by the Hills to be recorded in their monograph, *The Salabue Stradivari:* "It is a noteworthy instance of the fascination exercised by this perfect violin that no one of the successive owners of the splendid instrument, from Stradivari himself downwards, would part with it until called away by death." Not quite: Count Cozio sold it to Luigi Tarisio in 1827 and then lived another thirteen years. Tarisio never brought it to Paris, but talked about it to J. B. Vuillaume until Vuillaume could see it in his dreams; others were more skeptical about Tarisio's poetic descriptions of the perfect Stradivari. Tarisio continued to talk about the "Salabue" and to promise to bring it to Paris until Delphin Alard, Vuillaume's son-in-law, exclaimed in exasperation, "Monsieur Tarisio, your Stradivari is like the Messiah—he never comes." And thus the "Salabue" became the "Messiah" ("Le Messie"). The Reverend H. R. Haweis saw it in 1872 when it was exhibited at the South Kensington Museum in London, and wrote,

Unveiled in all its intact glory . . . stands this matchless new violin amidst its time-worn, rubbed, and fractured brethren. It is of the grand pattern; it is massive without looking massive; its strength is hidden beneath its grace. The back is in two parts; the wood very choice. The fine graining of the flat belly is remarkable. The holes are delicately cut, the left f a shade lower than the right; a practice so common it must have been intentional with Stradivarius, his fine eye not tolerating even there a suspicion of mechanical work. We see in this violin what the perfect Stradivari corners were. In almost every other known specimen the corners and the wood are both rubbed. The neatness of the purfling is incomparable, and over the whole instrument lies a thick rich red-brown varnish wondrous to behold . . . unworn by time and use. The brush seems to have left it about a week. The neck has been lengthened by M. Vuillaume. The head is light and graceful . . . the scroll thrown off like a ribbon lightly curled around the finger and drawn in . . . the lines of the scroll picked out with a thick rim of black varnish.

The last owners of the wonderful violin, Arthur and Alfred Hill, decided to bequeath it to the Ashmolean Museum in Oxford, but both men died before their wills were executed. Though it is there, the old superstition nevertheless proved true once more!

Printed labels, hidden inside violins, have created confusion in the violin world for the past three hundred years. Unlike names, which were almost never given to the instruments by their makers, labels are the maker's legitimate signature. Many paintings of that period are signed by their artist; in most books is printed the name of the author. The violin-makers had the right and the duty to place a label in the instruments or brand their names into it; some violin-makers used both labels and brands. Antonio Gragnani from Leghorn branded into his violins a crest with the letters A.G.; the Testore family in Milan branded a crown with a double-headed eagle.

Labels reveal much about the makers, and since we know so little about their private lives we are grateful for every hint. In principle the label shows the name of the maker, the place where the instrument was made, and the year. The label is almost always pasted to the back inside the violin, usually just below the middle part of the bass bar so that one can see it through the left sound hole. Some makers' labels show their modesty, others their promotional abilities: some realized early that the small piece of paper could be a signature, diary page, advertising, even an expression of piety, all in one. The label gave still-struggling makers a chance to mention their famous teacher—or use a famous name in hopes the customers would believe he was their teacher. If a man added to his name "alumnus Nicolai Stradivari," he would certainly get a higher price for his violin. Some makers proudly added "Cremonensis" or "Cremon.," though they had long left there. Matteo Gofriller, a fine maker who never worked in Cremona, wrote on his labels, "in Venetia al' Insegna di Cremona" ("in Venice, at the

Sign of Cremona"): anything to mention Cremona! Others stated their Cremonese origin with justification and pride "Petrus Guarnerius Cremonensis fecit Mantua," or "Petrus Guarnerius Filius Joseph Cremonensis Fecit Venetijs." Some labels are laconic, "Gasparo da Salo, In Brescia," but some are regular business cards: "Franz Simon, Hof-und bürgerlicher Lauten- und Geigenmacher zu Salzburg 1715" ("Court-and-city-lute-and-violin-maker"). Labels tell us about the cities where the Italian makers worked, and in some cases about their travels. The labels of J. B. Guadagnini indicate whether an instrument was made in Milan, Parma, Piacenza, or Turin; and on some labels he calls himself "Placentinus" ("from Piacenza"), which is correct, and on others "Cremonensis" ("the Cremonese"), which is stretching the truth, especially when "alumnus Antonii Stradivari" is added. Some makers wrote bold, powerful letters, others could hardly print the figures indicating the year. Jacob Stainer used handwritten labels which often contained orthographic mistakes, "Jacobus Stainer in Absam prope Oenipontum . . ."

Most Cremonese masters printed their own labels, often including misprints and spelling mistakes. Stradivari once printed a number of labels with one letter upside down, making "Antonins" out of "Antonius." Either he didn't care or he was thrifty and hated to throw things away; he used one of these labels in the "Muir Mackenzie" violin of 1694, and they are as valuable as the famous misprints of philatelistic rarities.

Many makers show definite idiosyncrasies in their labels. Nicolò Amati used a longish inscription, giving his whole family history: "Nicolaus Amatus Cremonen. Hieronymi Fil. ac. Antonij Nepot Fecit 16 . ." (". . . the son of Hieronymus and the nephew of Antonius"). The sons of Stradivari marked their jointly made instruments "Sotto la Disciplina d'Antonio Stradiuari F. in Cremona" ("made in Cremona under the supervision of Antonio Stradivari"), which was the exact truth. Antonio's son Francesco calls himself in one of his own violins, "Franciscus Stradivarius Cremonensis Filius Antonii," while Omobono, in his violins, printed incorrectly, "Omobonus Stradiuarius Filus (*sic*) Antonij Cremone . . ." Carlo Bergonzi felt he could stand on his own; his labels read, "Carlo Bergonzi fecit in Cremona."

Dishonest people have often tampered with labels to increase the price of violins that showed the influence of several makers, or were made by, for instance, a master and his assistant. It is relatively easy to alter a label—much easier than to alter an instrument—or the original label may be taken out and a forged label inserted. Until the late 1950s this was no crime, though never exactly ethical. A court in Switzerland has judged violin labels to be valid legal documents, "with the purpose of proving a fact of legal importance"; such legislation should be introduced in all civilized countries.

Labels don't prove the authenticity of an old violin; professional dealers and experts, unlike amateurs, look at the label only after they've made up their mind about an instrument. A genuine label increases the instrument's value and modern detecting methods (such as chemical analysis) may help to establish the truth about the age of the paper and the ink, but it is not easy to remove the label undamaged from an old violin.

Contrary to widespread opinion many violins made by famous masters still have their original labels, though sometimes a part—for instance, the date—may have been changed. Labels began to be falsified in Italy soon after the first violins were sold: in 1685 Tommaso A. Vitali, violinist at the court of Modena, complained in a letter to the duke that he'd bought for the price of twelve pistols a violin with a label of Nicolò Amati, underneath which he later discovered the label "of one Francesco Ruggieri, called 'Il Pero,' a maker of much less repute, whose violins at the utmost do not realize more than three pistols." Nicolò Amati had died only the year before, but unscrupulous persons were already taking advantage of his posthumous fame. Faked "Nicolò Amati" labels have been found in violins made by members of the Ruggieri family, by Andrea Guarneri, and by Goffredo Cappa. Lesser Gagliano makers occasionally copied a Stradivari violin, and for good measure put in a copy of a Stradivari label. In Germany there were hundreds—some people say thousands—of falsely labeled "Jacob Stainer" violins in the eighteenth century, when Stainer's fame was high.

In the early nineteenth century there was a regular renaissance of Andrea Guarneri's violins labeled "Nicolò Amati." Andrea had worked under Nicolò Amati and some of his violins have the Amati touch; the name Amati had more commercial value at that time than

Guarneri. Other Andrea Guarneri violins were sold under the name of Carlo Bergonzi and there is sometimes considerable affinity between the works of these two masters. When Del Gesù became the most famous Guarneri of all, violins made by his father, Joseph filius Andreae, or his brother, Pietro of Venice, were occasionally relabeled as works by Giuseppe del Gesù. The exception was Giuseppe's uncle, Pietro of Mantua, whose violins have such individuality that they were always recognized as his own.

Further complications ensued when collectors began to specialize in the labels alone, and were not ashamed to remove original labels from fine violins. Count Cozio di Salabue, an enthusiastic collector of labels as well as of violins, had a distinguished collection of stolen labels—Stradivari, Amati, Bergonzi, and others. Most of them were genuine, and Count Cozio realized he had to replace them in their instruments with false labels. It is possible that Luigi Tarisio helped him in this elegant racket. Some false labels were well imitated by such specialists as Pietro Giovanni Montegazza in Milan, an able violin-maker who did label-forging as a lucrative sideline. Charles Reade, who knew Tarisio well, also had a fine label collection.

Another enthusiast was Nicolò Bianchi, a nineteenth-century dealer and repairer who worked in Genoa, Paris, and Nice. An English cellist spent the winter in Nice and became friendly with Bianchi, and helped him arrange his collection of lovely labels; later the cellist gave Bianchi his Ruggieri cello for repairs, and received it back weeks later, minus its genuine Ruggieri label. Monsieur Bianchi had kept it as a souvenir, for his collection.

Many "false" labels were put in with no fraudulent intent. These instruments were sold as faithful copies, which included a faithful copy of the original label. Usually the copyists inserted their own labels elsewhere in the violin, for instance on the inside of the top. The greatest copyist of all, Jean Baptiste Vuillaume, often inserted copies of Stradivari labels in his copied instruments, but he dated all his Stradivari labels 1717. He never tried to reproduce the original label, though it would have been child's play for him. Often he also marked the number of his copy in the center of the back.

Unfortunately most people having to do with labels were less honest. The worst culprit was Luigi Tarisio, through whose hands passed many great instruments. He couldn't resist the temptation to get more for a second-rate instrument by putting a false label of Nicolò Amati or Stradivari. The practice was continued later in Paris and London.

In the case of Stradivari no one ever thought of removing or replacing a genuine Stradivari label, for no more precious label existed. But while any Stradivari label was good, some were better than others. Stradivari's work has been catalogued, more or less arbitrarily, into "epochs," and violins made during Stradivari's "best" years, between 1710 and 1720 say, were supposed to have more value: so why not change only the year on a genuine Stradivari label, making a 1716 out of 1706 or 1726? (My Stradivari has a genuine label with the date changed by a smart operator. The Emil Herrmann certificate says, ". . . the violin is in my opinion a work of Antonio Stradivari of Cremona, period 1729/1730, and bears a label 1716." The Rembert Wurlitzer certificate states that the violin was "made by Antonio Stradivari circa 1730. It bears its original label with the date altered to 1716.")

In most cases such "alterations" were made by inept swindlers. Experts know the characteristic manner in which Stradivari wrote out his figures, and cannot be deceived. But the swindlers were encouraged by the fact that Stradivari changed his labels several times during his long life. He had carved a block from which he printed his earliest labels, and this contained three printed figures "166 "; he wrote in the fourth figure; the rest of the text read, "Antonius Stradiuarius Cremonensis Faciebat Anno . . ." At the end he always affixed his monogram, a small cross above and between the A and S; the monogram was made on a separate block of wood.

When the 1660s ended and he still had a large supply of labels he simply wrote a "7" over the second "6," and in the 1680s he added a small circle to the second "6" to make it look like an "8." In the 1690s he devised several ways to turn the second "6" into a "9." It's done naïvely, and with great charm when one thinks of the highly sophisticated execution of his instruments.

Stradivari used this wood block until 1698, and then made the momentous decision to print a new set of labels in bolder letters. By that time he had good reason to be bold. The wording remained exactly the same, and the monogram with the cross between his initials. But he still hated to waste anything: the eighteenth century being just around the corner, he printed only the first figure ("1") and filled in the other three figures by hand. Thus the instruments made between 1698 and 1729 have the last three figures written by Stradivari's own hand. One doesn't have to be an expert to perceive his strong, impetuous "7," his unmistakable "8" with the upper circle always open like a tiny window toward the sky. "His "3" and "6" are also very characteristic.

In 1729, he made a last change. Using another, still heavier typeface—perhaps for his failing eyesight, since he was then in his eighties—he replaced the "u" in "Stradiuarius" with a Roman "v," making it "Stradivarius." Why he made that change, no one can say. The Hills have observed that the type in Stradivari's labels seems to somehow follow the style of his work. His finishing is less fine in his old age, just as the writing is also less fine, almost coarse. It may have been harder for Stradivari to write a label than to work on a violin; as a mellow octogenarian he made some wonderful masterpieces, but when he wrote "de Anni 89" ("at age 89") on a label the special effort is noticeable. He couldn't make the inscription "D'Anni 93," on one of his very last violins, "The Swan," in 1737—the year he died; he certainly worked on the violin, but the inscription on the label was made by his son Omobono.

Frauds and Stolen Violins

Well-made copies of masterpieces of all forms of art have been sold for centuries, and the violin is no exception. A fake Stradivari is even easier to sell than a fake Renoir, for there are fewer experts whose judgment is considered infallible. Ernest Doring writes about a good Guarneri del Gesù copy made by J. B. Vuillaume; Vuillaume never sold a copy as an original, but somehow the Guarneri got into the hands of a dishonest man, who was never identified, and it was accompanied by an impressive-looking "Royal Order of Presentation" from an obscure European ruler addressed to a Mr. Svendsen; there were also fake certificates from the Hills' firm and from a reputable German dealer. There are probably many such cases, but the unhappy buyers of fake instruments like to remain anonymous. Having been cheated, they don't want to be ridiculed.

A famous fake was the "Balfour" Stradivari, which was accepted by many experts as a genuine work. A London outfit, "Balfour & Company," even distributed a booklet entitled, "What Are the Broad Distinguishing Marks of a Stradivari Violin?" Even Willibald Leo von Lütgendorff, the German expert, was fooled, and included the instrument's false inscription in his famous encyclopedia of violin- and lutemakers. Eventually the fraud was exposed by Alfred Hill; the "Balfour" had been copied in London by William, Charles, and Arthur Voller.

The worst offenses were committed in the name of Guarneri del Gesù, whose erratic workmanship offered great possibilities for clever fakers. Doring points out that Horace Petherick's biography "contains an example of how badly a self-constituted expert may err . . . I could name other cases in which the memory of Del Gesù is similarly affronted."

Great violins are not only copied, they are also stolen, though the dealers have an old saying that it's easier to get rid of a baby than of a stolen famous violin. But great violins have always almost hypnotically attracted people who steal the instruments for themselves, not to sell them. Such a person hides the violin—and another instrument has disappeared.

Ludwig Spohr's beautiful Guarneri del Gesù was stolen in 1804. Spohr had received it as a gift from M. Rémi, an admirer in St. Petersburg. He loved the violin and told everybody he could give his best with it. After eighteen months in Russia, Spohr returned to Brunswick, where he was employed by the duke, and during a concert tour through Germany he visited Göttingen. There it happened: in his autobiography Spohr writes,

> The violin case with its contents was in my trunk, and the trunk was secured with strong leather straps to the back of my coach. I made the coachman stop from time to time to make sure that the trunk was still in its place. We arrived in Göttingen late last night. When we passed through the garden suburb outside the city walls, I stepped out of the coach for the last time to have a look at the trunk. Then I sat down again beside my accompanist, Beneke, and told him that my first step in Göttingen would be to get a strong iron chain and lock. We had to stop at the city gate. While Beneke told the sergeant of the watch our names, I asked one of the soldiers standing about to tell me if the trunk was still at the back. "What trunk are you talking about?" he asked, "I cannot see one."

> Mad with rage, I picked up my hunting knife, jumped out of the coach, and ran back along the road to the place where I had seen the trunk for the last time. There was no trace of the thieves. . . . The next morning I

was informed that an empty trunk and a violin case had been found in a field. In an ecstasy of joy, I went to the spot, hoping that the thieves had been content to take what was in the trunk, and left the violin in its case. But this was not so. My dear Guarneri was gone. It was small consolation that the thieves had not noticed a precious Tourte bow which had been fixed to the inside of the lid.

Spohr's Guarneri has never been found, and may have remained in the possession of some very private collector. Eventually it may have been destroyed. One night in 1908 the "Hercules" Stradivari made in 1732, which then belonged to Eugène Ysaÿe, was stolen from the artist's dressing room at the Maryinski Theater in St. Petersburg while he was onstage performing on his Guarneri del Gesù of 1740, his favorite violin. The "Hercules" Stradivari has never been seen since; its name was later given to another Stradivari.

A celebrated theft occurred in 1894 in a rooming house in New York where Jean Joseph Bott, a German-American violinist, kept his "Duke of Cambridge" Stradivari made in 1725. Bott had previously refused a check of $4500 for the violin from the Italian collector Ernest Nicolini (the husband of Adelina Patti), because Bott didn't trust checks and wanted payment in cash. Nicolini tore up his check in fury and told Bott to take his fiddle and beat it. Weeks later the violin was stolen. The police searched for it in vain, and the tragedy literally broke Bott's heart; he died the next year. A former friend of Bott, a New York violin dealer named Victor S. Flechter, was subsequently arrested, convicted of the theft by a jury, and sent to prison. Years later when Flechter was out on bail, pending a review of his case, the violin was found. It had been stolen by an unidentified man and sold to a pawnbroker for four dollars. By that time, Flechter was ruined financially, and a dying man besides.

In 1919 Bronislaw Huberman's famous "Gibson" Stradivari, of 1713, was stolen from his hotel room in Vienna. (It was named after George Alfred Gibson, a well-known English violinist.) Huberman's instrument was in a double case which also contained another good Cremonese violin and several bows. Within a few hours the Stradivari was offered to a Viennese dealer at a low price; the dealer suggested that the "seller" return later, and notified a detective agency; the thief was caught.

Huberman's 1713 Stradivari was stolen again in February, 1936, this time from his dressing room in Carnegie Hall in New York. No trace of the violin has ever been found, and Huberman collected insurance money of $30,000 for it. Huberman was pursued by more ill luck in October, 1937, when he was in an airplane crash near Palembang, Sumatra; his injuries ended his concert career. Many people wondered what happened to Huberman's Stradivari—perhaps it is still hidden somewhere in America, watched over by a fanatic who has no intention of ever putting it on the market.

How to Buy a Fine Violin

Reported prices for violins are often a skillful blend of fact and fiction. In 1967 it was widely reported that Heifetz had sold his "Dolphin" Stradivari of 1714 to a "West Coast syndicate" for "well above $100,000." "Like the old story about the fur business in St. Louis, it wasn't the West Coast and it wasn't a syndicate, and it wasn't even a hundred thousand dollars," writes Arnold Gingrich in *A Thousand Mornings of Music*. The "Dolphin," which the Hills called "a violin of high repute," was early acquired by Vuillaume who sold it to C. G. Meier for 6500 francs, then about $1300; Meier sold it in 1868 to the dealer George Hart for only £200, ($1000); Hart sold it to Louis d'Egville, but soon bought it back—maybe d'Egville didn't consider its repute high enough—and sold it in 1875 to John Adam for £625 ($3125), making a long-term profit of over three hundred per cent in seven years. In 1881 the Adam Collection was sold. David Laurie bought the "Dolphin" and sold it the following year to Richard Bennett for £1,000 ($5500) at a considerable short-term profit. In 1892 the

Hills acquired the violin "at an enhanced price," sold it to David Munro, a Royal Navy officer, later bought it back, and in 1950 sold it to Jascha Heifetz, who kept it seventeen years.

Dealers rarely reveal prices unless it is intentional—possibly to stir something up, or to set a high price for an instrument of similar value. But there was nothing secret about the world's most sensational violin sale: on June 3, 1971, at an auction at Sotheby's in London, the "Lady Blunt" Stradivari, made in 1721, fetched £84,000 ($201,600). This sum was nearly four times the highest known price paid for any violin in the past. Vuillaume had got hold of the instrument in 1864 "after it had lain undisturbed in a Spanish attic for a hundred years," and sold it for £260 ($1300) to Lady Anne Isobella Noel, better known as Lady Anne Blunt, a granddaughter of Lord Byron and a good amateur violinist (who had studied with Wilma Neruda). At that time this was considered a record price. With the violin there came a written guarantee by Vuillaume:

> I guarantee the perfect authenticity of this instrument which came into my possession with its primitive finger-board and without having been opened. Everything about it is intact, and I have not touched it except as is required by present day needs. I have had to change the bass bar and lengthen the neck to modern dimensions, but I have preserved the original neck. This fine instrument is therefore absolutely complete, and in an exceptionally rare state of preservation.

After Lady Anne's death in 1895, the violin was sold to a number of succeeding private collectors. In 1902 the Hills said the "Lady Blunt" was "remarkable for its fine state of preservation." It has never been owned by a professional violinist, and therefore has no scratches and almost the entire original light red-brown varnish. Eventually it came into the possession of Robert Bower, in England, who sold it in 1941 to Henry Werro, the noted dealer in Switzerland. Werro held it until 1959, then sold it for an undisclosed price to an American collector, Sam Bloomfield, of Palm Springs, California.

Prior to the auction in 1971 word had got around that something unheard-of might happen at Sotheby's. The place was jammed and the television cameras of the British Broadcasting Corporation were whirring when Howard Ricketts, a director of Sotheby's, described "Lot 21, a highly important violin by Antonio Stradivari, Cremona, 1721. . . ."

The instrument had its original label and the mortise with the initials P.S.—Paolo Stradivari, the maker's youngest son, who had kept it after his father's death until he sold it to Count Cozio di Salabue—and the violin was accompanied "by the maker's original fingerboard and bass bar," which Vuillaume had replaced in 1864. Ricketts started the bidding at ten thousand pounds. Within a few minutes, it was all over; Andrew Hill, of W. E. Hill and Sons, submitted the final bid of £84,000, topping the competition of London instrument dealers J. and A. Beare. (Not long after "Lot 74," a violin made by Carlo Landolfi in Milan in 1853, went for $9,120; this, many people thought, was a suitable anticlimax.) Surrounded by newspapermen and cameramen, Hill afterward admitted that he'd purchased the "Lady Blunt" for a collector; in the tradition of the house, he disclosed nothing more. (The collector was later identified as a banker in Singapore.)

It remains to be seen whether the fantastic price of the "Lady Blunt" was a unique curiosity (like the Velásquez *Portrait of Juan de Pareja,* which brought $5,544,000 at Christie's that year), caused by the inflated art markets all over the world. Thomas Hoving, director of New York's Metropolitan Museum of Art, which acquired the Velásquez, later rationalized, "When you have a combination of a great master at the full height of his powers, painting a subject he obviously deeply understands and enjoys, that has by luck come down 322 years in pristine condition, you have something that is really extraordinarily special." But the case of the two-hundred-and-fifty-year-old "Lady Blunt" Stradivari is different. If its price indicates a new trend most musicians have no hope of buying a very fine instrument; only wealthy collectors could do that. And at least a dozen violins on earth belong in the same exalted league with the "Messiah" and the "Lady Blunt."

One of the earliest references to violin prices is in an exchange of letters, quoted in the Hills' biography of Stradivari, between Galileo Galilei, the great astronomer, and Fra Fulgentius Micanzio, a Servite monk and former pupil of Galileo. On November 20, 1637, the astronomer, then in Arcetri near Florence, sent Father Micanzio in Venice "the amount of my small pension" and asked him to get "a violin, either of Cremonese or Brescian make," for his nephew Alberto, "a very good performer on that instrument." Father Micanzio replied on December 5 that he knew "Signor Monteverdi, Chapel-Master of St. Mark's, who has a nephew living in Cremona . . . The difference in the price will show you the superiority, for those [violins] of Cremona cost at the lowest *twelve ducats* each, whilst the others (Brescian) can be had for less than *four ducats*." On April 24, 1638, Father Micanzio wrote to Galileo that Monteverdi's nephew in Cremona had finally decided on "an instrument of exquisite work" which, however, couldn't "be brought to perfection without *the strong heat of the sun*." Evidently it was a recently varnished violin. However, there was available "an old one of superlative merit," at fourteen ducats; a month later, the price went up to fifteen. (The Hills believe it was a violin made by Nicolò Amati.) Obviously, less than a hundred years after the invention of the violin, a Cremonese violin was already worth three times the prices of a violin from Brescia.

The old masters may have thought about money but they left few written records. In 1685 Stradivari made instruments for Cardinal Orsini, archbishop of Benevento; the following year for the duke of Modena; in 1715 for the king of Poland. The transactions are confirmed but we don't know the prices of the instruments. Fétis quotes Pierre La Houssaie, a French violinist (1735–1813) who visited Cremona thirty years after Stradivari's death; he was told there that the price of a Stradivari was four *louis d'or*. (François Tourte in Paris got three times that much for one of his famous bows.) In a letter written on June 4, 1775, Count Cozio informs Paolo Stradivari that a certain Signor Boroni wanted to sell his Stradivari violin for eleven *gigliati*.

It is almost impossible to translate correctly the real value of old gold coins. Their exact purchasing power is unknown, and comparisons with modern currency are hypothetical. But one fact is certain: forty years after Stradivari's death an Amati violin cost four times as much as a Stradivari, and important violinists often preferred a Jacob Stainer to an Amati. Amati instruments were used generally by court orchestras, while Stainer violins were preferred by soloists for their sweet tone. Arcangelo Corelli (1653–1713), one of the earliest virtuosos, owned an Andrea Amati and a Matthias Albani. In 1756 the London *Daily Journal* reported that an old Cremona violin sold for 36 guineas "at the private sale of a deceased Gentleman's Effects in Bond Street." Prices were slowly going up.

In 1785 a writer in the *Encyclopédie Méthodique* in Paris considers Jacob Stainer the maker "of the greatest reputation," admitting that the violins of Cremona were "also renowned." Among the Cremonese he first mentions the Amatis, "Andrea Amati, the master of Stainer [*sic*], the brothers Antonius and Hieronymus whose admirable violins were much sought after and very expensive." Thirdly Nicolò Amati, whose violins were "of varying merit." Among the also-rans was Stradivari; "The merit of his instruments consists in their masculine, powerful and melodious tone."

Around 1780 the performing virtuosos began to create a new evaluation. In 1782 Viotti, the greatest virtuoso since Corelli, caused a sensation in Paris "by his admirable playing and the fine tone produced from his Stradivari instrument," according to M. Gallay; the sensation was later repeated in London. Viotti realized that he obtained a stronger tone and greater carrying power from a flat-model Stradivari than from a more highly curved, grand-pattern Nicolò Amati. Shortly after 1800 Count Cozio, then the great expert, wrote, "The best violin-makers are: Giacomo Steiner of Switzerland; Castagnery and Chapuy of France; Andrea, Antonio and Nicolò Amati; Stradivario Antonio; Guarnerio; and Rugeri of Cremona." He also praised "the admirable genius" of Giuseppe Odoardi. (Odoardi, 1746–1786, from Poggio di Bretta, followed the models of Montagnana, and was so widely admired and copied that his authentic instruments became genuine rarities.) At that time Count Cozio owned some of the greatest Stradivari violins, among them the "Messiah," but he ranked "Stradivario Antonio" in seventh place.

The important violinists of Count Cozio's time did not agree with him. La Houssaie, Kreutzer, Baillot, Rode, Habeneck, and others followed Viotti's lead and played on Stradivari violins. By 1805 Cozio had changed his mind, ranking Stradivari and his son Francesco first among the Cremonese, followed by the Amati family and, in fourth place, the once much-admired Stainer. Cozio considered the Guarneri family rather second-class and was especially critical of Guarneri del Gesù. He had many reservations about Del Gesù's earlier works—such reservations were later expressed by many experts—and thought that "most of the instruments he made afterwards, though he used the same pattern, hardly place him in the third category."

Around 1800 a Guarneri del Gesù rated about half the price of a Stradivari. But when Paganini began to perform all over Europe in the late 1820s on his "Cannon" Guarneri, Del Gesù prices rose; the best violins became about as expensive as the great instruments made by Stradivari. Ever since, Stradivari and Guarneri del Gesù have dominated the violin world with their flat-top models, while the curved Amatis and Stainer have fallen back. After 1870 many collectors showed increasing admiration for Stradivari. In 1902 the Hills wrote, "Today an average Stradivari violin cannot be purchased for less than six hundred to a thousand pounds, while a fine specimen is worth from a thousand to twelve hundred pounds." In 1902 a thousand pounds equaled $5,000. In 1968 the "Marie Hall" Stradivari was auctioned at Sotheby's for $52,800; the following year a Jacob Stainer fetched £1,350, or $3,250.

The violin market, always a special field, has often had ups and downs, though it is not as topsy-turvy as the art market. At certain times a fine violin has been offered at a ridiculously low price and has gone begging. At other times a great violin was not to be had at any price within reason.

Violins have always been bought by players, by collectors, and by those who buy them in the hope of making a profit. In the long run inflation and the steadily decreasing supply will drive up the prices of fine violins, for these are considered, like fine paintings, to have an absolute value, a hedge against the decreasing value of money. Speculators hoping to make a killing must develop a sixth sense for certain violin-makers whose works, they believe, will go up and up. In recent years there has been interest in violins made by Pietro of Mantua.

The dealer's first problem is to buy rare violins, and his second, to buy them at a price that will permit him to sell them profitably. But rare violins are not a commodity, they cannot be easily acquired. Celebrated violinists wouldn't think of selling the instruments on which they happily perform; wealthy collectors can afford to remain anonymous. The dealer must know the whereabouts of the greatest old violins that survive, numbering one or two thousand. He must keep up on deaths, divorces, and economic crises that involve the owners of rare violins, for any of these may mean a possible seller. He knows that he isn't alone; the race to get there first with the most will be spirited and ruthless. Dealers must study their customers in depth, correctly guess their wishes and needs (which the customers may not know themselves), and after sizing them up they must correctly decide which is the right violin for each customer. They must be prepared for protest. Their advice will not be appreciated, for violinists—amateurs as well as professionals—are often wishful thinkers whose self-evaluation is not always borne out by the facts. At some point of his career almost every fiddler dreamed of becoming a Heifetz. The illusion is often nurtured by doting parents and optimistic teachers. Sooner or later the average fiddler comes to realize the awful truth that very few violinists have the stuff a Heifetz is made of. But when they choose a violin, the wishful dreams seem to come back again. It is the job of the experienced and honest dealer to destroy these dreams without losing the customer. The best dealers know that the important job is not to sell the customer an instrument—any instrument—but to help him find the one that is best suited to him and to his means.

A good dealer knows that a man testing a violin gives himself away without knowing it. The customer, even a cold-blooded one, always loses the psychological contest against the violin. And few violin customers are cold-blooded, anyway; they are usually very hot-blooded. (Some get an acquisitive gleam in their eyes, the sort of gleam that is familiar to croupiers in Monte Carlo and to salesmen at Cartier's.) The customer takes the violin in his hands. He puts the violin under his chin reluctantly or defiantly—but always expectantly. He plays it, puts it down, looks at it, plays it again. He puts it away and tries the next violin. A good dealer soon knows that there is a violin which the customer likes best, though the customer may not know it yet. The customer has already lost the contest against that violin. He is licked. Somehow, even after testing three or four violins—which would seem the maximum for fifteen minutes—he instinctively reverts to one violin, whether he is aware of it or not. In nine cases out of ten, that is the violin for him.

There may be complications. A young violinist, less or more talented, comes with his teacher, more or less famous. The teacher knows "best," of course. The pupil likes a certain violin but the teacher doesn't. The dealer has to tactfully convince the teacher that the pupil is right, which will not be easy if the teacher considers himself infallible. Great teachers, of whom there are few at any time, often like to surround themselves with a halo—and shouldn't be blamed for it.

Another problem is the customer who bought an expensive instrument and has second thoughts about it. He's paid forty or fifty thousand dollars, yet somehow, suddenly, "the violin doesn't sound the way it should." Experienced dealers ask the customer to bring the instrument back and try it in comparison with other instruments in about the same price range. In nine cases out of ten, the first violin sounds fine again.

All dealers know that people act in certain ways when they pick up a fine violin. Some are so afraid of dropping it that they can hardly put a bow to it. They are awed by the thought that the small piece of varnished wood in their hands is worth more than a house, and it is almost always a heart-stirring experience. The only exceptions are a celebrated violinist, who for often unknown reasons wants to have "another instrument," or a rich collector, who buys the violin for complex reasons: he likes to have an instrument from a certain "period" of that master, or he wants to complete a set, or it attracts his fancy, or—if he is a real collector and loves the violin—he wants to save it for a few years from the ravages of time and violinists.

Unlike wealthy collectors, many musicians have only a limited amount of money to spend. Violin-lovers generally are a wistful group of people whose desire to gaze at, and handle, beautiful violins far exceeds their ability to pay for them. A shrewd dealer always asks a prospective customer how much he can afford. The dealer knows there is no sense in showing a person a forty-thousand-dollar Stradivari when he has only three thousand dollars. After playing the better fiddle, he won't like the less expensive one. In the end he may buy none, and the dealer has lost a customer.

When I became a prospective customer, Emil Herrmann told me not to experiment with violins for more than fifteen minutes. He said that more time makes even musicians with an expert ear lose their ability to discriminate. I didn't believe him, but of course he was right. As a rule, the last violin one plays always sounds the best—another inexplicable bit of the violin *mystique*. Also I know now that if you want to buy a violin you must never let someone else play it for you; one cannot judge the violin properly, one judges the player. It sounds different when one plays it oneself, but one must to get "the feel of it."

Dealers may try to dissuade their customers from taking violins home to test them. They concede that a man who is thinking of putting up thousands or tens of thousands of dollars for an instrument should be permitted to try it out in any reasonable way. But sometimes a customer takes home a fiddle he likes and plays it for relatives, friends, and kibitzers, and they find fault with it. After a while the customer is no longer so crazy about the violin. The violin hasn't changed, and he hasn't, but the kibitzers have raised all those objections: it is too shrill, too soft, too loud, too dull, too sharp, too whatnot. Violins never affect everyone the same way; even a great violin which is admired by most listeners is admired for a variety of reasons: that is one of its beauties. If they all agreed about its characteristics, it would prove to be a dull instrument.

Great dealers who consider their job a vocation feel happy when they sell a customer the violin that's just right for him. Back in 1914 Emil Herrmann chose for Jascha Heifetz, then thirteen years old, a Carlo Tononi made in 1735. Seven years later Herrmann was offered the beautiful Del Gesù called "Ferdinand David" after the concertmaster of the Leipzig Gewandhaus Orchestra, a former owner. By then Heifetz was already a great success, and Herrmann decided that this was the violin Heifetz ought to have. As Heifetz was then on tour Herrmann got in touch with the violinist's father. Heifetz *père* came to see him and bought the violin, solely on the dealer's recommendation; Jascha Heifetz had never seen it. Later Jascha wrote to Herrmann, "I have wanted to tell you how much joy my 'David' Guarneri is giving me. It is a most wonderful violin under any kind of playing conditions and I am continuously delighted with it. . . . I feel warmly toward you for bringing us together."

In 1929 Herrmann brought together Yehudi Menuhin, also thirteen years old, and the "Prince Khevenhüller" Stradivari, a magnificent violin made by the master in 1733, when he was eighty-nine. Herrmann lent young Menuhin the Stradivari to play a concert in Carnegie Hall; dealers often lend an instrument to a talented, impecunious artist, and not for entirely altruistic reasons. The young artist may find a benefactor who will lend him the money to buy the instrument or even pay for it outright. And in the audience that night was the blind Henry Goldman, the late New York banker and collector; after consulting with Adolf Busch and Fritz Kreisler, Goldman bought the "Prince Khevenhüller" for Menuhin. Years later, Herrmann sold Menuhin a Guarneri del Gesù of 1742. Menuhin wrote, "You can well imagine how happy I am with the Guarneri. It is useless to describe to *you* the glory of this instrument. It is fitting that I should find another lifelong friend through you . . . I know that now, with two of your adopted children in my possession, an ever greater attachment will ensue between us." Menuhin, a sensitive man, had well called the violins "adopted children" and spoke of "possession," not of "ownership"; possession is *temporary* ownership. The attachment later increased when Menuhin bought a third violin from Herrmann in 1952, the "Soil" Stradivari of 1714. Most concert artists swear by Stradivari or by Guarneri del Gesù; Menuhin swears by both. He has played occasionally two violins at the same concert, using his Guarneri for unaccompanied Bach and one of his Stradivaris for the rest of the program, a feat of adaptability not many violinists would attempt.

Most dealers love certain violins, and some dealers love them so much they refuse to sell them. These may not be the most famous or expensive instruments. Herrmann once admitted that the violin he loved most, among all the treasures he had ever handled, was a Nicolò Amati made in 1656—a beautiful "grand pattern" violin with double purfling and tiny rubies and emeralds inlaid into the wood, and an incredibly sweet and lovely sound. When Herrmann was forced to sell it, being a businessman, he felt that he had lost a dear friend. Mrs. Lee Wurlitzer Roth, whose firm owns some of the world's great violins, is likewise in love with the "Salabue" made by Francesco Stradivari in 1742. She cannot explain exactly why—which is the test of true love. She has refused all offers for it.

The prices of rare old violins, as of any work of art, will reflect the iron law of supply and demand, economic conditions, and the changing whims of popular taste. Fortunately, there will always be people

—violinists and collectors—who buy a violin for the best possible reason: because they fell in love with it. Such love usually guarantees a successful marriage between the possessor and his violin. No matter what he paid for it, it will be worth much more to him.

On Experts and Dealers, and the Violin War in Switzerland

Not many people on earth are genuine violin experts, able to judge the authenticity and merits of old instruments. It is no accident that there are so few people around who have the instinct and perception to "recognize" an old violin, and the knowledge and integrity to make their judgment stick. Even among the well-known dealers there are perhaps only half a dozen today whose judgment is accepted as gospel when tens of thousands of dollars are involved.

David Laurie, who was a genuine expert, wrote,

> To be a good expert requires three important gifts which must be inborn and yet require to be developed with much study. These three gifts are an unerring eye, a good memory, and a good ear. The two first are absolutely essential to enable one to distinguish the work of different makers . . .

> The third gift is not considered by any means necessary to the making of an expert, yet I think that a good ear plays an important part in the work . . . to be able to distinguish one tone from another and to decide which has the best carrying power and which is in most repute with the majority of musical folk, artists and amateurs alike.

Laurie, an expert with a sense of humor, wrote about people who kept their Stradivari violins in bed and slept next to them, "so they could get away with their fiddles in case of a sudden fire." He once discovered a Stradivari in the home of a musician in Paris who played second fiddle in a small theater, not knowing what he was playing on.

Another expert, Emil Herrmann (1888–1968), had seen most of the famous instruments during his long life and was able to recognize a fine violin he'd seen before, even if the previous encounter with the instrument was forty years back. He recognized a certain violin as surely as people recognize their friends. (But he could not always place the faces of men and women he knew, and often embarrassed his wife by asking her to introduce him to someone he had just met.) Herrmann's career answers the often-asked question, how one becomes a genuine violin expert: in Tauberbischofsheim, Germany, where he was born, his father had a repair shop and was a respected dealer in string instruments. Life in the Herrmann family revolved around violins. As a boy Emil spent much time at the workshop watching the craftsmen at work and "getting the feel" of violins, which is so important. His father wanted him and his older brother to become dealers rather than makers of violins; he started each son learning the violin by the age of six and told the boys that one could be a successful art dealer without being able to paint a picture but it was all but impossible to sell violins without knowing how to play one.

When Emil was eight his father began to explain the intricacies of the violin to the boys. The boys inspected a different undistinguished German violin every day for a year, and wrote a one-page analysis of it. The second year they had better French violins to study and analyze. Gradually they advanced to the good, then to the great, Italian violins. At the dinner table violins were always discussed, much as wine is always discussed at the tables of French viticulteurs. Whenever an old violin was brought into the shop Herrmann *père* would ask his sons to describe its characteristics in writing and try to deduce its country, date, and maker. Hard and often unexciting work, but it paid off; by the time Emil was eighteen his father had enough confidence in his judgment to send him out on the road as a buyer and seller. In Wiesbaden Emil sold a fine Nicolò Amati for twenty-one thousand marks ($5000), then a high price. His father was delighted, and the son began buying and selling violins all over Europe.

Throughout his life Emil Herrmann kept himself in practice by going almost every morning into the storage vault where the violins rested on their sides in velvet-lined compartments. To the left of the entrance there were rows of violins by Stradivari, the Guarneris, the Amatis, Bergonzi, Ruggieri, Montagnana; to the right were the less important violins, but they were often crowded by an overflow of Guadagninis, Gaglianos, and Gofrillers from the right. The hundred and eighty compartments built into the vault were rarely sufficient, and dozens of violins were stored on upper shelves. Alone and undisturbed, Herrmann would survey his rows of violins, indentifying each instrument by one detail or another of its appearance. He called this routine "playing a few scales."

Amateurs and connoisseurs are often fascinated by the behavior of prominent experts when they look at a beautiful violin: nine out of ten will first hold the violin in front of them, getting its feel and noting its shape. Once I stepped into the shop of Ludwig Tröstler, the leading violin expert in Vienna. He didn't know that I'd just acquired my Stradivari, and when I opened the case to show him my bow he just stared at the violin; then he took it out and held it up.

"How beautiful! I didn't know you had a Stradivari!" he said. I asked him how he could identify the violin in a few seconds. He was irritated by what he plainly considered a silly question. "Goodness, a Stradivari like this speaks to me, though it is silent. Why, the genius of its maker is all over it. . . . Admittedly, there are instruments when one isn't sure." Herrmann once told me that if he couldn't identify a reputedly good violin within a minute, the chances were that something was amiss.

In doubtful cases the intensive scrutiny begins with the back, where the expert examines the texture of the wood and the quality of the varnish. There follows a study of the front, the shape of the f-holes, the scroll, the sides, the ornamental purfling along the edges. Every prominent violin-maker has certain characteristics of design and execution; they may change slightly as his eyes get weaker in old age and his hands less sure. These peculiarities are as obvious to the expert eye as are the characteristics of a man's signature, as we have said, to an experienced bank teller: a man's signature may change in the course of the years, but the expert teller can always identify it.

Aberrations often provide a key, and the cutting of the scroll and the f-holes may be especially revealing. In his last years Stradivari made some beautiful-sounding masterpieces. Kreisler, Huberman, and Heifetz performed on violins that the old master made in 1734, when he was ninety. But the f-holes and the curves of most of Stradivari's last violins lack the dynamic sweep of his earlier ones, and the scrolls don't have the inspired flow.

Experts are fascinated by violins that display the touch of more than one important master, for those challenge their powers of detection. Often there is a story behind such an instrument. Some of the last instruments made by Nicolò Amati show the hand of Stradivari, who started out as an apprentice in Amati's workshop. George Hart wrote in 1875 that he was "not aware that there has ever appeared a Violin of Stradiuarius in which it is stated that he was a pupil of Nicholas Amati," but in a later edition of his book he changed his mind: "Having met with a violin by Stradivari (since the first edition of this work), dated 1666, it would appear that he left the workshop of his master at that time, or not later than the year of his marriage—in 1667." The late Alfred A. Hill mentioned a violin ". . . which we recognized as an early work of Stradivari, and great indeed was our pleasure and surprise when, on deciphering the original label, we found the words 'Alumnus Nicholai Amati, Faciebat Anno 1666.' " This label is the only existing admission by Stradivari that he was a pupil of Nicolò Amati.

The experts love to argue about some of Stradivari's last violins, made when he was assisted by his sons Francesco and Omobono. They also talk about certain Guarneri violins made after 1715, when Andrea Guarneri's son Giuseppe (Joseph filius Andreae) had several trained apprentices. His sons Pietro (later Pietro of Venice) and Giuseppe del Gesù, then twenty and seventeen years old respectively, were already in the workshop. The Hills consider it "quite possible" that Carlo Bergonzi, then thirty-two, was an assistant of Joseph filius Andreae; the conjecture is read out of Bergonzi's violins. The outlines, the placing of the sound holes, the purfling, mitres, blocks, and linings all show a certain affinity with the work of Joseph. Bergonzi's varnish is more similar to that of Joseph filius Andreae and Del Gesù than to Stradivari's. Yet for centuries Bergonzi was believed to have been "the favorite pupil" of Stradivari. But only the very greatest experts may play this refined game of detection.

Herrmann once identified an alleged Guarneri del Gesù as the work of Joseph filius Andreae. On the other hand Guarneri del Gesù used his own labels only after 1726, and some of his earlier, independently made violins use the label of his father, Joseph. Herrmann once showed me a violin labeled "Nicolò Amati, 1646," which was known to have been made by Nicolò's less gifted son, Girolamo; it was the favorite violin of Benito Mussolini, who always thought he had a genuine Nicolò Amati. No one disillusioned him.

Rudolph Wurlitzer started his great collection with a violin whose belly and label were by Stradivari, the back, ribs, and scroll by Alessandro Gagliano. Hill once bought a fine Stradivari of 1710 with a scroll by Guarneri del Gesù, and soon thereafter he came into possession of a fine Del Gesù with a Stradivari scroll. An anonymous violin-maker is believed to have had both violins in his shop for repair and switched the scrolls accidentally. All established dealers know of violins that were not made by the man who made the scroll. If the dealer can afford to wait, he puts such a violin in his vault and hopes for a minor miracle. Herrmann once waited twenty years until a relatively undistinguished instrument turned up with the fine Nicolò Amati scroll he needed for a better violin.

Important dealers treat their instruments as a clinic treats its patients, and for each instrument (i.e., patient) they make up a special file. Herrmann had records containing important details on many important instruments; every dealer has his own method. At Rembert Wurlitzer, Inc., America's leading firm, the "passports" and case histories of all important instruments are kept in binders that also describe the instrument's state of condition, preservation, and repair; the file contains the registered number of the instrument, the maker's name, date, and place where made, the label, all known former owners with dates of sale and prices paid if possible; dealers' certificates accompanying the instrument; articles and correspondence referring to it. This collection of data is followed by a minute description of the violin, with specifications of varnish, back, top, sides, model, sound holes, scroll, and the exact measurements of bouts, sound holes, ribs, and stops. On a special form is noted what cannot be seen from the outside —the number and the exact spots of patches, edges, underlays. Most old violins have a sound-post patch and half-edges because they have had to be opened for inspection, conditioning, and repair. The chart also contains an exact description of all patches, fill-ins, replacements of blocks and linings, and cracks. Like a patient's X-ray pictures, such a chart tells almost everything about the instrument, revealing its state of preservation.

On the basis of his experience, as well as such minute inspection, a dealer may issue a certificate. This contains a detailed description of the instrument and makes specific its state of preservation and repair. Some certificates give the instrument's measurements. There are reduced photographs of its top, sides, and back, and often actual-size reproductions of the f-holes and the scroll. Each photograph is signed by the dealer. The key sentence of the certificate reads, "The violin sold by me this day to . . ." The violin (or, "The violin in the possession of . . .") was made in our opinion by . . ." The reservation "in our opinion" was added in the early 1960s, when Switzerland and the international violin community had been badly shaken by the *liutomachia,* "violin war," that is still an unpleasant memory for dealers and experts everywhere.

The opening shot in this war was fired in the early 1950s by Commendatore Giovanni Iviglia, a former Italian consul in Germany during the Mussolini regime and later the general secretary of the Italian Chamber of Commerce in Zurich. Iviglia, who was always interested in violins, set up an "advisory council" that consisted of two Swiss violinmakers, a music historian, and a violin teacher. The members of this council considered themselves students of rare old violins, though none was an internationally known expert. Owners of old string instruments were invited to send them in for a "free inspection" but there was no assurance that the instruments might not be damaged when they were opened. It was said that any judgment would be rendered "without guarantee."

This was the sort of judgment that has always worried prestigious dealers. Each segment of the art world has its affairs and scandals, including the violin world; buyers of rare old violins are sometimes more emotional (and more gullible) than the buyers of great paintings, who may be cold-blooded investors. Violin enthusiasts fall in love with an instrument because it sounds beautiful, and thereafter they lose sight of the realities.

It is no secret that many violins believed to have been made by Stradivari, and shown in Cremona in 1937 at the bicentenary of the master's death, were later rejected by a committee of important experts as not made by Stradivari. Iviglia, in his preface to René Vannes' *Dictionnaire Universel des Luthiers,* quotes Franz Farga as his authority that "of two thousand instruments ascribed to Stradivari only forty were considered authentic." (Farga sometimes follows Fétis' method in blending fact and fiction: e.g., "As Stradivari never left his workshop during the day, other masters went to see him—serene, witty Carlo Bergonzi, wistful Ruggeri, temperamental Alessandro Gagliano, taciturn Domenico Montagnana, expected by friends to become a great master. They were all one big, happy family." Needless to say, there is no proof of the "big, happy family." On the contrary, the evidence from the Guarneris indicates that the common "family" had its share of professional jealousy and personal envy.)

Some collectors and musicians responded to Iviglia's invitation and sent their instruments to Zurich for a "free inspection." According to Iviglia, "nine out of ten" had to be told that their instruments were either copies or had been made by less prominent makers and later "promoted" to prominence often with the help of spurious labels. At that point, the Zurich police became interested in the affair. A "scientific police laboratory" was set up, subjecting the violins to "natural-science methods": microscopes, X-rays, fluorescence lamps, chemical analysis. Criminologists in money-conscious Switzerland are old hands at investigating counterfeit banknotes, and eventually Dr. Max Frei-Sulzer, the chief investigator, announced that in some cases "valuable violins turned out to be copies" and that he had discovered "faked labels bearing the names of Stradivari, Amati, Guarneri del Gesù."

There ensued bedlam. It was implied that many old violins might be forgeries. Henry Werro, a well-known Swiss violin-maker and dealer in Berne, and member of a respected family of luthiers, was accused of fraud and of falsifying labels which were now called "legal documents." Some famous violin experts were invited to testify before a grand jury in Berne. In the end the jurors were asked to decide the dilemma between the style-critical opinion of the violin experts and the "natural-science method" findings of the Zurich police. Neither the sometimes divergent opinions of the experts nor the results of the natural-science investigation by the police were sufficient to convince the jury and the court.

The experts pointed out that they needed no natural-science analysis to determine the authenticity of an old violin. They explained that the genuine expert recognizes the maker of a violin by an inexplicable mixture of instinct and intuition, training and experience, which no microscope or chemical analysis can supply. It is a fact that chemical analysis of wood and varnish are not infallible; the ingredients of old varnish have completely oxidized after the centuries and cannot be determined by natural-science methods. In several cases, fluorescence analyses made in 1954 and 1958 led to different conclusions. And the specific age of wood proves nothing by itself. Vuillaume bought up pieces of old wood from antique-dealers and beams from Swiss chalets and used such "aged wood" for the copies of his old Cremonese instruments (which he indicated as copies). Henry Werro, accused of twenty cases of fraud, was acquitted in eighteen cases; he was found guilty in two cases and given a fine of five thousand Swiss francs and a suspended sentence. The trial did not answer the important question, whether either the style-critical experts or the natural-science laboratory experts should decide the authenticity of an old instrument. On December 21, 1958, the prestigious *Neue Zürcher Zeitung* commented on the verdict, "It would have been presumptuous, after centuries of confusion in this sector of the antique market, to make decisions that would definitely *("endgültig")* solve questions of authenticity."

The most important decision reached by the court was that henceforth violin labels were to be considered "legal documents." Most violin experts are aware of the doubtful legal value of labels that had been tampered with centuries ago. "The court was also well aware that labels have created much confusion in the international violin market but it considered it significant that original labels are usually mentioned as such in dealers' certificates while facsimile labels are not specifically mentioned as such."

A work of art which is sold and bought as the product of a certain artist must be genuine; that is an accepted fact. Fine violins have been bought by some collectors as an investment, and this is subject to the same hazards as any comparable investment in a work of art. But an old violin is a work of art and also the tool of the violinist's trade. Suppose the practicing violinist, professional or amateur, is happy with the violin he lives with, and gets from it what he wants—easy response, beautiful tone, carrying power, a handsome appearance. He didn't buy the instrument as an investment. Does it matter to him whether the violin was made by a Cremonese maker in the seventeenth or eighteenth century, or by an able French maker a hundred years ago? A wise man knows the value of a certain amount of self-deception: he knows better than to investigate the past of the violin or of the woman he loves, or of his friends. As Paganini said, "Everybody has his secrets." Much of all that talk about a genuine rare old fiddle is the owner's vanity and snobbism. Some possessors of fine violins love their dealer's certificate more than their violin. A man who *really* loves violins enjoys a fiddle for what it gives him more than its noble origin.

The Story
of Great Collectors

Collectors and performers don't look at violins quite the same way. To a musician, a great old Italian violin appeals primarily for its acoustical qualities: beauty of sound, responsiveness, carrying power. A violinist wants a violin that speaks easily, has a well-balanced tone on all four strings, and can be heard, even when played in *pianissimo,* in the far corners of a large concert hall over the sound of the accompanying orchestra. In the opinion of many celebrated violinists, not many violins can do all that. When at last they find the violin that gives them nearly everything, they may stay with it for years, or forever. It is an unexplicable fact that certain great violins sound better when played by a certain great violinist than in the hands of another artist of equal standing. A violin is emotionally and spiritually the extension of a player's mind and feeling, breath and voice. It is pressed close to the chin and it vibrates with the player's heartbeat. It often reflects the artist's innermost feelings which he may not show even in his eyes or his face.

Great violinists sometimes own and perform on several instruments, each outstanding for some reason, but they may be unable to explain why they prefer one of their fiddles. The psychological and emotional rapport between a violinist and his violin is like the rapport between two human beings: a fine violin demands a lot from the player, but it gives him a lot in return. Important dealers know that even a celebrated violinist doesn't always sound so wonderful when he tries out a great violin in a dealer's study. No wonder: that intimate rapport with the violin is not yet established. "Few players are able to make all violins sound right, even all great ones," said Emil Herrmann, who had heard most of the great violinists of his time as they tried out fine violins in his study.

The average violinist approaches the purchase of a rare violin with as much thought as the average man devotes to buying a house. He hopes it will be the violin (or house) that he will keep for a long time. Violinists are interested in different instruments, depending on their financial position and their standing in the musical world. Amateurs, and chamber-music players generally, prefer beauty of tone to power of sound; they may find their instruments among the Amatis, a Ruggieri, a Pietro of Mantua. Orchestra players generally look for an instrument with powerful tone; they want to be heard by their fellow players over the din of the loud orchestra, which may be very loud when Wagner, Strauss, or Tchaikovsky are played. Their best bet may be a Guadagnini or Gagliano—instruments distinguished for power rather than delicacy. Soloists and great concert virtuosos need an instrument that has everything—including that mysterious something that makes their hearts beat just a little faster as they put the bow to a certain violin. In nine cases out of ten it will be a great Stradivari or a great Guarneri del Gesù.

Unfortunately, good violinists cannot always afford the instruments they deserve and ought to have. In earlier days the ratio between a concert artist's earnings and the price of a fine violin was more in the artist's favor. When Paganini gave a series of fourteen concerts in London's Covent Garden in the summer of 1832 he collected £8000 in ten weeks, almost $3000 a concert. Yet Paganini paid the equivalent of only a thousand dollars for his viola, made by Stradivari in 1731. He kept the beautiful instrument all his life. After his death his son,

Baron Paganini, sold it to Vuillaume; from Vuillaume it went to Otto Booth, an English collector; then to the Hills, to Baron Knoop (the famous collector), back to the Hills, to Robert von Mendelssohn (who bought it for the Joachim Quartet), and to Emil Herrmann, who reunited, incredibly, the Paganini viola with the three other Stradivari instruments that Paganini had owned.

This is one of the great stories of collecting. If there is anything better than to own a Stradivari, it is to own a Stradivari on which Paganini played. And if there could be anything better than that, it would be to own the quartet of Stradivari instruments that Paganini once owned. It should crown the achievement of a resourceful, obstinate, patient dealer—and of an enthusiastic and wealthy collector.

The task would seem almost impossible. The great instruments are scattered all over the world, and often owned by collectors who don't want to part with them. Emil Herrmann succeeded in 1949; he considered it, justly so, the high point of his career. To assemble a quartet of rare instruments by the same maker was his special delight because it carried an enormous challenge. Back in 1912 his father, August, had pointed out in a monograph, *Das ideale Streichquartett,* that only eleven Stradivari string quartets could be formed because only eleven Stradivari violas were then believed to exist.

Herrmann assembled one Stradivari quartet in 1937, which was played by the Musical Art Quartet. When the group disbanded the instruments were scattered. In the 1950s three other Stradivari quartets in the United States were owned by the Herbert N. Straus family, the estate of Felix M. Warburg, and the Whittall Foundation in Washington.

No one had been able to bring together the four Stradivari instruments once owned by Paganini: the "Desaint" and "Salabue" violins of 1680 and 1727; the "Paganini" viola of 1731; and the "Ladenburg" cello of 1736. Various dealers, among them Herrmann *père,* tried for years to bring the four instruments together but at best they could get control of two instruments at one time, never more. Herrmann got hold of the viola and the cello in 1935. In 1944, he acquired the "Desaint" violin after the death of David H. Walton, a Boston collector. And in 1945 he succeeded in getting the "Salabue," from Henry Hottinger, the New York collector. The "Salabue," a very beautiful violin in "a perfect state of preservation and almost fully covered with its original, dark-red varnish" (Doring), is one of Stradivari's instruments whose entire pedigree is known from the day it left the workshop of the maker.

The violin was part of the purchase made by Count Cozio di Salabue from Stradivari's youngest son, Paolo, in 1775. He considered it one of his finest possessions; it remains named after him. Count Cozio sold it to Paganini in 1817 for a hundred *louis d'or,* approximately four hundred dollars; the original bill of sale exists. Subsequent owners were: Paganini's son, Baron Achille Paganini; J. B. Vuillaume; the Comte de Vireille; the dealers Gand and Bernardel in Paris; the Italian collector Ernest Nicholas Nicolini; the dealers Hart and Son in London; the British collector Frederick Smith; W. E. Hills and Sons; the New York collector Felix Kahn, who brought the violin to America in 1914. Kahn later sold it to Helen Jeffrey, who sold it to Herrmann, who sold it to Hottinger, who sold it back to Herrmann to complete the Paganini quartet. During its tortuous career the price of the "Salabue" went up a hundredfold, to $40,000. Today it might be worth five times as much.

Hermann now had the Paganini quartet, and offered it to several affluent collectors, without success. He was already thinking of breaking it up and disposing of the instruments one by one (which, he admitted, would have almost broken his heart) when he met the Belgian cellist Robert Maas, once a member of the celebrated Pro Arte Quartet in Europe. Maas had come to America in 1944 and was trying to start a similar ensemble; he found three other players, but none of them had adequate instruments for such an undertaking. Herrmann showed Maas the Paganini quartet; Maas went to see Mrs. Anna E. Clark, a wealthy New York woman whose niece he had met in Europe; Mrs. Clark liked the instruments, and sent Herrmann a check for $155,000; she turned them over to Maas and his fellow players, who called themselves the Paganini Quartet.

Another famous quartet of outstanding Stradivari instruments is now the permanent possession of the Library of Congress in Washington, a gift from Mrs. Gertrude Clarke Whittall, the widow of a manufacturer in Shrewsbury, Massachusetts, who had been a lifelong admirer and collector of such instruments. In 1935 and 1936 Mrs.

Whittall gave the library of Congress five beautiful Stradivari instruments and five bows made by François Tourte; she also established the Gertrude Clarke Whittall Foundation for their preservation and care. The instruments are kept in the Whittall Pavilion, a large, beautifully furnished room with indirect lighting and air-conditioning. In a large glass case there are the instruments. The most famous is the "Betts" Stradivari made in 1704, "one of the great productions in Stradivari's life" (Hill), "a masterpiece of masterpieces" (Doring). The two other violins are the "Castelbarco" made in 1699, a fine example of the "long Stradivari" with a golden-orange varnish, and named for Count Cesare Castelbarco of Milan, a noted nineteenth-century collector; and the "Ward" of 1700, named for J. Ward, a London collector. Doring calls the latter "a perfect and beautiful specimen, unique in being possessed of its original neck, the label, as well as all other essential parts, as fresh almost as when the violin left its maker's hands." The viola is the "Casavetti" made in 1727, when Stradivari was eighty-three, and named for an early owner. The Hills comment on the master's old age, visible in "the stiffness of the curves and . . . the whole character." The cello, made in 1697, is also named for Castelbarco; though made from poplar wood, which is inferior to maple, Mischa Schneider, the cellist of the Budapest Quartet, was very satisfied with it.

Mrs. Whittall understood string instruments when she arranged for her generous gift. Like other collectors of such beautiful things, she had been saddened by the fate of Paganini's beloved Guarneri del Gesù, the "Cannon" of 1743, kept in a glass case in the Municipal Palace in Genoa and rarely played because the authorities are afraid to lend it. Mrs. Whittall stipulated that the Stradivari instruments must never leave the Library of Congress except for restoration and repair; she also stipulated that the income from her foundation must be used to pay distinguished artists to come to and perform at the Library of Congress so that the instruments would be "consecrated in perpetuity to vital public service" (William Dana Orcutt, in *The Stradivari Memorial*). At the Library of Congress the instruments would have a permanent home, "assured of security—insofar as it is humanly possible to foresee—and proper physical care, to be seen and admired in our nation's treasure house." Dr. Harold Spivacke, chief of the Library's Music Division, once told me that the generous bequest had created some unexpected problems. Not every artist cares to play on the instruments after only a few short rehearsals. String players like to be married (or at least engaged) to their instruments. "When the members of the Budapest Quartet gave their first concert here in December, 1938, they played well, but it was the old story—they didn't like to perform on unfamiliar instruments. This led eventually to our making them our quartet-in-residence, and the players had time to make friends with the beautiful instruments. For many years, the Budapest loved to perform . . . the Library was glad to have the outstanding quartet for twenty concerts a year; and the people of Washington could hear one of the greatest string quartets in all time, at a cost of twenty-five cents a ticket which is really a service charge. People would form long lines to get them on a first-come, first-served basis."

The two violinists of the Budapest would switch from one violin to the other. The risk was negligible, and in either case they would play a fine Stradivari. During a rehearsal I attended Joseph Roisman, the first violinist, played the "Ward," which had a soft, flexible tone; Alexander Schneider chose the harder-sounding "Betts." This beautiful, famous instrument has never been played much in its life, more than two hundred and fifty years; it was never owned by a practicing virtuoso who wore and tore it to pieces. That's why it is so beautiful today, and also sounds a little "hard."

Musicians often complain that wealthy collectors buy up fine instruments and put them away "where they do no one any good." The complaint is as old as the high price of fine instruments and the inability of gifted musicians to pay for them. (After the "Lady Blunt" Stradivari was auctioned off in London for $201,600, Mrs. Lee Wurlitzer Roth, president of Rembert Wurlitzer, Inc., was "shocked and saddened. The whole string world is upset to see such instruments out of the reach of people who use them as tools of their trade." Mrs. Wurlitzer Roth was right, though some collectors may not agree with her, figuring that the value of their own instruments has gone up too.) The argument will never be solved. Musicians agree that string instruments were created to be played on, not to be looked at or put away in bank safes. Talented, young violinists are often bitterly frustrated by their inadequate instruments, while many fine fiddles rest in elegant glass cases. But there is another side to the problem. We violinists must give credit to many collectors for preserving fine instruments that would otherwise have deteriorated or even vanished.

If all fine instruments had always been in the hands of musicians, especially professional musicians, there would be fewer instruments today. Amateur violinists usually treat their rare old instruments with affection and care. And some of the greatest artists—notably Kreisler, Heifetz, Francescatti, Menuhin, Milstein, and Stern—have always kept their violins in perfect condition. They clean them carefully, put them "to bed" (in their cases) after using them, and worry about the hazards of climate and traveling. But other players take shocking care of their instruments. They let them get scratched, expose them unnecessarily to heat and humidity, and don't always remove the rosin dust that eats into the varnish. (Gypsies and some old fiddlers believe that rosin dust on the top, in front of the bridge, gives a certain "distinction" to an old violin; this is as much nonsense as the mystique of dust on an old bottle of wine.) A drop of olive oil will safely remove the most stubborn rosin dust, but some people use alcohol, which kills the varnish altogether.

Experts have always complained about acts of vandalism performed by would-be repairers and restorers at the command of the owners of fine instruments. In 1872 Charles Reade wrote about several "noble tenors" made by the Brothers Amati that had been cut down: "These ruthless men just sawed a crescent off the top and another off the bottom, and the result is a thing with the inner bout of a giant and the upper and lower bout of a dwarf." The Hills complain that Stradivari's violas and cellos, of which there were never many, have suffered most. "They have been cut down and mutilated in the most ruthless manner; and this was done by violin-makers who, then as now, considered themselves thoroughly competent. . . . Under the cloak of restoring and improving, vandalism goes on as actively as ever." This is still true today, confirmed by leading experts and dealers. One famous violinist had his beautiful Stradivari ripped open so often that the beauty and tone of the instrument had been ruined for ever. Whenever an instrument is opened a tiny bit of the precious varnish is inevitably lost. "When a famous violinist feels that 'something is wrong with the violin' he ought to wonder whether something isn't wrong with himself," Herrmann used to say.

It is, of course, true that a violin should be played from time to time; if it is seldom or never played over a decade or two it becomes less responsive in its tonal qualities and vibrations, but after a few months of expert playing it sounds as good as before, sometimes better. The wood fibers, the varnish, the whole miraculous structure lovingly respond to the loving master. It is equally true that violins which are played too much get "tired" and need a rest, but just like human beings fine violins recuperate in a short time.

"We," the Hills write, "who have daily brought under our notice the ravages which time, and above all injudicious usage, have wrought upon so many fine instruments, cannot but pronounce in favor of those collectors who, by their care and reverence, have preserved, and are preserving for present and future generations, some of the masterpieces of the past." The Hills practiced what they preached when they bequeathed the "Messiah" Stradivari to the Ashmolean Museum.

No one—neither musician nor collector—should be permitted to believe that it is his privilege to mistreat a violin simply because he paid for it. For *it does not really belong to him.* Herrmann said, "People who have fine violins in their possession are merely trustees for future generations. Their ownership is temporary. They have the duty of preserving their instrument for posterity." The number of great old Italian instruments is limited, and can only get smaller every year.

No complete history of prominent collectors exists because quite a number always wish to remain anonymous. Count Cozio di Salabue was probably the first important collector, though he didn't collect violins merely because he loved them. He owned many of the finest instruments ever made, and though he was forced to sell many after 1800, he still left over sixty violins when he died in 1840. European collectors were prominent in the nineteenth and early twentieth centuries, but their numbers have declined steadily since World War I. The names of famous collectors remain household words among violin-lovers: Count Archinto, Count Castelbarco (both from Milan);

Marchese Menafoglio (Modena); the Duc de Camposelice (Paris); Count de Chaponay (Lyon). England had many noted collectors: in 1802 W. T. Parke, himself a collector, commented on E. Stephenson, a banker "who had perhaps the most valuable collection of Cremona violins of any private gentleman in England," adding, "Violins are frequently more esteemed on account of their scarcity, like strawberries in January, than their valuable qualities." Other important collectors were the Duke of Hamilton, the Duke of Cambridge, the Earl of Falmouth, the Duke of Marlborough, Lord Macdonald, and the Duke of Edinburgh, the brother of King Edward VII, who according to the London *Times* "played the violin on shipboard, as Admiral, and at the London smoking concerts."

Among nonaristocrats there was Joseph Gillott of Birmingham, a manufacturer of steel writing pens, who under the guidance of John Thomas Hart built up one of the largest private collections ever assembled; at one time he owned almost five hundred instruments. Others were R. D. Waddell, John Adam, and Messrs. Goding and Plowden. Elsewhere there were M. Wilmotte of Antwerp; Robert von Mendelssohn and other members of his family in Berlin; and in Vienna Theodor Hämmerle, Wilhelm Kux, Oskar Bondy, and various Rothschilds, Guttmanns, and Wittgensteins. Many collectors are remembered because their names are attached to famous violins.

The first important American collector was Royal de Forest Hawley from Newtown, Connecticut, who made a fortune in hardware, feed, and agricultural supplies; he loved playing the violin and invested part of his wealth in fine instruments. When he died in 1893, he owned twelve fine violins and several bows. The collection was acquired by Ralph M. Granger of San Diego, passed to an unnamed "business firm," and then became scattered. J. W. Coggeshall of Providence, a textile manufacturer, put together a fine collection. And Dwight J. Partello, a diplomat from Washington, played the violin, and after a visit to Hawley's home he began collecting in a modest way. In Vienna he bought "for a high price, and with a written guarantee" a violin said to be a Joseph Guarneri filius Andreae, which turned out to be the work of an unknown Venetian; Partello learned from his discouraging experience. When he died in 1920 his beautiful collection contained four Stradivari violins, three made by Nicolò Amati, a Guarneri del Gesù, a Bergonzi, a Stainer, a Ruggieri, a J. B. Guadagnini, and several Tourte bows. He bequeathed the collection to the Smithsonian Institution but his heirs succeeded in breaking the will, and the collection was sold to Lyon and Healy in Chicago, and dispersed.

John Wanamaker, the merchant prince, and his son Rodman also built up a fine collection. They often arranged musical soirées at their houses, and the name of the Wanamaker "Capella" appeared in golden letters on the cases and trunks in which the instruments were transported. When the collection was sold in 1929 to Rudolph Wurlitzer it was said to be "the most valuable ever put together in America": five Stradivaris, a Guarneri del Gesù, seven Guadagninis, four Gofrillers, and many others.

But perhaps the finest private collection in recent times was that of Henry Hottinger, a New York investment banker and amateur violinist (who long remained anonymous).

Hottinger bought his first Stradivari in 1935, and kept new acquisitions inconspicuously in the closets of his New York apartment. Thirty years later the astonishing collection, assembled under the guidance of Emil Herrmann, consisted of: an Andrea Amati (1566, "King Charles IX of France," probably the oldest Cremonese violin in the United States); a Nicolò Amati (1658, the "Hämmerle"); a Girolamo II Amati (1686, the "Pearl"); twelve Stradivari violins (1679, the "Hellier"; 1688, the "Derenberg"; 1693, the "Harrison," perhaps the finest *allongé* specimen; 1708, the "Ruby"; 1711, the "Earl of Plymouth"; 1712, the "Viotti"; 1714, the "Dolphin"; 1716, the "Cessole"; 1716, the "Booth"; 1722, the "Chaponay"; 1727, the "Venus"; and 1737, the "Lord Norton"); a Francesco Stradivari (1742, the "Salabue"); a Pietro Guarneri of Mantua (1703, the "Wertheim"); a Joseph filius Andreae (1717, the "Ritter-Zahony"); six violins by Guarneri del Gesù (1716, the "Serdet"; 1726, the "Stretton"; 1737, the "Joachim"; 1740, the "Ysaÿe"; and 1743, the "Carrodus"); a violin by Pietro Guarneri of Venice (1743, the "Baron Knoop"); a Francesco Ruggieri (1698, the "Kirstein"); a Vincenzo Ruggieri (1735, the "Bloch"); a Carlo Bergonzi (1733, the "Earl of Falmouth"); an Alessandro Gagliano (1710, the "Rotondo"); a Camillo Camilli (1730, the "Rudolph"); a Domenico Montagnana (1749, the "Steinheil"); a J. B. Guadagnini (1767, the "Wilhelmj"); a Carlo Landolfi (1770, the "Dahl"); an Enrico Ceruti (1858, the "Topaz"); and a Jacob Stainer (1659, the "King"). Hottinger's favorite violin was the "Hellier" Stradivari, followed by the "Rotondo" Gagliano.

In 1966 Mrs. Lee Wurlitzer Roth managed to get the magnificent collection for Rembert Wurlitzer, Inc. Money is a subject rarely mentioned among great collectors and prominent dealers, but in this case it was "around or above" one million dollars. An armored truck was sent to Mr. Hottinger's home and the precious cargo was taken from the closets to the vaults of the Wurlitzer Company.

Incomprehensibly, there is no violin museum anywhere on earth. Herrmann once said, "Painters, sculptors, furniture makers, tapestry weavers, art dealers, and others have plenty of opportunity to study the works of the great masters. But for violinists and violin-makers there is no place in the world where great instruments can be studied. Dealers and collectors should get together and pool their treasures, at least some of them. The violins, violas, and cellos in such a museum needn't be the most famous in their field. The exhibits should be typical specimens, not necessarily outstanding ones. In the case of Stradivari, for instance, there should be an Amatisé violin of his early period, a long-pattern model of the following, a violin of the Golden Period, and one from his last years. Students could follow the evolution of the master. Attached to the museum there should be a workshop where an experienced repairer would keep care of the instruments, and perhaps teach younger people what seems to become a vanishing art. There will always be new factory fiddles made but how many people on earth will be making fine violins, bows, pegs, and bridges in fifty years, or in a hundred? And it should be a living museum, loaning out its assets to gifted young artists."

It was a great idea, and perhaps it will come true when a wealthy collector, convinced of the importance of such an establishment for the future of violins and violin-making, will start it; perhaps others might follow. Until now violin collectors have been less public-spirited, less aware of their responsibility to the future, than the great collectors of painting and sculpture. Admittedly the great art collectors were richer. And no Lord Duveen, no Wilhelm von Bode has come along yet to persuade rich collectors to donate some of their treasures to such a museum.

Interlude:

The Mystery of Violin Sound

Violinists love to play great violins "against each other," hoping to find out why one violin sounds different from another. Each great violin has something special in its sound, but exactly what is it? Such experiments can be carried out only in the shop of a prominent dealer, or in the home of an affluent collector, where the violinist finds an adequate supply of great instruments of different provenience.

In 1963, "a unique attempt [was made] to explore the mysteries of violin sound via the techniques of modern recording," wrote Israel Horowitz, who produced the Decca album, *The Glory of Cremona*. In the accompanying text the late Rembert Wurlitzer wrote, "Fine violins were made, both in Cremona and elsewhere, but none since that time [the 1740s] has quite matched the extraordinary playing and tonal qualities of the earlier great instruments. The reason remains, even to this day, a mystery, and although self-acclaimed geniuses continued to produce instruments, some of great merit, the artists and virtuosos, after these two hundred years, still seek the great violins of Cremona." Even the leading violin experts, of whom Rembert Wurlitzer was one, cannot explain the mystery of the violin. "The violin," wrote Eugène Ysaÿe, one of the greatest violinists, "is a poet whose enigmatic nature may only be divined by the elect."

The "unique attempt" was simple and ingenious. Rembert Wurlitzer brought together fifteen carefully selected violins. This took some doing, since they belonged to different people, and it took some daring, considering the hazards of traffic and safety in Manhattan. The instruments were adequately insured, but all the money on earth could not have replaced them in case of loss. They were then valued at about $750,000; today their worth might be two or three times that much.

Eventually the fifteen great violins were placed on large tables in the New York studio of Decca Records and made an unforgettable sight for the violin-lovers there. The color photograph on the cover of the album shows the violins lying in a large, lovely circle but does not convey their full beauty. For no reproduction can give the mysterious inner life of a great violin.

Also at the studio were Ruggiero Ricci, the noted violinist, and Leon Pommers, his pianist. Ricci would play "under controlled conditions" each of the fifteen violins "in selections carefully chosen to present each instrument in music sympathetic to its individual qualities." The violins, too, were carefully chosen to convey accurately "the glory of Cremona." Among them were two of the oldest violins known to exist. The "King Charles IX of France" was made by Andrea Amati— the first major creator of our modern violin—between 1560 and 1570 for the court of France, as one of a set of twenty-four instruments; only four have survived. The second oldest violin was made by Gasparo da Salò between 1570 and 1580. "Indeed he was long believed to have been the originator of the modern violin." (Rembert Wurlitzer, like all experts, instinctively avoids the word "inventor" when the violin is concerned. One invents a machine or an engine, but not a violin.)

Among the other violins to be tested there was a Nicolò Amati made in 1656 for the court of France under Louis XIV; a great Carlo Bergonzi dated 1731; six Stradivari violins; and five violins made by Guarneri del Gesù. Rembert Wurlitzer had assembled specimens from the various periods of the two greatest makers. The Stradivari violins ranged from his early period (the "Spanish," made in 1677, when he was thirty-two) to the "Rode" of 1733, on whose label the master wrote in a bold hand, "Fatto De Anni 89" ("made at the age of 89"). The five Guarneri del Gesù violins are among his greatest, including the "Gibson" made in 1734, an especially fortunate year. It was once the concert violin of Bronislaw Huberman and is now Ruggiero Ricci's concert violin.

The selections to be played matched the character of the instruments. For the Gasparo da Salò, a *Largo* by Veracini; for the Nicolò Amati, a *Praeludium* by Vivaldi; for Ricci's Guarneri, the *Hungarian Dance No. 17* by Brahms; for the "Ernst" Stradivari of 1709, *Song Without Words*, Opus 62, No. 1, by Mendelssohn-Kreisler. And so on. The recordings were made under controlled conditions. ("Once a proper recording balance was achieved, Mr. Ricci's position in the studio was marked and he held to it for the entire series of recording sessions. Microphoning and control-board settings, once arrived at, also remained constant.")

But for the truly inquisitive student of violin sound, one variable remained: a different selection was played on each instrument. So a seven-inch "comparison record" was added, with Ricci playing the same phrase—the opening solo statement from Bruch's Violin Concerto in G minor—on each of the fifteen violins. The phrase is perfectly suited for such a test; it begins on the open G string and goes over all four strings to the E string, demonstrating the balance of sound on all strings.

After listening repeatedly to the "comparison record" I was able to distinguish the sweet, velvety, nasal sound of a Stradivari from the sensuous, rich, brilliant sound of a Del Gesù. Stradivari made me think of a Raphael *Madonna,* Del Gesù had something of the titanic impetuosity of Michelangelo. But it was far more difficult to distinguish among the Stradivari violins, and among those made by Guarneri. It was relatively easy to separate the sound of the early Stradivari (1677) from that of the magnificent "Ernst" made in 1709; it was almost impossible to distinguish between the "Joachim" (1714), the "Monasterio" (1719), and the "Madrileño" (1720). And the violins of Guarneri del Gesù were even more difficult to keep apart; they had been made between 1734 (the "Gibson") and 1744 (the "De Bériot"), and sometimes I guessed right but I was never quite sure. I guessed best if I didn't listen more than five minutes and to no more than three violins; after that they all began to sound wonderful, and somewhat alike. I thought, wistfully, I would be glad to have any of them.

Gradually I made more advanced tests. Setting down the needle at random, with my eyes closed, I would try to guess which violin was being played. It was relatively easy to pick the dulcet, tender sound of the Nicolò Amati, or the rich, dark tone of the Gasparo da Salò. But again I began to fail after five minutes: once I was convinced that the "Ernst" Stradivari was a resonant, sensuous Guarneri—proof that Stradivari could create sensuous sound when he so desired!

Ricci, after playing all these wonderful fiddles, wrote,

> In their preference for instruments violinists have long been divided into two main camps: Stradivari and Guarneri. Those who prefer a velvety, more organ-like tone quality choose Stradivari. This group includes almost all the German masters, such as Joachim, Spohr, Busch and Wilhelmj, as well as Kubelik and Sarasate. In our day Elman, Francescatti, Menuhin, Milstein, Morini and Oistrakh have chosen Strads. The Guarneri is more often the choice of the artist who makes more excessive demands of his instrument. Paganini, Vieuxtemps, Sauret, Wieniawski and Ysaÿe all used Guarneris, and in our time it is the vehicle for Heifetz and Stern. Kreisler was a notable exception; he used both.

Actually many artists who played primarily on a Guarneri usually own a fine Stradivari also, but those who use mostly a Stradivari seem to be happy without a Guarneri. "There are many intangible factors," Ricci says, "For instance, who is to say why one instrument demands more *vibrato* than another? Generally speaking, the more output and resource an instrument has, the more difficult it is to handle. Ultimately, it is the player who must adapt himself to his violin if it is to respond to its best advantage." (Isaac Stern told me that he uses less *vibrato* on his "Alard" Guarneri of 1737 than on his second Guarneri, made in 1740.)

After repeated listening to the "comparison record" I became convinced that no violin fulfills everybody's demands. Even some of the greatest fiddles are not right for some of the greatest fiddlers. "The best a violinist can do is to find an instrument which most nearly suits his individual temperament," Ricci said. And Rembert Wurlitzer wrote,

> The merit of these great violins lies not only in the beauty of their sound but also in many other subtle differences which acquire great importance to an artist. These differences are not so apparent to the listener: the speed of response to each note, that is the articulation of the instrument; the greater dynamic range and quality of tone at any level of sound; the evenness and balance of the voicing of the instrument throughout its registers; and finally what might be described as the efficiency of the instrument—the amount of energy required of the player to give the result he is seeking.

Though the experiment was not, strictly speaking, scientific it provided the most searching analysis so far of the mysteries of violin sound. Scientific analysis has failed to clarify the enigma. The frequency, pitch, and energy of the overtones were determined with the help of electronic measurements; the quality and intensity of the tone of a Stradivari were analyzed, and the resonant frequency band of the violin was found to be between 3,200 and 5,200 cycles. But this doesn't explain how the soft wood of the top and the hard wood of the back are "tuned" to one another, whether the aging of the wood changes the relationship, and exactly in what way a soft or hard varnish affects the color of the tone.

How would a great violinist sound on a cheap factory fiddle? Answer: he would sound like himself, more or less. His unmistakable tone, comparable to the timbre of a singer's voice, would be there, but the timbre of a great violinist is filtered, beautified, and magnified by a great violin. Heifetz will remain Heifetz on any violin. But if Heifetz, Oistrakh, Milstein, Menuhin were to play the same violin, one after the other, the violin would sound different in each case, as it communicated the player's personal tone. It is not the violin that makes the performer, it is the performer who makes the violin. If the violin were the thing, as many people seem to believe, a great Stradivari or an outstanding Del Gesù would make a first-rate player out of a third-rate one. We all know that this isn't the case.

But the influence of a fine fiddle must be neither overrated nor underrated. Great performers who instinctively sense the secret of their own tone often search among the great fiddles for the one that they hope will become their perfect voice. Some think they have found it, but after a while they change again; perhaps it wasn't the perfect marriage after all. Some remain happy with the violins they've played for a long time, like men who are happy with the women they found long ago. As in a marriage, the relationship between the artist and his instrument is delicate and intricate, includes give and take. The artist knows that the violin cannot adapt itself to him, and he should also know that there is no "ideal" violin tone. There is only the best tone for a certain person. The tonal quality of a violin depends on three factors: beauty of sound; carrying power, sometimes referred to as volume; articulation, the speed and easiness with which the violin responds to the performer. Carrying power and articulation can be established without much difficulty, but beauty of sound remains problematical. It is easy to distinguish a violin with beautiful sound from one without it but most violinists will not agree about which among several violins has the most beautiful sound, because that must be instinctively felt and cannot be rationally explained.

Violinists act emotionally when they approach a violin. They often love its sound and are dissatisfied with its volume: "It doesn't carry far enough." They may like both the sound and the volume but find fault with its responsiveness. When a man knows he may have to spend a large sum for a violin he easily becomes hypercritical, perversely looking for hidden imperfections. Often he believes he has found the perfect instrument only he learns that it isn't for sale. All these reactions are human; in the end he may make a compromise and get the second-best violin, but if he is an artist and gives himself and the violin a chance, he may make it into the best instrument for him. The great masters understood such peculiarities. Stradivari knew that the musical-minded members of the high clergy and aristocracy considered ideal the dulcet, soft, feminine tone of the "small pattern" Amati and even after 1710 he occasionally made smaller-type instruments for them, though he was altogether sure of his best models by that time. In 1716—the year he made the perfect "Messiah"—he also made a violin that was only 13^{15}/$_{16}$ inches long and had relatively less sound.

Stradivari and the other great makers knew that a good violinist cares more about the quality of his tone than the quantity (volume). Violinists have lasting fame for the beauty of their tone—Nardini, Sarasate, Vieuxtemps, Kreisler—not for the bigness of their sound. Some celebrated artists have a smaller tone than do less famous ones, who try so hard for the big tone that they sacrifice the aesthetic principles of a pure tonal beauty. What produces a big tone remains a mystery even to the best teachers. It seems to have little connection with the player's physique: small, slight violinists may draw a big, round, powerful tone from their instruments while strong, large men manage only a relatively small tone. Were it only a matter of bow pressure it could be taught: but it seems also a matter of inner conviction. Every concertgoer knows that the artist who gets carried away during a performance plays with a tone that is increasingly big, both in volume and intensity.

The experienced soloist playing a concerto never stands too near the accompanying orchestra, to avoid hearing distracting echoes. (The sounds of percussion instruments continue for a while after being made; woodwinds are slower in their attack than strings.) But when he plays sonatas with the piano he stands close to the pianist because the two instruments have different tone qualities, and neither interferes with the other; it is also hard to blend the different tones unless the pianist plays the piano almost like a violin, with feeling and a sense of adaptation.

Quality of tone is indispensable for the good player; unfortunately, it cannot be taught. Tone is a natural gift, though it may be improved by intelligent study: the player must learn to listen to himself. Quality depends first on the charm and beauty of sound; next, on the ability to play long, sustained notes, and to tie notes together without noticeable breaks; last, to give the notes a certain breadth of value which extends beyond their actual value of sound. An artist's standing is not so much determined by his ability to play many notes fast—that is, sheer virtuosity—but by the sustained, even tone he produces, and, naturally, by the spiritual content of his performance. The seemingly simple things are the most difficult ones: to lead the bow imperceptibly from one string to the next; to start a *pianissimo* in such a way that the audience doesn't notice the bow touching the strings.

When famous violinists try out a violin, they always test it for its carrying power. They know that a violin must never be forced, and they try how far they can go to get volume as well as charm and beauty of tone. The tone should be so produced that the strings will continue to vibrate after the bow has left them; if the strings are attacked with too much force the vibrations may be muted or checked altogether. When a good violin is played less power of attack as a rule means more carrying power, for it's the quality of the instrument that carries. A happy medium must be found, though; good violins need a certain power of approach. Even well-known violinists admit (not always publicly) that it took them a long time to get the maximum efficiency out of certain instruments.

Famous violinists rarely talk about the art of violin-playing (the exceptions only underscore the rule). They are even more reticent about the tonal qualities of the great fiddles on which they perform. Though they know the importance of having the violin that suits their artistic temperament, tone, and technique, they are reluctant to analyze their instruments. It has always been like that. Dittersdorf, Spohr, Szigeti, or Flesch—in none of their books have they written about the mysteries of violin sound. Spohr's account of how his "splendid Guarnerius" was stolen is amply detailed but he never tells us how it sounded. Great performers must have a considerable artistic ego, of course, to succeed and go on succeeding, and everybody is supposed to know how they sound. One doesn't talk about it, for words are anyway inadequate to describe exactly the sound of a tone or the taste of a wine. Perhaps great performers don't like to divert attention from the way they sound to the tonal qualities of the violin that helps them sound that way. In my frequent discussions with famous violinists I have noticed a general reluctance to discuss their violins. They let you look at them, maybe even let you play on them (I advise strongly against this; the violin never sounds for you as it does when the great artist plays on it), but they don't like to talk about their intimate characteristics. Nearly all of them play on old Italian violins.

Years ago, Dr. Frederick A. Saunders, then professor of physics at Harvard, made various tone tests of string instruments, recording their vibrations. Once he tested behind a screen the "Nightingale" Stradivari of 1717 and two modern violins. He concluded that "the new violins are harder to play . . . this mechanical difference produces effects of great importance to the player. When he comes to the end of a bow-length he turns and begins to put force on the string. The old violin begins to sing a small fraction of a second before the new one. In a rapid passage where the note may last only a fraction of a second, the least balkiness on the part of a violin may determine whether a player fails or succeeds in producing the tone. Hence to the player . . . the ease of response may be more important than anything else, even the tone quality. To him the expensive violin is worth what it costs. To the listener who is unaware of the difficulties it means less. A violinist acting as a listener may, if he is keen enough, hear the easy start of each note, and appreciate the help which the old violin gives to the player. To such a rare listener the violin may be worth a high price. But the average listener, whether musical or not, appears to be unable to say whether he is hearing a masterpiece of Cremona or a good modern violin."

Amateurs and collectors who don't perform professionally may have other reasons for acquiring an expensive old violin: the touch of the master who made it centuries ago, its historical background and pedigree, and above all the charm and beauty that only time can give to a work of art. That even its tone is covered by a certain patina, is beyond doubt. A person's evaluation of the violin tone will change, like everything else, as he gets older. As a youth I was particularly impressed by the brilliant, soaring sound of the violin's upper string, the stirring, exciting tones high up on the E string. Nowadays when I test a violin I instinctively turn to the lower strings, especially to the high tones on the D string: they seem the real proof of a violin's tone quality. They must not be weak; they should have a woody, dark, soulful sound. The G string is also very important, the foundation of the tonal structure. Ideally there should be no breaks between the strings, as between the registers of a good singing voice. The violin's sonority and balance should be unbroken from the empty G string to the highest tones on the E string. Not all old violins have such tone.

The Wonderful Art of

Violin Playing

Evolution,
and the Early Virtuosos

After playing the violin for more than fifty years—first as a hopeful pupil, later as a discouraged professional, and now as an enthusiastic amateur—I am ever more fascinated by the instrument. My fascination has gone through various phases—a common development among violinists, I suspect. During my early phase I was preoccupied with technique and admired the great violinists mostly for their virtuosity. Then gradually I learned that technique doesn't make the artist. Technique is simply a means of overcoming the physical difficulties of the art of playing, and of freeing the artist to reach the outermost limits. The technically perfect artist (assuming that such a specimen exists) can do anything with his violin and bow; the true artist will strive to re-create the very spirit of the music.

Here we have come upon one of the mystifying aspects of performing. The printed score of a piece of music remains always the same, but its inner meaning changes constantly because it reflects the personality of every performing artist, and that will vary within the framework of style and taste in his time. Playing the violin has much in common with speaking or singing; the slightest inflection of the violin voice may change the meaning of the musical words. Beethoven's Violin Concerto—one of the greatest of all compositions for violin and orchestra—has been performed on the concert stage by every destinguished violinist since 1806, when Beethoven wrote it. Many have played it beautifully, but no two have played it alike.

Right away, the opening passage in octaves is played differently by every important artist, though Beethoven indicated precisely what he wanted, a sixteenth note followed by a quarter note. This hasn't deterred noted artists from adding their own crescendos and accents, or from playing straight double stops in octaves if they felt it that way. It is a very difficult beginning and some violinists adjust the score to fit the limits of their abilities rather than trying to play it as Beethoven wrote it. Certain printed editions of the work have foolishly tried to "improve" Beethoven, and some editors, among them noted artists, have dared "correct" Beethoven. Any artist who plays the Concerto as Beethoven wanted it played has unquestionably attained interpretative greatness—but can he be sure exactly how Beethoven wanted it played? Yet Beethoven was no dogmatic; severity is contrary to the true spirit of his art, and D. F. Tovey considered it "a mistaken form of piety" to adhere strictly to Beethoven's metronome marks.

As a small boy I heard the Beethoven Concerto performed by Eugène Ysaÿe, the great Belgian artist. He was then an old man, and his performance was not impeccable technically. Ysaÿe's left hand was still in fine shape, but he had some trouble with his bow. (Elderly singers with good voices often have breath problems.) Yet the performance was unforgettable for its spiritual and emotional depth. Even Beethoven might have been pleased (if he was ever pleased). Ysaÿe didn't play the notes or even the phrases, he played the music of Beethoven. Though I didn't know it then, Ysaÿe was the first important violinist to play with *vibrato,* then a relatively new addition to modern violin technique that is considered indispensable today.

In 1835 A. F. Servais, the Belgian cellist who with Charles de Bériot created the celebrated Belgian school of string-playing, was criticized in London "for the unusual manner of producing his tone . . . by that intense pressure of the fingers." This described what we now accept as *vibrato,* and we couldn't do without it, though Servais was said to use "a not altogether creditable trick." Eugène Ysaÿe was probably the first great concert violinist who used the not altogether creditable trick, though his father strictly forbade him to use *vibrato* in the 1860s: "You are all over the place like a bad tenor. *Vibrato* will come later, and you must not deviate from the note. You will speak through the violin." Ysaÿe never forgot the admonition. His early recordings, made in 1912, prove his chaste, noble *cantilene,* his artistically impeccable *vibrato.*

Since I heard Ysaÿe, I've heard nearly all contemporary masters of the violin perform the Beethoven Concerto. I remember, among many other qualities, the emotional intensity of Huberman, the classic nobility of Adolf Busch, the warm charm of Kreisler, the pure style of Szigeti, the masculine tenderness of Milstein, the intellectual force of Stern, the true humanity of David Oistrakh, the flawless perfection of Heifetz. The same piece of music—the same notes, played at the same tempo, with almost the same strength of bow—may be perceived by sensitive listeners to convey not only different shades of feeling but different feelings.

Alan Tyson has pointed out some fantastic distortions in the Beethoven Concerto, beginning in 1808 with the first edition. The Concerto was first performed in Vienna by Franz Clement (1750–1842), whom Beethoven admired; the Concerto was composed for him. Clement received his solo part only two days before the performance on December 23, 1806; he must have been a first-rate violinist. The critics thought the Concerto was "good in parts" but "unbalanced." Tyson believes that the haste with which the work was presented accounts "for the impression that Beethoven was partly still composing the Concerto while he was writing it out." The autograph manuscript at the Nationalbibliothek in Vienna gives the impression of haste; it contains passages where one feels that Beethoven had not yet quite made up his mind, for he was a slow and painful worker, always revising. Tyson has done real detective work on the autograph: there is "the case of the missing bar" (bar 217 in the Rondo, at first left out and later put in), and the engraver who mistakenly read Beethoven's "espressivo" as "sempre fsimo" (*sempre fortissimo*). Tyson reached the conclusion that

Beethoven was not bothered about this or the other detail, leaving it hopefully to style-conscious performers to find the solution. Years ago George Szell, a most style-conscious conductor, said, "The composers want us to be imaginative in the direction of their thinking, not just robots who execute an order." The danger, which Szell admitted, lies in a performer's being *too* imaginative.

Great composers who did not completely understand the violin have often asked their violinist friends for practical advice. Mendelssohn had Ferdinand David when he wrote his violin concerto, and Brahms and Bruch discussed their problems with Joseph Joachim; Saint-Saëns consulted Pablo Sarasate. But Brahms and Saint-Saëns continually thought in terms of the piano, and their violin concertos contain enormous violinistic problems. Performing artists admit that they can always play the Beethoven or Mendelssohn concertos even if they haven't worked on them recently, while they feel they must study the Brahms or Saint-Saëns again before every performance.

This doesn't meant that the celebrated violinists were always helpful to the composers. When Brahms made the mistake of showing his Violin Concerto to Henri Wieniawski, at that time one of the most famous violinists, the arrogant Pole declared that the concerto could not be performed on the violin. Leopold Auer refused to study and perform the Tchaikovsky Concerto, though he later recognized his mistake and made his star pupils, Elman and Heifetz, study it. Alberto Bachmann writes, "The fact is that the violinists themselves have been the greatest obstacles toward progress and development in violin technique."

Violin-playing is a relatively young art—some four hundred years old. We cannot separate its history from that of the violin itself; both came into being during the mid-sixteenth century, but there is no agreement about who actually "invented" the violin nor about how the technique for the new instrument was evolved. Both the violin and the art of playing it originated in Italy, probably in Cremona. Andrea Amati, the most influential among the earliest makers of the violin, was born in Cremona around 1500. Claudio Monteverdi was born there in 1567, and he was the first man to realize the technical possibilities of what has been called "the noblest instrument of all." Monteverdi, himself a competent violinist, probably played an Andrea Amati. Being so close to a great violin-maker and to violins, Monteverdi naturally became interested in the possibilities of the new and fascinating instrument.

The violin was not yet a solo instrument; the oldest violin music is one part in an orchestral score. In a sinfonia written in 1591 by the great Roman madrigalist Luca Marenzio, the soprano part is given to the violin. Composers began to notice the new instrument, though the technique of violin-playing was still rather rudimentary. Monteverdi's operatic scores already indicate *tremolos, portamentos,* and *pizzicatos* for violins, also the direction *"questa ultima nota va in arcata morendo."* Flourishes, quavers, and other features were cautiously pioneered by the early violinists, who taught them to their pupils as "secrets." Gradually double stops, chords, octave jumps, and tenths were attempted. Some fiddlers specialized in reproducing animal sounds— the barking of a dog, the song of a lark, and the mewing of a cat. They were much applauded by that part of the audience which has always loved such "attractions."

The art of violin-playing evolved slowly. Almost three hundred years separate the invention of the violin, in the first half of the sixteenth century, from the full glory of violin-playing that came with Paganini in the first half of the nineteenth century. There is a long way from the early *pizzicato* effects that Monteverdi used in his opera scores, to the fantastic *pizzicato* runs that Paganini composed in his great *Caprices.*

The violin was not immediately accepted as a noble instrument, in the sense of the older viol. Anthony Wood, historian of Oxford University (1632–1695), wrote about chamber music there,

> The Gentlemen in private meetings which I frequented played three, four and five parts with viols, a treble viol, tenor viol, counter-tenor and bass, with an organ, virginal or harpsicon joined with them; and they esteemed a violin to be an instrument only belonging to a common fidler, and could not endure that it should come among them for fear of making their meetings to be vain and fidling.

But the violin was established in England by 1660, because John Jenkins (1592–1678) then issued his Twelve Sonatas for Two Violins and a Base, with a Thorough Base for the Organ or Theorbo. This is believed to be the first chamber music for violin written in England.

By that time the Italian composers Salomone Rossi (1587–1628) and Biagio Marini (c. 1597–1665) had already written and performed their trio sonatas. Later in the seventeenth century talented violinists emerged everywhere in Italy: Giovanni Legrenzi (1626–1690) from Venice and Giovanni Battista Vitali (1646–1692) from Cremona both performed and composed sonatas for two violins or flutes with figured bass. New techniques were added. In 1627 Carlo Farina from Mantua (c. 1580–1628) published works that demanded a new virtuosity: the playing in several positions, double stops, *pizzicato, tremolo, sul ponticello* ("very close to the bridge," which creates a strange, disembodied effect), and *col legno* ("with the wooden part of the bow").

But only Arcangelo Corelli, the first genuine violin virtuoso, made the violin generally accepted as the most important instrument in early chamber music—louder, more brilliant, and more expressive than the older, more respected viol—and, later, as a prominent solo instrument. With the composition of his magnificent sonatas and concerti grossi Corelli created a whole new world for the violin. Using a variety of new bowings, he evolved a wide range of styles, feelings, and new musical forms, from songlike *cantilene* to brilliant cadenzas. "Corelli established the violin as one of the most important instruments," the Hills conclude; the violin never lost its importance.

Stradivari was nine years old when Corelli was born in Fusignano, near Bologna, in 1653. "Every art depends on its means of expression, and it is no accident that the great Italian School of violin composition flourished at the time when Stradivari, having finished his apprenticeship, found his own style," writes Paul Henry Lang, praising "that unsurpassable grandeur and symmetry which made the very name of Stradivari a symbol." Corelli was trained as a soloist, went to Rome in 1672, and later worked in Bavaria at the service of Elector Maximilian II. Back in Rome he supervised the musical academies at the palace of Cardinal Pietro Ottoboni. He also worked as conductor for ex-Queen Christina of Sweden; she loved opera and music, and after she abdicated she converted to the Roman Catholic faith and arranged concerts and opera performances in her Roman palace. After 1683, Corelli became known as a composer. His influence on Johann Sebastian Bach is part of musical history. Corelli had no use for the often labored, polyphonic writing of the Germans though he admitted their immense depth of feeling. Unlike his German contemporaries Heinrich Biber (1644–1704) and Georg Johann Pisendel (1687–1755), who wrote fine solo sonatas well known to Bach when he wrote *his* magnificent solo sonatas and partitas for violin, Corelli was an Italian, and the ideal of all Italian musicians and instrument-makers was the human voice. Giuseppe Tartini, his successor, would tell his pupils, "To play the violin well you must sing well." Italian composers have always treated violin music, and music generally, as vocal music. (Verdi's *Requiem* is great vocal music; so is his string quartet.)

Corelli expressed feelings that range from chaste nobility to sensuous passion. His charm, lyrical beauty, and unfailing sense of style and balance made him the master composer of the classical age of violin music in Italy. His *La Follia*, a beautiful Adagio with variations, is still much performed, and in his Forty-eight Trios for Two Violins and Bass he is the precursor of chamber music. (Joseph Haydn's first string quartet, Opus 1, No. 1, the very first string quartet ever completed, was composed in 1755, some seventy years later.) In 1712 Corelli's twelve concerti grossi were published, originally to be played in church. With their changing moods, tempi, and styles they are almost melodramatic ("operatic"); they are lasting masterpieces of baroque music. Corelli died in 1713 (when Stradivari made some of his greatest violins). He is buried in the Pantheon in Rome, next to Raphael.

Corelli probably played on some Stradivari violins but we know only of two violins he owned. His solo instrument was an Andrea Amati made in 1578, then over a hundred years old and probably sonorous and mellow. As an orchestra leader he used a contemporary violin made by Matthias Albani from Bolzano (Bozen). His artistic heir was his most talented pupil, Pietro Locatelli from Bergamo (1693–1764), who furthered the technique of violin-playing. Locatelli's twelve concertos were published in 1733 as *Twenty-four Caprices;* each contained two solo cadenzas, and the works were a century ahead of their time. (They presaged Paganini's celebrated *Twenty-four Caprices,* which also opened new horizons for violin-playing.) Baffled violinists tried Locatelli's *Caprices* and couldn't play them, so rumors spread that Locatelli had "an operation performed on the ligatures connecting the fingers of the left hand." Whenever less gifted fiddlers get beyond their depth they spread malicious gossip about those who can swim.

The stage was set for the distinguished Italian violinist-composers of the eighteenth century. The first was Francesco Maria Veracini (1685–1750), who called himself "Il Fiorentino" after his birthplace, Florence. He was a gifted, unhappy, restless man; from Venice, where he'd played as soloist at San Marco, he went to Dresden, where his Twelve Sonatas for Violin and Double Bass were published in 1725. From there he went to Prague, back to Italy, and in 1736 to London as conductor of the Haymarket Theatre orchestra; George Frederick Handel was its manager. In 1744, when Handel began to write his great oratorios, he made Veracini his orchestra conductor. When Handel went bankrupt in 1746, Veracini left London. Though shipwrecked in the Channel, he survived, but his two beloved Marcus Stainer violins, named "St. Peter" and "St. Paul" were lost. Veracini died in 1750 in Pisa, a poor man.

Antonio Vivaldi, born in Venice about 1676, was first a priest but later became a violinist and musical director of the Conservatory della Pietà, in Venice. Bach thought so highly of Vivaldi's work that he transcribed six of his violin concertos for the piano and two for the organ. Vivaldi's operas—about thirty—are now forgotten, but his double concertos for two violins are performed, for they are masterpieces. His four concerti grossi grouped into *Le Stagioni* (The Seasons) influenced Haydn in his oratorio *Die Jahreszeiten* (The Seasons). Vivaldi was one of the few great violinists who died happy, much admired, in Venice, in 1741.

The greatest violinist after Corelli was Giuseppe Tartini. He was born on April 8, 1692, in Pirano, Istria. In Padua, where he studied law, he became interested in fencing which he thought was much more fascinating (he was right, of course). His father cut off his allowance, but the gifted young fellow had learned to play the fiddle and soon supported himself giving violin lessons. Among his many pupils was the fifteen-year-old niece of Cardinal Cornaro: when the inevitable had happened Tartini didn't bother to ask a blessing of His Eminence, but secretly married the girl. Sued by the cardinal, Tartini ran to the Franciscan monastery at Assisi, where he found a protector, *"il padre Boemo."* The "Bohemian father" was Bohuslav Czernohorsky, who returned to Prague and became the teacher of Christoph Willibald Gluck, the great reformer of opera.

Tartini stayed several years in Assisi and emerged a great violinist and composer. According to an unconfirmed story, when he played in church concerts he would perform behind a screen to avoid the cardinal's spies and informers who still sought him. (Important violinist-composers of this time often performed in churches.) Eventually the cardinal relented, and Tartini returned to his wife in Padua. But when he heard Veracini perform beautifully he became depressed and went off to Ancona where he practiced the violin, especially bow exercises. Emerging from his hideout onto the concert stage, he was soon Italy's greatest living violinist. He spent three years in Prague, where he met Father Czernohorsky again, but finally he settled in Padua to teach and occasionally to perform.

Tartini had a beautiful tone and a masterly style of bowing. He would use two bows alternately, playing only one third or one quarter of the bow. His left hand was also admired; he could play the fastest notes with complete accuracy. He discovered the phenomenon of the "Tartini tones": when any two notes are played simultaneously with intensity, a third note is produced whose vibration number is the difference between the number of vibrations of the two notes. Tartini wrote useful exercises for perfecting the intonation, and made changes in the violin bow. He wrote about a hundred and fifty violin concertos, and almost as many sonatas; these contained new technical innovations. He invented the musical form "air with variations" that has had lasting popularity; his own variations on a Gavotte by Corelli are magnificent. His most famous composition is *The Devil's Trill* Sonata, with beautiful melodies, that has the passionate mood of a masterpiece; it's much more than an exercise in virtuosity, though it contains the most famous double trill in all of violin literature. Not surprisingly, there is a legend about its intriguing title. Tartini, a man with a sense of public relations, liked to tell his pupils that he'd had a vision of the Devil playing a strange sonata on Tartini's violin. He couldn't remember the melody but the strange double trill was still ringing in his ears when he woke up. If *The Devil's Trill* is performed by a great violinist, it really has a mysterious, sinister quality; it's also devilishly difficult. Tartini died on February 16, 1770, in Padua, and his funeral was "almost as splendid as that of Palestrina in St. Peter's."

For a long time, Tartini's masterwork was heard in "edited" versions that only passed for the original. This case is no exception; other works have fallen into the hands of "editors" who make up distorted, abridged, or otherwise mutilated editions. "Of all editions of *The Devil's Trill* Sonata at present available," Joseph Szigeti has written in *Szigeti on the Violin,* "only two have preserved the original double-stopped statement of the lovely, Siciliana-like first movement; and as these two, Hubay's (Bosworth) and Tivadar Nachez (Schott), are less used than those of Joachim, Kreisler (Edition Peters) and others, we take for granted the suppression of the necessary and enhancing accompanying musical voice." *The Devil's Trill* was first published in 1798 by Jean Baptiste Cartier (1765–1841), who used the original manuscript that was lent to him by Baillot. But the next edition, by Henri Vieuxtemps (1820–1881) and published by André in Offenbach, suppressed the double-stopping version and offered accompaniment "for either piano or string quartet." In the Allegro, Vieuxtemps—known as a musician of taste and style—added his own cadenza (!) and took various other liberties. And so it went. Only since the days of Gustav Mahler, Toscanini, and later Bruno Walter and George Szell, has absolute fidelity to the original score become required of the instrumentalist who is serious about style and execution.

Genealogical tables for the various schools of violin-playing have been set up, but they are often arbitrary; the succession of teacher to pupil to pupil's pupil, and so on, does not necessarily mean a musical succession. Joseph Szigeti, one of the most thoughtful violinists of our time, believes that "the so-called genealogical tables showing how twentieth-century violinists descend from this or that illustrious *chef d'école* of the past are not as dependable as the authors would like to make them seem." A great player is not only his teacher's pupil; musically he represents the substance of what he's been taught, what he's heard, and what he has observed in other players. With this reservation, it can be stated that Corelli created the art of playing, that after him there was Giuseppe Tartini (1692–1770), and then Gaetano Pugnani (1727–1803), the pupil of both. Pugnani was the teacher of Giovanni Battista Viotti (1753–1824). So far, so good, but now the succession gets doubtful. In the case of Ysaÿe, for instance, Alberto

Bachmann establishes a "genealogy" of Viotti–Kreutzer–Massart–Wieniawski–Ysaÿe; in the case of Kreisler he believes the antecedents are Viotti–Kreutzer–Massart–Kreisler. It may be the truth, but certainly not the whole truth.

The last great Italian violinist of that great era was Giovanni Battista Viotti, born on May 23, 1753, in Vercelli, Piedmont. As a virtuoso he surpassed Corelli and Tartini, and he became a prolific, fine composer. He influenced the structure and melodic line of Paganini, as a composer, and it's not surprising that there is now a worldwide Viotti revival. A prodigy, he studied with Gaetano Pugnani, an excellent musician, and astonished everybody by playing very difficult pieces at sight. When Viotti was twenty-six he gave his first concerts; he was a handsome young man, and Pugnani, who accompanied him, was grotesquely ugly. The contrast was dramatic, and the people everywhere loved them both.

Viotti was the greatest violinist B.P. (before Paganini). His tone was noble, his *cantilene* bewitching, his left-hand technique formidable, and his bowing so perfect that one hardly noticed it. He was triumphant in St. Petersburg, Paris, London. In Paris he became director of the Théâtre de Monsieur, later known as the Théâtre Feydeau. Pierre Rode and Pierre Baillot, later great French violinists, were Viotti's pupils, and his assistant at the theater was young Luigi Cherubini (Haydn called Cherubini one of the greatest composers, and even Beethoven was awed by him and studied his scores).

After the French Revolution Viotti went to London, but he was suspected of being a secret French agent and left in a hurry for Hamburg where he wrote and composed. In 1801 Baillot invited his former teacher to perform at the Conservatoire in Paris. Afterward, wrote Baillot, "Everything seemed to flow effortlessly yet powerfully. His tone was magnificent, as though the tender bow were handled by the arm of Hercules."

Then something strange happened to Viotti: after several financial disasters he went to London and became a wine merchant. Artists have occasionally been commercial-minded, and violinists are no exception. Locatelli, for example, was a part-time string-dealer; Geminiani sold paintings as a sideline; W. T. Parke described Felice de Giardini, the eighteenth-century virtuoso and composer, as selling "inferior instruments at a large price to gentlemen who, in his hands, admired the beautiful tone, though they found afterwards, to their great surprise, that they could draw forth very little." (No wonder, for an inferior instrument will sound good in the hands of a virtuoso.) Domenico Dragonetti, the famous double bass player, sold fine Cremonese violins in Paris and London; Paganini was often involved in buying and selling violins, and so was Arthur Betts, the English violinist and pupil of Viotti, after whom the "Betts" Stradivari is named. Charles de Bériot stipulated that his students must buy their violins through him; prominent fiddlers should be forgiven for taking advantage of their fame. The Hills write that Ole Bull, the Norwegian virtuoso, was "notorious" for such activities; dealers naturally take a dim view of the competition, sounding as though a question of ethics were involved.

Viotti did not succeed as a wine merchant. He was rescued by his former assistant, Cherubini, who asked Louis XVIII to make Viotti manager of the Paris Opéra. Viotti stayed three years in Paris, went to London again, and died there penniless and forgotten on March 3, 1824. But now he is very much remembered: his twenty-one concertos and other compositions, once considered useful material for unhappy violin pupils, are today, especially certain concertos, performed by leading artists. They have great beauty, and lovely melodies, elegance, and passion; the best are masterpieces. Viotti was the last of the great Italian violinists in the classic manner, and his orchestration seems influenced by Haydn. He treated the violin as a voice part, and truly made it sing. His pupils in France continued his teachings: historically, Viotti is the founder of the great French school.

Next to Viotti, the other predecessor of the French school was Jean Marie Leclair from Lyon (1697–1764), who studied in Turin with Giovanni Battista Somis, a Corelli pupil. He wrote graceful sonatas of great originality, and is sometimes called "the Couperin of the violin." French violinist-composers of the early eighteenth century had first been influenced by the sonatas of Corelli and Tartini, but French "sonatas" were more loosely connected dancing pieces: usually two faster movements would be separated by a quiet, melodious movement. It was brilliant rococo music; Leclair's best-known work is the charming *Tambourin* sonata. (Leclair was mysteriously assassinated on October 22, 1764.)

Another early French violinist was Pierre Gaviniés, from Bordeaux (1726–1800). His father, François, was a respected violin-maker; his instruments had a beautiful yellow varnish, but their tone was somewhat nasal and people said he'd made only one fine violin, his son. Pierre Gaviniés was the first professor for violin-playing at the Paris Conservatoire. His twenty-four *Caprices*—always the tradition of twenty-four—known as *Twenty-four Matinées,* are studied everywhere.

Obviously, the French were ready to take over the hegemony of violin-playing after the inevitable decline of the classic Italian School. The Italians had been first, and they understood that the violin must be primarily a "singing" instrument, as close as possible to the human voice. This was not the French ideal but they brought to the art of violin-playing their native elegance and a particular *légèreté* of the bow. It is no accident that the greatest bow-maker, François Tourte, was from Paris; the French contributed most to the design and the technique of the bow.

The oldest of the trio of great French violinists was Pierre Marie Francois Baillot de Sales, born in Paris in 1771. He studied the violin with Viotti, and harmony and composition with Cherubini. His *Études* are a standard work for study; he also wrote ten concertos, and was himself a noted virtuoso. His friend, Pierre Rode, born in Bordeaux in 1774, was the second member of the great trio. Rode performed all over Europe and was considered in a class with his teacher, Viotti; some people said he had even more feeling. Rode stayed five years in Russia; he had no real competition there and became careless. In 1811 he came to Vienna. Beethoven asked Rode to perform Beethoven's new G major Sonata, Opus 96, at the Palais Lobkowitz, with Archduke Rudolf of Habsburg playing the piano part. Beethoven was not satisfied with Rode; two years later Ludwig Spohr heard Rode in Vienna and wrote, "I was greatly looking forward to Rode's perfection. But . . . I missed his former élan in sumounting difficulties. His E major variations proved to me that he had lost his previous self-confidence. He had simplified for himself the more complicated passages . . . The audience was very cool." Rode is remembered for thirteen violin concertos, his violin method, and brilliant *Twenty-four Caprices.*

The third of the French trio of violinists was Rodolphe Kreutzer. He was born in 1766 in Versailles, where his father, a French army musician, had come from Silesia. The young Kreutzer studied with Anton Stamitz in Mannheim, and with Viotti, and became concertmaster at the Paris Opéra. Napoleon appointed him assistant to François Antoine Habeneck, the excellent concertmaster; Habeneck and Spohr became the first genuine "conductors" of symphonic music. (Weber and Spontini were the first modern conductors of opera.)

Kreutzer was a good composer. He wrote forty operas, most of them performed, and chamber-music works and nineteen violin concertos. The concertos have a certain grandeur, the slow movements often beautiful. His operas are now forgotten but his *Forty-two Études* remain famous, presenting technical violin problems in a highly musical, imaginative way. (Small boys hate them, but great violinists often use them to polish up technical weaknesses. Arnold Rosé, the Vienna Opera's concertmaster and first violinist of the celebrated Rosé Quartet, regularly practiced the Kreutzer *Études* as an old man.) Kreutzer was a fine violinist with a noble tone and beautiful *cantilene,* but his bowing was more monotonous than Viotti's and less elegant than Rode's. In Vienna Beethoven expressed his admiration by dedicating his finest violin sonata, Opus 47, to Kreutzer, thus bestowing a certain immortality upon him (Tolstoy later wrote a story entitled *The Kreutzer Sonata*). Kreutzer didn't like Beethoven's sonata and exclaimed, "The old man's crazy," when he first heard it; later, many of Beethoven's contemporaries believed he was crazy when they heard his late, great string quartets. How could they know that the works were written for future generations, not for them?

In 1810, Kreutzer broke his left arm and had to give up his career as a soloist at the age of forty-four. He continued to teach, compose, and conduct, and died in 1831 in Geneva. He belongs to that remarkable group of nineteenth-century violinists who were technical masters of their instruments and also excellent musicians.

The importance of the Italian school and later of the French school of violin-playing often conceals other important contributions to the art of the violin that were made elsewhere. Johann Stamitz, one of the founders of the great Mannheim school, created a style of orchestral violin-playing that was new in its time and has had far-reaching effects. Dr. Charles Burney, the eighteenth-century English musicologist, reported that the Mannheim Orchestra was the first to use uniform bowing, and was also distinguished by its elegant phrasing and by observing all dynamic signs. Ignaz Schuppanzigh (1776–1830), an excellent Viennese teacher and conductor, remains famous among chamber music aficionados as first violinist in the Schuppanzigh Quartet which gave the first performances of many of Beethoven's string quartets. It must have been a fine quartet, for Beethoven was happy with them. Ludwig Spohr, born in Brunswick in 1784, was an outstanding German violinist who is now better known as a composer. He began as a gifted performer. It was his bad luck that Paganini was still around. Every performing violinist of that era was measured against Paganini.

 Paganini

Nicolò Paganini (1784–1840) is still the most famous fiddler of all time, and remains the most mysterious. Hector Berlioz called Paganini "a comet. . . . Never did a flaming body appear so unexpectedly in the heavens of art, or excite in the course of his long orbit greater amazement mixed with a sort of terror before it disappeared forever." It was Berlioz's great regret that he'd never heard Paganini play; they did not become friends until the last years of Paganini's life, when the great artist was no longer performing.

Paganini's accomplishments remain a source of wonderment to violinists everywhere, and the facts of his life have become inseparable from the legends that were created by his magic personality. Fortunately Paganini's compositions are very real. His *Twenty-four Caprices,* composed primarily for himself, are proof of his prophetic genius; they open up new vistas in the art of violin-playing.

The Paganini legend starts early. It is said that one night in Leghorn, when he was only fifteen, he lost everything, including his

Andrea Amati, in a wild gambling bout. He had to give a concert the next day, so he spent the next morning looking for a suitable instrument at the local dealers but finding none. Then Livron, a wealthy French music-lover, heard of the boy's embarrassment and lent him his Guarneri del Gesù for the concert. Now comes the Paganini touch: he reportedly played the violin so beautifully that at the end of the concert Livron, "overcome with emotion, embraced young Paganini and gave him the Guarneri, making only one condition: Paganini must never let anyone else play it." (According to a letter written by Paganini in April, 1839, shortly before his death, a Guarneri del Gesù was given to him by a close friend, General Pino from Milan; but this must be another Del Gesù.) Paganini eventually owned a magnificent Nicolò Amati, two violins by Paolo Maggini, and several fine Stradivari instruments, but he loved most his Del Gesù and he kept his promise to M. Livron. No one else played the Guarneri, and he bequeathed it to Genoa, his native town. It is now exhibited, under glass, at the Palazzo Municipale. He called the Guarneri his "Cannon," because of its sonorous, powerful tone. Professor Arturo Codignola, the author of the biography *Paganini Intimo* and Genoa's leading authority on Paganini, told me he had never understood why Paganini gave his beloved violin to Genoa, for they had treated him badly whenever he was in trouble (which happened often). In Genoa he wasn't deemed important enough to rate even a small statue, though the Austrian emperor appointed Paganini court virtuoso, the king of Prussia named him Konzertmeister, and in Westphalia he was given the hereditary title of Baron.

Paganini was born on February 18, 1784 (some people won't be surprised that Kreisler and Heifetz, too, were born in the sign of Aquarius). His parents, Antonio Paganini and Teresa Bocciardi, liked music without being musical. At the age of five Nicolò began playing the guitar under his father's guidance; eventually he played it as brilliantly as the violin—mainly, it is rumored, to please an aristocratic lady friend. But stories about his love affairs in high circles are almost as numerous as reports about his virtuosity on the violin.

He was seven when he was first given a small violin. "Within a few months I was able to play any music at sight," he said later, probably stating a fact. He appeared in public for the first time at the age of eleven, at the Teatro Sant' Agostino in Genoa, during a concert given by the singer Teresa Bertinotti and the famous castrato, Luigi Marchesi, the star of the evening. After performing several pieces by Corelli and Tartini, little Nicolò played his own variations on the revolutionary song *La Carmagnola,* and instantly became the star (the year was 1791).

He studied with three well-known composers, Alessandro Rolla, Ghiretti, and Ferdinando Paër, learning harmony and composition. He gave youthful concerts in Milan, Florence, Pisa, and Leghorn; his father went too and was strict with the boy, perhaps too strict. Paganini later said he'd been forced to practice "from dawn to dusk," sometimes ten hours a day. He studied the entire repertory from Corelli to Viotti, and began to compose his first *Caprices.* They were so difficult that he could play them only "with some effort"; no one else could play them at all.

At seventeen Nicolò ran away from home, and went to Lucca. The following years were wild: playing the violin, gambling, women. The Paganini legend that is best known is not supported by evidence: allegedly he killed an unfaithful mistress and spent several years in prison. In another version "he suffered an imprisonment of eight years for assassinating a rival." It was reputedly in prison that he acquired his incredible skill on the G string, "the only string left on his violin." This legend may not be true but it certainly is *ben trovato,* for his skill on the G string was no legend; it's proved by Paganini's compositions for the G string alone, such as the *Variations on the Prayer from Rossini's "Moses."*

In his biography there are long gaps when he seemed to disappear from public life for years. These gaps were later conveniently filled with legends. He was said to have spent several years at the country home of an aristocratic lady; with typical reticence Paganini mentions in his autobiographical notes that he became interested in "farming and guitar-playing." If he was half as good at farming as at guitar-playing, he must have been one of the best farmers on earth! Another time he was involved with Elisa Bonaparte, Napoleon's sister, later the grand duchess of Tuscany, "who fainted remarkably often during his concerts." She was not the only one; women were often carried out when Paganini performed. He lived several years with Antonia Bianchi, a well-known singer, who bore him a son, Archillino, in Palermo in 1825. (Note that the nineteenth-century family of violin-makers called Paganini—Luigi, Giuseppe, Alba, Maria—who lived and worked in Forlì, are no relation to the great violinist.)

Paganini first left Italy in 1828, when he was forty-four; in Rome he had met Prince Metternich, who invited him to come to Vienna. Paganini arrived in the city that was then "the world capital of music" on March 16, accompanied by Signora Bianchi and the three-year-old Archillino. He gave his first concert on March 29, at the Imperial Ballroom (today's Redoutensaal) of the Hofburg. It was a fantastic success, and the beginning of his world fame. There had been great excitement preceding the event, the cheapest seat was five guilders and five-guilder notes became locally known as "Paganiners." Paganini played almost exclusively his own compositions: his Violin Concerto No. 1, in D major, Sonata Militaire for the G String Alone, Variations on *Non più andrai* from Mozart's *Figaro,* and Variations on an Aria from Rossini's *Cenerentola.* The audience was as in a trance. The critics were unable to express their enthusiasm—words failed them, which happens rarely in Vienna. The only dissenter was M. G. Saphir, who gave Paganini a bad review but it was said that he was angry not to get free seats. The second concert was attended by all of the Imperial family. Scalpers made a land-office business.

Paganini gave twenty concerts in Vienna, "and even dethroned the giraffe which the Pasha of Egypt had just presented to the Court" (Franz Farga). Pastry cooks made petits fours in the shape of tiny violins, and somebody offered a special Paganini goulash. Without a doubt, Paganini had arrived.

During the following years he performed in the other European cities. In 1830 he paid into his Viennese bank account 169,000 guilders. He came to Paris in 1831 during an outbreak of cholera, but the people's enthusiasm surpassed their fear of infection: "Paganini had so forcibly struck the imagination and heart of the Parisians that he made them forget death hovering over them," Berlioz wrote later. Paganini gave eleven concerts at the Opéra, earning 165,741 gold francs. The French impresarios asked him to play French music in addition to his own compositions. Paganini disliked making this concession but the Parisians expected it. He would play duets with Delphin Alard, a fine

French violinist and Vuillaume's son-in-law; Alard later confessed to David Laurie, the English violin expert, that he dreaded these appearances, for Paganini didn't bother to rehearse their duets—Alard was convinced that Paganini never looked at them before he strode out on the platform. Occasionally Paganini was accompanied by a small chamber orchestra, but during the fast moment he played so rapidly that the orchestra players couldn't keep up with him and finally refused to perform. Laurie, who never heard Paganini, writes, "A Scotch friend of mine who went to hear him left the hall before the concert was halfway through, crying like a child. Such was the power of this marvelous man over the emotions of his hearers."

Yet Paganini remained remote and mysterious, seeing almost nobody. (He was lucky he didn't live in an earlier century. They might have burned him at the stake.) Even Vuillaume, who occasionally repaired Paganini's violins and bows, knew little about him. One day Paganini brought Vuillaume a bow that was broken near the head. There were rumors about this bow, such as that Paganini played his fantastic *staccato* runs because "the bow was hollow, filled with small leaden bullets which would run up and down when required to do so." Vuillaume didn't believe this absurd story, but with the broken bow in his hands he couldn't resist cutting off the hair at the head where the bullets were said to be inserted; there were only the two rough ends of a broken stick. "Paganini smiled grimly and said he hadn't thought Vuillaume to be such a fool as to believe the tales about the bow," Laurie remembers. Many historians tell the story about how Paganini brought his "Cannon" to Vuillaume for repairs. Presented about a week later with two identical-looking instruments he was unable to recognize his Del Gesù, but he never claimed to be an expert, he just loved beautiful violins. The Hills own a Paganini letter concerning the purchase of a Stradivari from Count Cozio di Salabue for 100 *louis d'or,* then approximately $400. Paganini also owned a complete quartet of Stradivari instruments (see p. 192).

In Paris his only diversion was playing the guitar with an obscure German violinist named Sina. Paganini composed several duets for these occasions. The two spent quiet evenings making music and having fun. He also wrote sonatas for violin and guitar, and six string quartets for violin, viola, guitar, and cello.

Paganini gave a series of fourteen concerts at Covent Garden in London in the summer of 1832. A typical program, for Friday, August 17, lists among Paganini's "favorite pieces":

> **Grand Sonata Militaire** in which will be introduced Mozart's Aria, *Non piu andrai,* followed by a **Tema,** with brilliant Variations (to conclude with GOD SAVE THE KING!), composed and to be performed on ONE STRING ONLY (the Fourth String) by SIGNOR PAGANINI.

In 1834 he returned to Italy, to the Villa Gaiona near Parma. The *Journal des Artistes* reported on June 29, "The celebrated Paganini has just invented an instrument which will cause the astonishment and admiration of all *dilettanti.* The great artist has long sought to produce a sound that offers similarity with the human voice. He believes to have achieved this with the help of an instrument that he named the Contraviola Paganini. It is to the viola what the double bass is to the cello. Paganini fears no rival who could handle the Contraviola."

Paganini was already suffering from tuberculosis of the larynx. According to modern research he also had a serious disease, probably a result of his wild way of life. He died in Nice on May 27, 1840, leaving an estate of 1,700,000 francs. He did not receive extreme unction, and the bishop of Nice refused him a church funeral. Rumor said that he was an infidel, "suspected of dealings with the devil." Only many years later were his mortal remains transferred to his homeland. He was buried in Parma, one of Italy's most music-loving cities. (Verdi and Toscanini also came from the region.)

Paganini's achievements as a virtuoso remain unsurpassed to this day. During a performance he would tune the strings up and down for special effects; he would play two-octave jumps on a single string, confounding the experts. (He would touch the lower tone first as in a very short grace note, then almost simultaneously play the upper note one octave higher. The Viennese papers reported that he performed incredible octave runs and tenth passages; arpeggios executed with half the bow yet "played as powerfully as on a large harp"; racing up semiquavers (the first note played *pizzicato,* the second bowed); double stop harmonics; and "a long run across four octaves, played *staccato,* in a single stroke of the bow." The reports suggested that the leading

Viennese violinists, Joseph Mayseder and Joseph Böhm, considered Paganini "the greatest violin virtuoso of all time"; Ignaz Castelli, the poet, wrote *Paganiniana,* imaginary dialogues with "the God of the Violin."

Paganini's very appearance hypnotized his audiences. All pictures of him convey this impression: the drawings by R. Hamerton and the lithographs by Daniel Maclise made in London in 1831; the lithograph by Maurir; and especially the beautiful painting by Eugène Delacroix in 1832 when Paganini was in Paris, now at the Phillips Collection in Washington, D.C. It shows his haunted and haunting presence: a tall, gaunt man with a pale, longish face, a long nose, and deep, burning eyes, his long hair falling down on his shoulders. His left hand easily reaches up to the highest positions on the violin; his right hand holds the bow slightly above the frog.

He was a fascinating artist, but his success wasn't due solely to his charisma. He seems to have had the perfect physique for a great fiddler. A few years after Paganini's death Francesco Bennati, an Italian physician who had treated Paganini for many years, wrote in the *Revue de Paris* in a physiological study that Paganini had very elastic shoulder muscles, unusually powerful knuckles, and forearms and fingers "as strong as iron cudgels." His fingers were extremely flexible. He could play in the third position without moving his hand from the first position, thanks to his long, hard fingers. Above all he was blessed with exceptionally acute hearing. His left ear, close to the violin, was especially sensitive; during a performance he reacted with split-second speed, making instinctive, infinitesimal adjustments with somnambulistic certainty when the strings went down in pitch. All critics and even his "competitors" commented on his perfect intonation—truly remarkable since his violin strings, gut strings only, were less reliable than today's steel strings. And in Paganini's compositions, with their terrific *pizzicato* passages, the strings would go down fast while he was playing. He compensated for the decline as a matter of routine, but this takes supreme concentration and automatic reaction.

People who had never seen him might chuckle when he stepped out on the platform. Tall and emaciated, "he looked almost like a skeleton." His posture while playing was highly unorthodox: he would stand with his left shoulder pushed forward (which any teacher will consider absolutely wrong) so that the violin rested securely on his collarbone. He needed neither chinrest nor shoulder pad, and this intimate contact with the violin made it truly an extension of his body.

Some early authorities, describing the phenomenon that was Paganini, suggested that he was a sleight-of-hand practitioner achieving "magic" effects because his hands were quicker than the eyes of his audience. This was nonsense. Paganini simply played the violin better than anyone else ever had. His supremacy among the greatest violinists can be compared only with that of Enrico Caruso among the greatest singers. Spohr, who should have known better, made sarcastic remarks about Paganini; others called him a charlatan because they failed to understand him. In addition to his technical accomplishments he was a very great musician; otherwise he couldn't have made such an impression on some of the greatest musicians of his time, for virtuosity alone would not have sufficed.

Schubert borrowed money to attend one of Paganini's concerts in Vienna and left "as in a trance." Meyerbeer followed him around, trying to understand "the mystery of his incredible talent." Sensitive reviewers made the point that Paganini's violin "had become his soul," that "he lived through his instrument." Rossini, rarely enthusiastic about other musicians, was said to feel for Paganini a "devotion mingled with fear." (Exactly as Berlioz wrote in Paganini's obituary: "an amazement mixed with a sort of terror." The underlying fear was always there; Paganini must have seemed weird to many.)

Chopin was said to have been "completely overcome with emotion" when he first heard the virtuoso in Warsaw—the romantic of the piano sensed an affinity with the romantic of the violin. Chopin remained a lifelong admirer of Paganini and made piano transcriptions of some themes from Paganini's beautiful Second Violin Concerto. Another great romantic, Robert Schumann, wrote, "Paganini's compositions contain the purest and most valuable qualities, such as can be brought out effectively on the piano," and made piano transcriptions of twelve of Paganini's *Caprices*. Liszt wrote to a friend, "*Quel homme, quel violon, quel artiste! Dieu, que de souffrances, de misères, de tortures dans ces quatre cordes!*" ("What a man, what a violin, what an artist! God, how much of suffering, misery, torture is in those four strings.") In 1840, the year of Paganini's death, he too made bravura piano transcriptions of the *Caprices*. Brahms in 1866 published Variations on the last *Caprice*. All musical romantics had unbounded admiration for Paganini, who personified romanticism in his personality, appearance, and style of life, and in his music. The romantics were great improvisers; the laws and order of classicism seemed alien, and improvisation expressed the romantic idea of "instantaneous creation." during his recitals, Paganini would not play the scores of his own compositions exactly as he'd written them. He freely improvised when he was "in the mood," and this gave his performances a spontaneous, "magical" effect. Later, Liszt's performances of his own Rhapsodies were full of improvisation, similar to Paganini's playing style. Liszt too had a "demoniac" effect on his listeners. Today, audiences wouldn't accept this rhapsodic style of playing. We demand, and get, *Werktreue,* fidelity to the score—but I suppose we miss a great deal.

Paganini so far surpassed the other prominent violinists of his time that it must have been frustrating to be a prominent fiddler in the 1820s. There were fine artists—Rode, Kreutzer, Viotti, Baillot, Spohr. They continued the tradition and technique of Corelli and Tartini, and extended the emotional expression that could be achieved on the violin. Most of them made valuable contributions by way of melody, left-hand technique, or bowing technique. But somehow they all resembled one another.

Paganini was different, a devil, seemingly in control of supernatural phenomena. He could play more notes faster and more accurately than anyone ever had; he never played a wrong note; his mastery of harmonics has apparently not been surpassed to this day. He must have had his own technique for playing harmonics, and he certainly had his personal system of practice, like nearly every great violinist. When people asked him about his "system" Paganini would smile mysteriously (some said maliciously), saying, *"Ognuno ha i suoi segreti"* ("Everybody has his secrets"). The "system," if there was one, wouldn't have helped others without his physique and strong nerves. His attitude—remote, sarcastic, always defensive—created rumors that he was arrogant and mean. He was said to care about saving money—most prominent artists do—and his nickname was "Paganiente" ("Pay-Nothing").

His fees were the highest ever paid to any violinist. But in return Paganini gave his listeners more than had anyone else who played the fiddle in public. When his contemporaries reported that "the violin became his soul," they unveiled the true secret of the great artist, his ability to identify himself perfectly with his art. Dr. Bennati wrote that prior to a concert Paganini often felt terribly tired, but as soon as his bow touched his strings "a spark seemed to revive his body, his brain, his nerves." There must have been a glorious freedom in his performance. He was an artist who knew no restriction; he was not afraid to venture out into new, strange, unknown worlds. Jascha Heifetz, who is the nearest to Paganini among all violinists today, once told me he wished there could have been some Paganini recordings. All prominent violinists share this wish, though not all admit it. They sense instinctively that Paganini was more than a great performer.

For a long time Paganini the virtuoso performer outshone Paganini the composer, but in recent years there has been a growing appreciation of his music. His Opus 1, *Twenty-four Caprices,* is now justly acknowledged a musical masterpiece. They contain everything a violinist needs to attain a flawless technique, yet they are more than mere études. Paganini managed to express technical problems by way of artistic beauty. Nearly always the melody and musical substance equal the valuable technical exercise. The third *Caprice* is the first important violin composition using the double quaver; the fourth has devastatingly difficult double stops and high-speed passages; the seventh covers almost the entire scope of the violin; the ninth evolves the sound of other instruments, the flute and the English horn. The range of Paganini's genius was not really apparent until 1946, when the original text of the *Caprices* was edited by M. Abbado and published by Suvini-Zerboni in Milan (where the manuscript had been in the possession of G. Ricordi and Co.). "It is only now that we see how the many accretions and simplifications have falsified the picture we had of these masterpieces of instrumental ingenuity" (*Szigeti on the Violin*).

Paganini's *Moto Perpetuo* is a veritable tour de force—3,040 semiquavers played *presto* and *staccato,* a formidable finger-and-bow exercise. Paganini could have written a wonderful "school of violin playing." The *Witches' Dance* takes a theme by Mozart's pupil, Franz Süssmayer (who completed Mozart's *Requiem*), and makes variations on it, each more difficult than the preceding one. Paganini's *Variations on "God Save the King"* are rarely performed, not because great violinists have anti-monarchist sentiments but because the fourth variation has enormous difficulties where the melody on the G string is accompanied by demisemiquavers, *pizzicato,* on the highest string. The finale is one long, terrifying, *staccato* arpeggio.

The first two violin concertos by Paganini have been in the repertory of the leading violinists since they were published posthumously. Number 1, now usually played in D major, was composed in E flat; No. 2 is in B minor. No. 4 in D minor, was not discovered until 1954; apparently Paganini's distant heirs continue his policy of secrecy. Many Paganini compositions remain unpublished, though the manuscripts exist. In some cases the heirs have refused publication, or asked for extravagant sums of money. Violin Concerto No. 5 in A minor, was found in 1969 by the violinist Franco Gulli. And No. 3 in E major, long believed lost, was brought before the public by Henryk Szeryng in 1970, almost a century and a half after it was written. The most popular concertos, first and second, combine a classical structure in the style of Viotti, with a deep, romantic sweep. Both concertos have fine melodious inventions and definite originality; only Paganini could have written them. Both are very difficult technically, but technical exhibition is an organic part of the compositions, not their aim. Neither seemed difficult to Paganini when he wrote it—this was the music he heard in his inner ear and wrote down. The Rondo in Concerto No. 2 was later transcribed by Liszt, who called it *La Campanella* and often played it at the end of a recital, fascinating his audiences. Some day all of Paganini's work will be published, and it will confirm his stature as a great composer.

In 1832, during his first visit to London, Paganini bought a Stradivari viola to complete his quartet of Stradivari instruments. The "Paganini" viola was made in 1731, brought to England later in the eighteenth century, and sold by John Betts to E. Stephenson, a banker and collector. Then it passed to George Corsby, a dealer, to whom Paganini paid 1000 francs for it. The viola is large and handsome, with a one-piece back of beautifully patterned maple; the red-orange varnish is almost completely preserved.

Paganini's friend Hector Berlioz later wrote, "Paganini came to me [in 1833] and said, 'I have a marvelous viola, an admirable Stradivari, and I wish to play it in public. But I have no music *ad hoc*. Will you write a solo piece for it? You are the only one I can trust for such work." Berlioz first contemplated using a theme, *Les Derniers Instants de Marie Stuart* (*The Last Moments of Mary Stuart*) but fortunately changed his mind, and wrote the Symphony *Harold in Italy* with a magnificent solo part for the viola. Paganini didn't approve of the part and never played it: he allegedly said it contained "too many rests." This complaint was never confirmed by Berlioz, who wrote that he hadn't really expected Paganini to play the viola part. The first performance was in Paris in 1834, the noted French violist Chrétien Urhan performing the solo part. In December, 1838, Paganini attended a performance of *Harold in Italy* and the *Symphonie Fantastique* by Berlioz, and wrote to the composer, "Beethoven is dead, there is no one but Berlioz to carry on." As a token of his admiration, Paganini asked his Paris banker, Baron de Rothschild, to send 20,000 francs to Berlioz so he could continue composing. Berlioz later wrote, "I do not even consider it necessary to take notice of the stupid insinuations to which Paganini's noble act gave rise." Paganini wrote, "I did it for Berlioz and for myself. For Berlioz, because his genius was wearing himself out fighting against the jealousy and ignorance of his fellow men; and for myself because posterity will thank me for what I did."

In his *Evenings with the Orchestra* Berlioz writes how Paganini and he were in Paris, "when the sun gave him the desire to go out." By that time Paganini had completely lost his voice, so Berlioz had a notebook and a pencil. Paganini would write down in a few words the subject he wanted to talk about. Berlioz would discuss it, and Paganini would write in the notebook his reflections "that were often highly original in their laconic brevity." This is unusual praise from Berlioz, a great musician and a highly original writer: "The deaf Beethoven used a notebook to take in his friends' ideas; the mute Paganini used it to convey his own."

Berlioz, himself a romantic phenomenon, understood Paganini better than all who wrote about him. In a letter to Carlo Conestabile, the author of *Vita di Nicolò Paganini da Genova,* in which Berlioz considered himself treated "most unkindly," he wrote,

> I can neither pass upon the historical merits of the book, not being in a position to know the truth of the facts it reports; nor upon the style of the author, since the niceties of the Italian language are necessarily beyond my grasp; nor upon the correctness of the author's estimate of the great virtuoso's talent, for I never heard Paganini play. I was in Italy at the time this extraordinary artist was turning everyone's head in France. When I knew him later, he had already given up playing in public; the state of his health no longer permitted it, and it will be readily understood that I did not dare ask him to play once more for me alone. If I conceived so high an opinion of him, it is, in the first place, because of his conversation; because of the radiance which seems to emanate from certain distinguished men, and which surrounded Paganini with an aura of poetry; and second, because of the ardent and reasoned admiration he inspired in certain artists in whose judgement I place implicit trust.

Paganini extended the boundaries of violin virtuosity. Prior to him, audiences were satisfied when a performer could play well in the fourth position. Paganini was the first who made full use of the range of the violin in its entirety. He was a practical virtuoso and at the same time a visionary. He had the idea of what could be done and the ability to do it. Paganini's genius is proved by the astonishing fact that no one has since extended the range of violin-playing—just as no one since Stradivari has extended the range of violin-making.

Paganini's crowning masterpieces are the *Twenty-four Caprices.* They are immensely difficult, but violinistic; they are playable because they were written by an artist who understood the deepest "secrets" of the violin. (Liszt, who almost did for the piano what Paganini did for the violin, remained committed to Paganini; so did Chopin.)

Some day a new Paganini may appear who will go even further. Some violinists today—though not the best ones—take a dim view of Paganini and think of him as a "technician," a "virtuoso." They are in the precious company of esoterics who have little respect for "caprices" and "bravura pieces" because they lack "depth" and "dimension"; if you want to play solo violin music, they say, play Bach. But *both* Bach and Paganini made the art of violin-playing what it now is. Bach, never a precious esoteric, would have admired Paganini, perhaps even envied him, though the two great musicians couldn't have been more different. In analogy with violin-makers, Bach makes you think of Stradivari, and Paganini of Guarneri del Gesù. I haven't met a fiddler yet who wouldn't want to own a Stradivari *and* a Guarneri del Gesù, though he may prefer one to the other.

After Paganini— Until Today

For a long time after the death of Paganini every violinist was measured up against him. The comparison was probably unfair, and certainly unfavorable. Anyone who had heard Paganini or talked to someone who had heard him, was prejudiced; it wasn't only Paganini's miraculous technique that was so vividly remembered—technique alone could not cast such a spell posthumously—it was the haunting, "demoniac" personality of Paganini, his unforgettable image. Obviously he had been more than the greatest violinist of all time. An artist with a true and flaming passion, Paganini turned everything he did into a reflection of life itself. Few performers have achieved this, at any time. Apparently Liszt could do it. Caruso did—and half a century after his death tenors are still measured against the past presence, and recordings, of Caruso. There is a thrill in hearing his best recordings even though his voice is electronically changed and filtered; it retains that undefinable quality that *does* something to people.

Even the critics who were expected to show some impartiality remained under the spell of Paganini. They were cautious in their praise of later violinists, though these certainly included some excellent ones. Yes, the critics said, *but* . . . Many great violinists feel exactly the same today, and some even admit it; because any artist reflects the taste and style and feelings of his time, some who were great in the past might be out of step with the times were they to come back today. But the greatest artists—both creative and re-creative ones—have a passion and power that is timeless.

Virtuoso violinists have written more good music than most other virtuoso instrumentalists. Almost all important composers have played the piano, but only the exceptional few were virtuoso performers: Mozart, Chopin, Liszt, Ravel, Rachmaninoff. Mozart was a great improvisor on the piano; in 1787 he played it at a "Big Musical Academy" in Prague where he spent a few happy weeks. Franz Xaver Niemetschek, his biographer, later wrote, "At the end of the Academy, Mozart improvised alone on the pianoforte for half an hour and heightened our fascination to the highest degree. In fact, his improvisations surpassed everything that one could imagine about piano-playing."

In contrast, many great violin virtuosos have needed an outlet for their musicianship, and have composed. Apparently playing the violin, however brilliantly, did not satisfy their musical needs. Corelli, Tartini, and the Italian virtuosos of the eighteenth century started the trend. Bach, of course, is a special case: He was above all a master performer on the organ, but he played the violin and understood it so well that his genius turned the violin into an instrument of majestic polyphony, never surpassed.

Paganini, Vieuxtemps, Spohr, Kreutzer, Sarasate, and Wieniawski are among the violin virtuosos who became important composers, in some cases now remembered mostly as composers. Some wrote for the violin; others wrote operas, treating the human voice like the violin voice. Many wrote excellent manuals, études, and caprices, trying to pass their accumulated experience on to future generations and widen the horizons of the art of violin-playing.

Ludwig Spohr (1784–1859), from Brunswick, Germany, was never considered brilliant as a violinist but he wrote operas that were performed in Vienna, where he was a conductor at the Theater an der Wien, and became a famous educator and orchestra builder. In Paris François Habeneck, the noted concertmaster, used to conduct with his bow, using it to play the violin with the orchestra when all was going well. (Johann Strauss later created a virtuoso technique in Vienna, conducting and playing the fiddle at the same time.) But the concertmaster who had charge of the orchestra was, of course, accepted at a much earlier date. In Mannheim, Dresden, Vienna, Berlin, Paris, and London the concertmaster drilled his musicians, occasionally also acting as conductor. A homogeneous technique and uniform use of the bow became standard demands. Spohr as a concertmaster-violinist used a small ivory stick while conducting, to keep German-style discipline; the people didn't like Spohr's stick in London, but he prevailed.

As a composer Spohr is unfairly rated as a second-class Romantic by some, and as a "Biedermeier" composer of *gemütlich* music by others. His operas and symphonies belong with the minor Romantics but he had strong influence on Mendelssohn and Schumann. And there is nothing second-rate about his violin concertos; with their melodic sweep and genuine passion they are fine music. The Concerto No. 8, called *Gesangszene* (Singing Lesson), is a masterpiece of poetic power. Spohr understood the affinity of singing with violin-playing as eighteenth-century Italians did before him.

Today we take an objective view of the great violinists in the era following Paganini. (If we had records made by Paganini we might be less objective.) There were many outstanding violinists. Spohr's pupil, Ferdinand David (1810–1873), was concertmaster of the famous Gewandhaus Orchestra in Leipzig, professor at the Leipzig Conservatory, a good composer and a noted soloist; Mendelssohn dedicated his Violin Concerto to David. His *Hohe Schule des Violinspiels* long remained an admired pedagogical work; style-conscious artists now prefer original manuscripts of the composer to any "edited" versions. As an editor, David committed many distortions and deviations from the original manuscripts or first editions, and he was an autocrat who tolerated no opposition.

August Wilhelmj (1845–1908) was at one time known as the best German violinist. Richard Wagner offered him the job of concertmaster in Bayreuth, and he made the string section of the Festspielhaus a model of musical homogeneity. Wagner was so delighted that he embraced Wilhelmj in public. As a soloist, his tone was said to be beautiful and his technique splendid. He wrote original works, transcriptions, and a *Modern School for the Violin.*

About the middle of the nineteenth century Belgium became a major power in the world of the violin. The Romantic Belgian school began with Charles Auguste de Bériot, born in Louvain in 1802; he played a Viotti concerto in public at the age of nine. In Paris he was introduced to Viotti, who told the boy "to listen to every good violinist but to imitate no one." De Bériot never forgot this advice. Later he was famous for his elegant violin-playing—and for his love affair with Maria Malibran, the reigning prima donna; the couple dared live together, even toured together for six years, and their audiences were thrilled; they became a public legend. Madame Malibran's beautiful mezzo soprano was often compared to the sound of De Bériot's Paolo Maggini violin. In 1833 they had a son and three years later they were married, but soon after Maria Malibran fell from a horse in London and died, only twenty-eight years old. Charles de Bériot never recovered from the shock. After years of melancholy, he began teaching at the Brussels Conservatoire and found time to compose; his ten admirable violin concertos are melodious and exciting. He wrote a brilliant violin manual, duets, and eleven *Airs Variés* that became popular virtuoso pieces.

His most celebrated pupil was Henri Vieuxtemps (1820–1881), who surpassed De Bériot as a virtuoso, and as a musician became a Belgian symbol. When he first heard Beethoven's *Fidelio* in Frankfurt he was overcome with emotion, unable to play the violin for several days. In Leipzig he met Schumann, who wrote about "the magic circle" which Vieuxtemps drew around his listeners. In London he heard Paganini and he was not critical (as Spohr had been), he was overwhelmed. "Everybody willingly submitted to his art. I understood the enormous intensity of his playing although I did not understand his technical resources. From that day on, Paganini was my model, both as a violinist and a composer." Vieuxtemps met Paganini, and his admiration increased. In Paris Vieuxtemps became a friend of Chopin, Liszt, and Berlioz, the exacting critic who remained one of Vieuxtemps's ardent admirers.

As a composer Vieuxtemps followed Paganini: he, too, could turn technical brilliance into melody and music. Only a virtuoso can perform his seven violin concertos with the needed elegance, but their technical difficulties do not merely show off the player's virtuosity. Concerto No. 3, in A major, is melodious and exciting. Number 4, in D minor, is Vieuxtemps's masterpiece, with its beautiful, moving Adagio and fascinating Scherzo. Number 8 remains unfinished. His concert pieces are still performed: the magnificent *Ballade et Polonaise, Fantaisie-Appassionata, Old-Style Suite,* and *Concert Études.*

The Belgian school reached its zenith with Eugène Ysaÿe, born in 1858 in Liége. (Liége remains a violinists' city. Massart was born there, and in the vicinity Léonard and Marsick.) Ysaÿe remains the greatest Liégeois of all. He came at the right time: Paganini was slowly being forgotten. Ysaÿe studied with Massart, Vieuxtemps, and Henri Wieniawski. He had the good fortune to live in Paris at the time of César Franck, Debussy, Flaubert, Zola, Manet, Degas. He met Franck at an evening of chamber music in Vieuxtemps's house, and they became friends. Ysaÿe was a big, strong man who loved life and music and approached both with gusto. He became concertmaster of the Bilse Orchestra in Berlin, but his Belgian temperament and French training didn't conform with the strict German standards; the critics considered "shocking" his performance of Beethoven's Violin Concerto. Joachim after listening to him said archly, "I've never heard the violin played in that manner." Unwittingly, he'd hit it; Ysaÿe was ahead of his time, as Paganini had been. Ysaÿe became a professor at the Brussels Conservatoire, founded the "Ysaÿe Orchestral Concerts," and began to tour Europe, and after 1894, America. Everywhere but in Germany he was a success; there the critics didn't forget Joachim's verdict. He had his own string quartet, and after he gave up his career as a soloist he began teaching. He became an American citizen and in 1918 conducted the Cincinnati Orchestra. He died in Brussels in 1931.

Ysaÿe pioneered many advances in violin technique and style. He developed the *vibrato,* a most important contribution. He dared perform Bach as we do now—as a timeless genius, living and creating in the early eighteenth century. César Franck, who understood Ysaÿe, dedicated to him his masterpiece, the Violin Sonata in A major. When the age of the gramophone began, Ysaÿe made some recordings in 1912.

They have deeply stirring qualities—beautiful tone, impeccable technique, love of music. He was one of the greatest violinists.

The Romantic age of violin-playing extended all over Europe. Henri Wieniawski (1835–1880), the greatest Polish violinist, was a true Romantic, like so many Poles, passionate and elegiac, elegant and unpredictable. He had sensuous tone and a splendid technique. (Poland's first great violinist was Charles Lipinski, 1790–1861, an excellent musician who had his own quartet and conducted the Dresden Court Orchestra for many years. It was his bad luck to be only six years younger than Paganini; sometimes they played duets together. Paganini was quoted, "I can't say who the greatest living violinist is but Lipinski is certainly the second."

Wieniawski studied with Massart in Paris and was influenced by the Belgian school. He lived in the romantic manner: wine, women, and gambling. Once, like young Paganini, he was forced to sell his Pietro Guarneri to pay for an urgent gambling debt, but he had no M. Livron to give him a Guarneri del Gesù. Wieniawski was a modern artist: he played Mozart in the style of Mozart and Viotti in the style of Viotti, resisting the temptation to make them all sound like Wieniawski. He was especially successful in Russia and America, once earning $25,000 in a few weeks. Later he suffered from heart disease and was forced to remain seated while playing. He succeeded Vieuxtemps as professor in the Brussels Conservatory, and died in Moscow.

Wieniawski's fame as a composer has endured. His Concerto No. 2, in D minor, is a beautiful work, still popular; his Concerto in F sharp minor is also very fine, though less often performed. In structure and melodic line his concertos come close to Paganini's. Every violinist has played Wieniawski's *Légende,* and his *Russian Carnival* is a stunning tour de force. His teaching works are among the best in the literature: the *École Moderne* and the virtuoso *Études-Caprices.*

The Polish Romantic had a rival—in Spain. Pablo Sarasate, the greatest Spanish violinist, was born in Pamplona in 1844. His family was very poor but Pablo, a child prodigy, was sent to Paris and became the protégé of Delphin Alard, the noted violinist and Vuillaume's son-in-law. As a foreigner Sarasate couldn't become a regular student at the Paris Conservatoire, but he was such a good player that he won the Conservatoire's Grand Prix a year later and gave his first concerts.

Sarasate was a great violinist and a fine musician. The critics loved his "incredibly sweet tone," his style and taste, "and perhaps the best bowing technique since Paganini." He had an impeccable ear. Pablo Casals, who remembers Sarasate, has said that the great violinist sometimes didn't bother to tune his violin exactly when performing with an orchestra, but his intonation was always absolutely pure—he would make minute adjustments of his fingers at split-second speed. Édouard Lalo wrote for Sarasate his beautiful *Symphonie Espagnole* and Max Bruch his romantic *Scotch Fantasy*—Sarasate played them both for their first performances. His audiences were sometimes puzzled by the passion of his performance in contrast with the impassive, almost remote expression on his face; some people said he was "cold."

His compositions are played by violinists everywhere today: *Gypsy Airs, Romanza andalusia, Malagueña, Tarantella,* fantasies and paraphrases. He has taste and a sense of poetic melody and, always, of rhythm. He died in Biarritz in 1908, rich and famous, leaving his fortune to charities and his Stradivari violins, of 1714 and 1724, to the Paris Conservatoire and the Madrid Museum. Pamplona, his native town, was given a Vuillaume copy of a Stradivari; when Sarasate played it everyone was convinced he was performing on one of his Stradivaris.

The third great Romantic of the epoch comes from northern Europe; Ole Bornemann Bull was born in 1810 in Bergen, Norway. He is not remembered in the same way as Wieniawski or Sarasate because he never composed. Bull's parents wanted him to be a clergyman, but he studied in Cassel with Spohr and in 1829 he heard Paganini: the impression was overpowering. Bull followed Paganini to Paris to hear him more often, and began to study what he thought was Paganini's technique. After a dramatic interlude—Bull's Stainer violin was stolen, he jumped into the Seine, was rescued and "adopted" by a wealthy woman—he began trying to imitate Paganini. He had a Hieronymus Amati with an especially flat bridge and very thin strings which helped him to play fast double stops without imperfection, and even double stops in harmonics (which Paganini did so brilliantly). He was said to play Paganini's works very well; he had beautiful *canti-*

lene and exquisite bowing technique. He was very successful in Germany, the Scandinavian countries, and America. He died in 1880 (the same year as Wieniawski) in his home town, where his favorite violin, a beautiful Gasparo da Salò, is preserved in the town museum.

The Romantic school of violin-playing ended in the early years of this century. Gustav Mahler and Arturo Toscanini began to do away with "the arbitrariness of the romantic approach" (as George Szell later defined it); instead they wanted the artistic truth.

Audiences were growing up, distinguishing between a "virtuoso," admired above all for his technique, and an "artist," who used technique as one means toward expressing the spirit of the music. People were no longer impressed by lush *cantilene* or bravura fireworks. Technique was downgraded, often too far; a great violinist must have great technique, though he need not show it off.

The advent of phonograph recording ushered in a new era. We can only wistfully imagine the tone of Paganini, Vieuxtemps, Wieniawski, Sarasate; we can hear that of Ysaÿe, Kreisler, Thibaud, Huberman, and Heifetz.

Joseph Joachim, whom many people considered the typical German violinist, was nevertheless born in 1831 in Pressburg (Bratislava), at that time in Hungary, and trained in Vienna. But he is hardly an exponent of the Vienna school. He soon left for Leipzig, became concertmaster in Weimar under Liszt, and went to Berlin in 1866 as director of the new Music Academy. Richard Wagner predicted that Joachim would "favor" Beethoven and Brahms instead of Wagner, and he was right. Brahms and Joachim were close friends. Joachim taught for almost fifty years in Berlin and became the musical czar. Though he was not primarily a soloist, his performances of the classics were famous. The Joachim Quartet (with De Ahna, Wirth, and Hausmann) was said in its day to be the best in Europe. Joachim was extremely popular in England, and the Victorian critics loved him. His English admirers presented him with a fine Stradivari made in 1715 though he already had four other Stradivaris. Bruno Walter, who as a young man heard Joachim shortly before the violinist's death, remembered the "simplicity and greatness"; while one of Joachim's quartet associates said that to play with Joachim was "difficult, always different tempi, different accents . . ." Joachim died in Belin in 1907.

The Czech school of violin-playing developed relatively early, around the middle of the eighteenth century. Many instrumentalists from Bohemia and Moravia went to Mannheim and Vienna. Had Vienna had a telephone directory at the time of Mozart and Beethoven, it would have read much like the equally nonexistent Prague directory, full of Czech-sounding names. "Czech musicians" were justly famous all over Europe.

The first virtuoso of the Czech school was H. W. Ernst (1814–1867), from Brno (Brünn), Moravia. He studied in nearby Vienna as a teenager and at fifteen he played for Paganini. Paganini was impressed— and may have regretted it later, for Ernst declared he wanted to be "another Paganini." (How many of us wanted to be "another Heifetz"?) Once he rented a hotel room next to Paganini's rooms and listened to Paganini practicing; he had a formidable musical memory, and after making a few notes he wrote down some of Paganini's unpublished compositions, which were then played only by Paganini himself: *Carnival in Venice, Nel cor più,* the *"Moses" Variations.* Ernst performed these pieces in public; Paganini was said to be annoyed and no wonder. Ernst's own compositions in the style of Paganini are now forgotten. He died in Nice in 1867, twenty-seven years after Paganini's death in the same town.

Otakar Ševčik (1852–1934), from Pisek, Bohemia, became one of the greatest teachers in violin history, evolving his own system of study. (It will be discussed on p. 297 in the chapter on teachers and students.) His star pupil was Jan Kubelik (1880–1938), famous for his beautiful tone and fantastic technique, a very great virtuoso. Another important pupil was Jaroslav Kocian. Later Váša Příhoda continued the Czech virtuoso tradition: I remember him as the Paganini of my childhood, especially for his performances of Paganini's Second Concerto and the *Caprices.* The country of Smetana and Anton Dvořák, who was also a good viola-player, was full of fine quartets: the best were the Bohemian Quartet and later the Ondřiček Quartet. Josef Suk, the second violinist of the Bohemian Quartet (and Dvořák's son-in-law), is now recognized as an important composer, and Josef's son, also Josef Suk, has become Czechoslovakia's greatest violinist. He plays the Dvořák Violin Concerto with beauty, passion, and an impeccable sense of rhythm: Grandfather Dvořák would be well pleased.

In Hungary, also an important violin country, Jenö Hubay (1858–1937) from Budapest studied with his father, and in Berlin with Joachim. He was a friend of Vieuxtemps, taught at the Brussels Conservatory, and succeeded his father as professor at the Budapest National Academy of Music. The Hubay-Popper Quartet was one of the finest in its era. Hubay's best pupils were Steffi Geyer, Franz von Veczey, and, especially Joseph Szigeti, born in Budapest on September 5, 1892. Szigeti takes an intellectual approach to his art. He taught at the Geneva Conservatoire, as the successor of Henri Marteau, and is a great, scholarly artist who has lived up to the dictum of his friend, Ferruccio Busoni: "May your art satisfy you: others will rejoice in it, but the former is more important." Szigeti plays Bach with strength and style, and builds his programs with almost scientific thought. Bartók, Bloch, Prokofiev, and Ysaÿe dedicated compositions to him. Szigeti is much more than a great violinist: he is a very great musician.

The same was also said of Adolf Busch (1891–1952) from Siegen, Westphalia. His father was a music-lover and minor violin-maker, and two brothers—Fritz Busch, the conductor, and Hermann Busch, the cellist—also became famous. The Busches were musicians in the finest German tradition, striving always for the spiritual essence of the music, never for effect. In 1917 Adolf Busch succeeded Henri Marteau at the Music Academy in Berlin, originally Joachim's post. With his brother Hermann Busch as cellist, he formed the great Busch Quartet. In 1931, he performed the Beethoven Concerto with the New York Philharmonic, under Toscanini, and the two became musical and personal friends. When Hitler took over Germany the Buschs, who were not Jewish, left their homeland; Adolf became a Swiss citizen in 1935. He was a great violinist in the classical tradition. With his son-in-law Rudolf Serkin at the piano, he performed the Beethoven and Brahms violin sonatas with admirable purity of style and beauty of phrasing. (*The New York Times* called the Beethoven performances in the 1940s "the highest ideal of ensemble playing.") And the Busch Chamber Players made beautiful recordings of Bach's Six Brandenburg Concertos. Busch's nobility as man and musician is remembered by everyone lucky enough to know him.

His contemporary Bronislaw Huberman was also a great artist, and a very different one. Huberman was born in 1882 in Czenstochowa, Poland, and for a while studied with Joachim in Berlin. At age fourteen, in 1896, young Bronislaw performed the Brahms Concerto at the Musikverein Hall in Vienna; Johannes Brahms sat upstairs in his box, and was said to be very pleased. Huberman has remained a beloved artist in Vienna, and in many other places. Looking intent and gloomy like a latter-day Beethoven, Huberman would transform all the music he played into something very alive; his intensity was enormous, and his artistic passion made every note he played an animated miracle of tone. I heard him for the first time in Vienna, in 1920, and now, after half a century, I still hear as though it were yesterday his playing of a certain phrase of Sarasate's *Jota Navarra*. That happens very rarely, and the truly soul-stirring sound is what I mean by a "miracle." He died in 1947.

Such playing was, of course, not acceptable to everybody. Huberman's critics accused him of "gross overplaying" and "too much emotionalism," and many pointed out that his intonation was not always faultless, that his bowing was often noticeable. All this was true, but Huberman also injected his love of music into everything he did.

Mischa Elman (1892–1967), from Talnoye, in the Ukraine, also began as a child prodigy and later studied at the Imperial Music School at Odessa. He became a favorite pupil of Leopold Auer in St. Petersburg. After his debut in London in 1905, and in New York three years later, he maintained a triumphal success with his admirers. He, too, was accused of "emotionalism" and "sentimentalism"; the critics said that he applied "the Elman tone" to everything he played, from Bach to Tchaikovsky, and doubtless the almost legendary sweetness of his tone was better suited to his temperament than to the works of German classicism. But with the "Elmanites," of whom millions bought his recordings, Mischa Elman could do no wrong. When he died in New York many people mourned the great Russian-Jewish fiddler.

Jacques Thibaud (1880–1953) from Bordeaux was the great French violinist of the era. He studied in Paris with Marsick, was concertmaster of the Orchestre Colonne, became a great soloist, and was always a very fine musician. In many ways Thibaud was the antithesis of Huberman and Elman; his tone was pure and noble, his passion controlled, his performances elegant rather than emotional. His Bach and Brahms were very different from the way Huberman and Elman played these works; Thibaud applied his French style and clarity to everything he did, and the performance was intellectual, completely musical. Where he and Huberman and Elman met one another was in the spirit of music; each reached it his own way, and each way was somehow right. The great trio Jacques Thibaud–Pablo Casals–Alfred Cortot made musical history. Ysaÿe once said, "There are two great violinists from whom I can always learn something—Thibaud and Kreisler."

Fritz Kreisler was born in Vienna, on February 2, 1875. (Jascha Heifetz was born the same day in 1901.) Kreisler remains the last great representative of the Western European school of violin-playing, a somewhat vague term that includes Italian, French, Belgian, German, Czech elements. Kreisler, one of the great fiddlers of all time, is still remembered with deep affection by people who heard him. His tone was sweet and warm, his intonation nearly always impeccable; his bowing was very special and fine, and he was a superb musician. "Those who are interested in nothing but their own art are not great artists," he once said.

After a brilliant early start, things at first went wrong with Kreisler's career. His success began only in 1899, in Berlin. Soon he impressed his audiences and critics with his interpretations of Bach, Beethoven, and Brahms. Kreisler became admired by most of his fellow violinists and loved by his audiences, but he was not loved by musicologists and assorted experts and critics. For years he performed a number of "transcriptions" from the works of Vivaldi, Couperin, Francoeur, and others. One day in 1935 Olin Downes, music critic of *The New York*

Times, tried to trace the origin of Kreisler's "transcription" of Pugnani's *Praeludium and Allegro;* Kreisler had claimed that he'd discovered these rare manuscripts in "old monasteries in Europe," and no one had expressed any doubt. But that day Kreisler cabled Downes that the entire series of "classical manuscripts" were his original compositions "with the sole exception of the first eight bars from the *Chanson Louis XIII* by Couperin. . . . Necessity forced this course upon me thirty years ago when I wanted to enlarge my programs."

Legally Kreisler had fooled everybody for thirty years. Ethically he'd done no wrong: the music had enchanted hundreds of thousands of people, who loved it for how it sounded, not for its composer. But the experts were bitter; they had written thousands of words about these "classical" masterpieces, and now this! Kreisler later explained that he'd performed his pieces under his own name when he was young, but no one had cared for them. When he programed them under the names of great composers of the past, everybody cared. Which proves the eternal snobbery of experts, and the fact that Kreisler was an excellent copyist-composer, not unlike Vuillaume, whose copies of Stradivari violins cannot be recognized by the average fiddler. Actually Kreisler was a very good original composer: only a born-and-bred Viennese could have captured the local charm in *Liebesfreud, Liebeslied, Schön Rosmarin,* and *Caprice Viennois.* They are as good in their way as the waltzes by his fellow Viennese, Johann Strauss. Kreisler died in New York in 1962, and a violinistic epoch died with him.

For no good reason many people seem to think the violin is "an instrument for men." A woman's place in playing music is said to be behind the piano, or maybe the harp. Who wants to see a woman performing on the violin or, God forbid, the cello? And if she plays the trumpet, these people say she should go to the Reeperbahn in Hamburg, where the sailors come on shore leave and not for love of music.

The fact is that some women have played, and are playing, the violin more beautifully than most men. No one would know the difference if experiments were made behind a screen.

Wilma Neruda (1839–1911) from Brno, Moravia, who became the wife of Sir Charles Hallé in 1885, was certainly one of the finest violinists of the second half of the last century. Vieuxtemps admired her and dedicated his Violin Concerto No. 6 to her. Sir Henry Wood writes in *My Life of Music,* "The nobility of Lady Hallé's style reminded me of Joachim but, to be quite candid, I thought her tone more musical than his; certainly her intonation was better."

Ginette Neveu, born in 1919 in Paris, might today be one of the great violinists had she not died in an airplane crash in the Azores, in October, 1949, when she was just thirty years old. (Her Stradivari, of 1730, was found in her arms, broken but not burned.) A pupil of Flesch, she early became famous for her musicianship; her technique was a means to create the music. *"L'art d'un artiste est de toujours créer les oeuvres maîtresses de la littérature musicale et l'instrument dont il se sert n'est qu'un moyen d'accéder a ce but"* ("An artist's art is to create continually the masterpieces of musical literature; the instrument that is used only provides a way of reaching that end."), she once said. She played Bach, Beethoven, and Brahms beautifully, often accompanied by her brother Jean, an excellent pianist—who died with her.

Erika Morini, the Great Jewish-Austrian violinist who has remained famous in America since her debut in 1921, was a child prodigy, and studied with Ševčik. Her first important performance was in Leipzig with the Gewandhaus Orchestra under Arthur Nikisch. Among her recent ones were appearances with the Cleveland Orchestra under George Szell, a fellow Austrian who greatly admired her art. She is justly famous for her beautiful tone, her sense of style, her technique and taste.

These are three great artists (and there are others), but women in the violin world are often treated like the women of Kuwait and Liechtenstein—permitted to perform but not to vote. It is an atavistic notion, and we men ought to change these ways of thinking, before the women violinists start their own Woman's Lib movement.

Today the greatest violinists live either in the United States or in the Soviet Union. On both sides of the Atlantic Ocean the "Russian" school dominates. Its breeding grounds are Vilna in the north; Odessa in the south; and some places in between. The Budapest String Quartet, the finest around the middle of our century, had two players from Vilna (the brothers Schneider) and two from Odessa (Roisman and

Kroyt), and that's no accident. Jascha Heifetz comes from Vilna; David Oistrakh and Nathan Milstein come from Odessa, where Elman studied; Isaac Stern comes from Kreminiecz, not far from Odessa; Menuhin was born in New York, but his parents came from Russia. None of this is accident.

Most of the prominent violinists now performing are Jews. This does not mean that the violin, invented in Cremona and highly treasured by princes of the Church, has become a "Jewish instrument." (Kreisler, Busch, and a few others were not Jews.) But the violin became popular with the Jews in the nineteenth and early twentieth centuries as a result of ghetto life in Czarist Russia, and the persecution of the Jews almost everywhere. From a practical point of view a fiddle was cheap—smaller and cheaper than a piano or a Wagnerian tuba. Who would want to study the tuba, upsetting the neighbors and keeping the family in a state of tension? And maybe you didn't even have to buy a fiddle, there was one lying in the attic, and perhaps even a bow with it. And a fellow who could play the first three positions— the "teacher"—maybe he lived around the corner. Lessons would not be expensive.

Also, the violin is an instrument for sensitive, melancholy people, people with a "soul," because the violin has a soul of its own. It was the perfect instrument for the ghetto Jews who were sentimental, sensitive, melancholy. The violin would express their sadness and joy, their hopes and disappointments. Relatively few eighteenth- and nineteenth-century violinists were Jews. Only in the twentieth century did the violin become the instrument of many Jewish artists.

Today's violinists belong in this book only insofar as they have contributed to the story of the violin or violin-playing. The perfection of Jascha Heifetz is here because, by the almost unanimous judgment of his peers, the great violinists, he is considered the greatest living violinist. In the Soviet Union David Oistrakh is the dean of the new faculty of violin teachers who are great artists. Great contemporary fiddlers are mentioned in this book here and there. Thank God there are always some great fiddlers, and there will always be. But just as we Jews are still waiting for the Messiah, we fiddlers are still waiting for another Paganini.

The Great Performer's True Secret

M ost books about the art of violin-playing deal primarily with its technical aspects. The best of them offer no "secrets," no "formulas," no nonexistent shortcuts to virtuosity; instead they give sound advice on the change of finger on identical notes repeated in a phrase, the importance of tone color, the specifics of bowing. A certain way of doing a *staccato,* the special articulation of a phrase, a highly personal *portamento*—these form the violinist's "handwriting," similar to the painter's brushstroke. Listen carefully to a particular phrase in the Brahms Violin Concerto as recorded by Heifetz, Milstein, Oistrakh, and Stern and you will realize that each of them has his own unmistakable handwriting. Only important violinists develop a clear handwriting of their own.

Violinists are incorrigible optimists, almost like gamblers. They just can't help hoping that some day they will come upon a magic formula enabling them to perform impossible feats on their instrument. The hope is encouraged by teachers and relatives, and also by editors and publishers trying to sell books containing gimmicks and "improvements." These range from "new studies in tenths," which can be dangerous for the muscles if practiced too many hours, and something called "perpetual motion in fingered octaves," to such outlandish promises as "fifteen minutes' practice a day will guarantee a brilliant left-hand technique." Others offer mysterious exercises for the bow arm that "guarantee"—the key word—a *detaché,* a *staccato,* a *spiccato.* Even M. P. J. Marsick, the excellent teacher of Flesch and Thibaud, published his *Eureka* manual, exercises guaranteed to reduce the time of daily practice to "a few minutes." Unfortunately well-intentioned though misguided violinists sometimes believe such promises; by the time they find out the bitter truth, they may have lost valuable years.

Books on the art of violin-playing rarely deal with the intangibles and complexities of the spirit of the music. But the spirit of the music poses the real enigma, not the fine nuances of the *vibrato* or the method of executing a *staccato*-arpeggio that may temporarily baffle the practicing violinist. Music is a living art, heard differently by each generation. Music is communication, and each generation has its own way of communicating. There are many ways to play a phrase, not just one right and many wrong ways: many ways of playing it can be equally valid if they are done artistically and convincingly. Would Mozart have liked the slow movement of one of his violin concertos played with *vibrato?* Whether the answer is yes or no, today no other way of playing it is possible.

It is difficult to realize how Bach's solo works for the violin sounded during his lifetime, but for all we know they may have sounded to his hearers not unlike the way they sound to us, because so many proportions were reduced: the sound of the instrument, the size of the hall, the listeners' sense of hearing. Certainly Bach's greatness always came through. In 1890 G. B. Shaw, who understood music and musicians, wrote about Joachim's performance of Bach's C major Fugue,

> Joachim scraped away frantically, making a sound after which an attempt to grate a nutmeg effectively on a boot sole would have been as the strain of an Aeolian harp. The notes which were musical enough to have any discernible pitch at all were mostly out of tune. It was horrible, damnable . . . Yet we all—I no less than others—were interested and enthusiastic. The dignified artistic career of Joachim and the grandeur of Bach's repu-

tation had so hypnotized us that we took an abominable noise for the music of the spheres.

Comparisons with the past are irrelevant. They are also impossible, for two down-to-earth reasons: first, one would have to answer the question "Which past?" and that is unanswerable, for the great violinists of former days used instruments the way their makers had made them; there were different bows and hairs, and smaller bass bars, for instance, so that violins didn't have the tonal power they have today —and didn't need it. Beauty and sweetness of tone were alone important. Second, the masters of the violin have seldom been articulate about their art. Many great violinists are introverts; other great performers have played seemingly by instinct, and been unable or unwilling to explain how they brought off their miracles. Others have been reluctant to talk, though they have given a great deal of thought to what they are doing. In this respect, nothing has changed since Paganini. Great violinists, it seems, are either so introspective that they can express their true selves only through their music, or so outgoing that they regard music mainly as a means of exhibiting their unusual gifts. Certainly many of them have more to say about playing their instrument than about making music.

Among the exceptions is the American violinist Isaac Stern, who once told me, "The worst crime is to play notes instead of making music. Playing the violin must be like making love—all or nothing." Stern spoke openly of his strengths and weaknesses. "My main strength and my main weakness are that my mind works constantly while I perform. I never play instinctively. It's a more dangerous way to live, but it's infinitely more rewarding. Every single moment has a meaning. There can be no real performance without inner tension, and every man must find his own way of resolving the tension. The automatic performer masters the difficulty by becoming a sort of machine. He may do this so well that many people in the audience don't realize what is happening. With me, the mechanism is always subject to the dictates of the intellect. The thinking performer constantly faces all the possible dangers. His mind sees more than the mind of the unthinking performer. The automatic performer shields himself as with a suit of armor. But if the armor doesn't fit him properly, it starts to rattle, and that may have a bad effect on the music."

Stern remembered a performance, years ago, of Mozart's A major Concerto with the Cleveland Orchestra under George Szell. "Playing with them was like playing a quartet. Szell had his point of view, and I had mine, and we argued, but our disagreement was not basic. Had it been, there could have been no music. We had similar musical tastes, and we both had good taste." Taste is very important. On February 12, 1785, Haydn and Leopold Mozart were both at the home of Wolfgang Amadeus and heard three of the string quartets which Mozart had dedicated to Haydn, "a very celebrated man." Haydn said, "Before God and as an honest man, I tell you that your son is the greatest composer known to me either in person or by name. He has taste and, what is more, the most profound knowledge of composition." An authentic genius, Haydn considered taste a primary element of artistic creativity.

In Mozart's A major Concerto the slow movement contains many small things and imperceptible changes; it moves along seemingly at the same pace, yet there are always little differences. If played too slowly it becomes too long and boredom may replace serenity. The borderline is indeterminable; the artist must sense it, for no one can tell this to him. This is the true secret of the great performer. Stern called it "the real mystery in this music, something that cannot be explained. It occurs when the orchestra sings out with a voice of its own and reaches an intense moment, and then I come in with my beautiful melody. The transition must be psychologically believable to be absolutely right. Then the solo violin and the orchestra move along with tranquillity, and there is distilled emotion. . . . This is one of the rare moments when I am absolutely, perfectly happy." Afterward the third movement should be played rather slow, but with an inner elegance and a sort of lilting pace. The melody comes back five times, each time different; with Mozart nothing is ever the same twice, even if it seems written the same way. To bring out these incredibly subtle changes, the performer must understand them thoroughly. It is perhaps a matter of perception, of love. It may result in a classic performance, done in a modern way. The performer's task is to build the bridge from the classic creation to its modern presentation, in the style and taste of our era. Not many performing artists are able to build such bridges.

Perception is the ability to see deeply, to perceive as much as possible. This perception together with the love of music, give the inner glow, the real mystery, the content of the music. They cannot be taught and practiced like technical problems of *staccato* and *spiccato*. Perception makes the artist extremely sensitive to the era's cross currents of ever-changing style and taste, matters that are imperceptible to the average person.

Great artists have recorded the same violin concerto more than once in the course of their career. Stern performed the Brahms Concerto in 1952 with Sir Thomas Beecham and in 1960 with Eugene Ormandy; each time, the artists concerned were completely convinced that they were playing the music the only way possible. But when one compares the two versions, one realizes that they are quite different. Great artists are usually convinced that each version is right in its own way. It isn't so much that taste has changed. Taste, of course, is never absolute, but the present moment's reflection of something beautiful. Once taste is temporarily established, however, it delimits what can be done and, more importantly, what cannot be done. As long as the artist keeps within the limits he is making beautiful music, and within the limits there may be ten ways of playing a phrase, all of them beautiful, all reflecting an artist's training, his ideas, his feelings, his ethical approach —his whole life.

This is what George Szell, the most uncompromising musician in matters of style and taste, called "the artistic truth"—the supreme simplicity that came from his deep conviction that what he was doing at that moment couldn't be done any other way. Only then was he able to convince his musicians, and, through them, his audience. A true artist's performance is the expression of his innermost feelings and convictions at the moment of performance. His basic artistic convictions remain unchanged, but it would be a mistake to believe that the performance of a certain work remains unchanged. The artist's devotion to the composer and to the fidelity of the work—this is a matter of artistic discipline. But as an artist becomes older, great music matures in his mind as a great wine matures in the barrel, and later in the bottle. No two bottles of the same wine are identical, and neither are two performances of the same work.

While technique must be taken for granted because it gives the performer the tools to accomplish the job, it is technique and taste together that establish the conditions for the making of music—the bringing out of the spiritual essence, the creation of that special throb that comes from the performer's soul and heart and touches the listener's soul and heart. No one can determine how it is done and no one can teach it. Certainly, talent alone is not enough. More people have talent than is generally assumed, yet there are also more bad musicians than there is bad music. It has been said that talent is what you possess and genius is what possesses you. To re-create the spiritual essence of a work of music, talent must be blended with the artist's humanity, decency, and his whole belief in art.

As the thinking artist performs, his mind is always a fraction of a second ahead of what he is actually playing. He thinks of the work in its totality, and as he "sings" on his violin, his mind sings too—always a little in advance of his fingers. While his ears listen to what he is playing, his mind listens to what is coming next. It is this perpetual awareness that gives his performance what George Szell has described as "depth, intensity, and artistic concentration"; Eugene Istomin, one of Stern's trio partners, has described it as "a new, modern approach to emotion, an inner feeling rather than old-fashioned flamboyance." Stern himself has described it as:

> "the sweep of the long phrase. . . . Take the beginning of the solo part of the Brahms Violin Concerto. It's very difficult. It goes on and on, still on and on, until it reaches a wonderful climax. Unless the long phrase is musically developed in every detail, the performance will not be artistically convincing. The phrase must glow with an inner life. Even in the fast notes, the singing line must always remain audible. Playing the violin is like changing the register of one's singing voice, with the voice going up and down all the time. Very few artists can do it. Ysaÿe could do it. Kreisler could do it. Heifetz can do it. Oistrakh can do it. When it's well done, it is magnificent. When it is done by somebody trying to imitate a great artist, it can be horrible. A truly great artist expresses in one long phrase his whole musical viewpoint, his musical breeding, his musical convictions. . . . So does the imitator—his phrase is artificial, without inner structure. The phrase may still seem to the casual listener to have the same tonal

and dynamic values, but it has no inner meaning. It isn't "soulful," as the Germans say. It's soulless, and doesn't express the inevitability of the music."

Some of the greatest modern musicians believe in "the inevitability of the music." Toscanini did, Bruno Walter did, Szell did. When Casals plays Bach on his cello he plays the phrases simply, one might almost say, normally. That's the way a great violinist tries to play the solo sonatas by Bach. Albert Schweitzer, who himself strongly believed in the inevitability of the music, once told me that Bach must have been an accomplished violinist who knew a lot about the technique of violin-playing. "If he didn't, how could he have written all that great polyphonic music in his violin sonatas and partitas?" A true artist must have that sense of inevitability, no matter what he performs. Otherwise he wouldn't believe in his own performance, and how could he convince the audience if he cannot convince himself?

In every generation there are very few performers whose performances are carried by the inevitability of the music and glorious in their absolute freedom. These are the artists who can do no wrong. Their tempi are almost always right, and so is their phrasing. Their approach is never forced. They seem to do everything naturally. It seems so simple, yet this simplicity is the hardest thing to achieve. There exists a recording of Mozart's E flat major Concerto which Ysaÿe made early in this century. Recording was then in its infancy, but Ysaÿe's greatness comes through: an artist who accepted no restrictions, except those set by bad taste and faulty style. Many people feel that way today about Pablo Casals.

The intellectual performer (as contrasted with the instinctive one) has a mental picture of the music before his eyes. He knows the amount of space in which he can safely operate without reaching the limits of taste. He knows the limits of his instrument, his intonation, his bowing, and these limits must never be exceeded. But when Casals plays Bach he extends these limits. He can see farther than most other musicians and he still knows the limits clearly. This is his greatness. Casals makes the margins larger but at the same time controls the whole area and organizes it into musical thoughts. He does it by greater perception, by his deep love of Bach's music, and by his constant search for wider possibilities. At this point, the performance truly becomes a "re-creation" of the music, perhaps adding a dimension to it which wasn't even intended or thought of by the composer. Who can say? Stern has compared Casal's playing of Bach to "opening a door and seeing a beautiful garden. How far you will walk out into the garden is controlled by your talent. But you must be able to open the door and see the garden. Not many can do that."

There are some famous performers today—instrumentalists, singers, conductors—who hold that the artist must remain emotionally detached, always in control of one's technique. They perform with cold, intellectual brilliance instead of with soul. Famous singers who perform without inner emotion are known to last longer than those who "give" a lot. The classic *prima donna assoluta,* Nellie Melba, gave her farewell concert at the age of sixty-seven, still dazzling her audience with her brilliant technique. Melba, temperamentally or instinctively, had always shied away from emotion on the stage, and even as a suffering heroine, she never suffered personally. Caruso, by contrast, suffered before and during the performance and perhaps this hastened his death at the age of forty-eight. Likewise some celebrated violinists seem "proud" of being able to remain emotionally detached while they perform. They may not know it but they miss a great deal: the exhilaration, the supreme happiness that comes from giving everything and building that wonderful bridge between the music and the audience. Admittedly they are also spared the misery of the emotional performer who has tried to give everything and knows that he failed. The emotionally detached performers are the ones Leopold Mozart had in mind when he wrote to his son Wolfgang, "How often will you hear a violinist who is much admired, for whom you feel only pity."

History seems to prove that so far as violinists are concerned, the emotionalists are winning over the emotionally detached ones. The great violinists that are lovingly remembered are the ones that gave their audiences everything they had: Paganini, Sarasate, Ysaÿe, Kreisler, Huberman. People instinctively sensed that Fritz Kreisler's great love of music seemed to envelop everything he did and ennobled it. Huberman's performance was an emotional experience. And I was never deceived by Heifetz' aristocratic remoteness while he performed. He may have looked detached but he wasn't. His musical passion is in every phrase he played, in his sensuous vibrato. Some people say that

Heifetz is "cool." They just are not sensitive enough to feel his emotion.

Let us listen to Charles O'Connell, who supervised the recordings made by great musicians since the old Victor Talking Machine Company days, and for thirteen years directed for RCA Victor Red Seal records. In *The Other Side of the Record* he writes,

> Of [Heifetz'] personal and artistic integrity, almost unique in the whole world of musicians, I need not speak. But he is also careful, meticulous, precise, scrupulous, and ethical in everything he does. . . . Heifetz cold? If you mean that every move of bow and arm and wrist and finger is absolutely controlled, exquisitely calculated, if you mean that he never abandons himself in emotion, or tears a passion to tatters, if you mean that his approach to music is objective, that he brings upon music intelligence and intuition of singular power and penetration—if by "coldness" you mean these things, I'll agree that Heifetz in his music is cold. . . . I know no artist who can afford to abandon himself to emotion; I know no musician who ever does. Such abandon is a luxury the audience pays to enjoy. The performer has other things on his mind, and must have. Emotion is certainly the motive power of art, but emotion isn't art, it's nature . . . You do perhaps observe a face of Oriental impassiveness, but I think that this expression, or absence of it, comes about because Heifetz pours into his playing every last iota of concentration, of nervous and muscular strength, of a co-ordination of mind, heart, and hand so exquisitely adjusted and so precise that even a smile or a frown would disturb it.

I never respected famous artists who pretended they were not keyed up prior to a performance. True artists are nervous, suffering, trying to overcome their tension; many are literally sick with stage fright. I've heard performers say that only children and idiots are not nervous. Some artists are known as *routiniers,* and to be a *routinier* is to be mediocre, uninvolved, second-class, uninterested, and egotistic. The real artist lives with his tension, but overcomes it and performs well. Heifetz, the perfectionist among the great violinists, once explained it to me in simple mathematical terms. "The performing artist must have one hundred and thirty per cent in himself when he is playing alone, in his study. During the performance thirty per cent will get lost by climate, acoustics problems, audience resistance, and, of course, the initial nervousness. After overcoming all these handicaps, the artist must still give a one-hundred-per-cent performance. If he were prepared only one hundred per cent, he might wind up with a seventy-per-cent performance, which isn't enough . . ." The credo of a great artist who gives everything he has. Everybody knows the story of G. B. Shaw allegedly telling young Heifetz, "Nothing must be perfect in this world, or else the gods become jealous and destroy it. Please make a habit of playing one wrong note every night before going to bed." A witty aphorism, no doubt, but it fails to hit the mark. Perfection is so rare in our imperfect world that we must be grateful if somebody with the needed equipment tries to prove that perfection still exists.

Every performer has his own way of attempting to relax before a performance. Some sleep, some read mystery stories, some walk the streets, some drive a racing car, some terrorize their families. All performers agree that they must not get overtense; they must keep some control of their nervous pressure, for too much tension is as bad as not enough. The violinist's right arm reacts like a properly inflated automobile tire; the pressure should be just right.

Every performer aims for the best possible performance. It is never the definitive one; no matter how good it was, the true artist feels that it could always have been better. Some performers may be elated about their performance but the finest musicians are elated about the music, not about their own performance. Most of them can sense how it will go the moment they step out on the platform. The audience may be good or rather slow. The artist may, or may not, try to go after the audience; he may prefer to make the audience come up to him, which is harder. Today's audiences know a great deal, owing to recordings and radio. Technical bravura no longer makes a musical performance. Technique must be blended with psychological and emotional excitement. Playing all twenty-four Paganini *Caprices* is a terrific technical accomplishment, but not necessarily a musical one. Szigeti, a true artist, admits that he never played more than five at one recital but he played them so well that he could face "gramophone recordings at a time when no correction, no tape slicings were possible." The great test of the violinist comes with the music that solves all human problems: Bach, Mozart, Beethoven, Brahms, Bartók. Playing all of Bach's solo sonatas and partitas for unaccompanied violin in one evening is a terrific technical *and* musical accomplishment.

It has been said that Bach is incomparable, Mozart the greatest composer who ever lived, and that there is only one Beethoven, the giant. Very true. Playing Bach is a healthy, cleansing experience. (Herbert von Karajan once said that conducting Bach's B minor Mass was like "stepping into a light-filled cathedral and getting cleansed.") Bach's solo works for the violin are the greatest violin music ever written. Paul Henry Lang calls these six works, "Fantastic preludes, completely developed fugues, and cyclopean variations alternating with graceful dances . . . Creative imagination fetes in them its absolute triumph over all restrictions and limitations imposed upon it by form, material, and medium of expression." In the Chaconne in D minor Bach conjured up "a whole world" for Schweitzer.

Musically Bach's solo works pose problems that the average performer can never hope to solve completely. Only a very great artist can do justice to Bach's sense of beauty, his architectural conception, and his variety of mood ranging from classic serenity to baroque exultation and to strange, dark smolderings. Presenting an evening of Bach's solo works is something that practically all contemporary violinists aspire to do but few are able to achieve. (Performing a Bach solo work is the requirement generally accepted at international violin competitions today.) The interpretation of these works as undergone many changes since Simrock published the first edition in 1802, fifty-two years after Bach's death. Even great musicians who admired Bach often misunderstood his intentions. Schumann and Mendelssohn considered it necessary to provide piano accompaniments. Violinists often used a single movement from a solo sonata or partita as a technical showpiece, played as fast as possible for effect! Nonviolinists such as Albert Schweitzer and Ferruccio Busoni understood the structure of these "colossal edifices" better than many violinists, who are not all born polyphonists.

Some very great artists perform the entire D minor Partita without pausing between the movements—an astonishing achievement. The five movements are based on dance rhythms but Bach's genius erects on these simple melodies a masterpiece of musical architecture. The D minor Partita consists of an Allemande followed by the Courante, the Saraband, and the Gigue, and winds up with the glorious Chaconne, probably the greatest single piece of music written for the solo violin. An artist who never pauses between the movements to tune his violin may face serious musical and technical problems. By the time he reaches the Chaconne, with its terrifyingly difficult double stops, some of the strings may have gone out of tune. A great violinist is able to adjust—almost automatically, one might say—to the open strings, a feat demanding excellent hearing, perfect left-hand technique, and, above all, strong nerves. If one string is completely out of tune with the three other strings, one must try to play it as little as possible, either changing the fingering or permitting the bow to rest on it for the shortest possible time. (Strings may go flat under strong bow pressure, and steel strings may go up sharply in an overheated hall.) Such a feat might be compared to dancing on a tightrope with closed eyes after dropping one's balance pole. Playing Bach is primarily a musical problem, however; the audience must not be made aware of technical difficulties. A violinist needs strong self-discipline and economy of movement in order to reserve his emotional and physical resources for the overpowering climax at the very end of the Chaconne. (Stern said he'd trained for it "like a prizefighter for the world heavyweight championship . . . The important thing is not to panic when danger stares you in the face but to sustain the melodic line and preserve the architecture of the music.")

Musical notation is, at best, limited; the score is only a blueprint. The classical composers often conducted their works and knew the performers personally, and didn't bother to write down elaborate directions. Haydn conducting in Eisenstadt or Mozart in Vienna could always tell an orchestra how he wanted his music played. Their scores usually indicate only the effects, without specifying how those effects were to be achieved. (A good trumpeter knew that when a *forte* was called for, in his part of a Mozart symphony, he would produce the right sound if he played *mezzo piano*.) Toward the end of the nineteenth century, as orchestras became larger and composers less often conducted their own works, there was an increasing need for careful notation. Wagner started a new trend. Instead of indicating only the desired effect and leaving the method of achieving it to the individual player, he noted the effort required. The most exact markings are in the scores of Gustav Mahler, a virtuoso orchestrator.

Richard Strauss, another master orchestrator, said, "A musical score is always something that is not apparent on the page." Strauss called the music page "an imperfect blueprint of conception, a lifeless diagram that awaits resurrection by the interpreter" who has "the final judgement just as long as his re-creative powers remain relevant to the spirit and the substance of the work." Though Strauss always tried to make the score as clear as possible, he was aware of the abyss between the music as he heard it in his imagination and the way it turned out when translated into musical notation. He admired Mozart enormously because he knew that the scores of Mozart often offer various ways of interpretation, provided the spirit and the substance of the music are expressed. We don't know how Mozart played his music, but we know that contemporary composers—Strauss, Ravel, Prokofiev, Hindemith, Stravinsky—did not consider their scores to be sacrosanct. Furthermore they have not always performed the music in the same way, but added subtle touches and exquisite changes that must have occurred to them in the moment of the interpretation, because they are not in the score. Generally, however, the composer's intentions must be respected even when they seem stylistically or temporarily unfashionable. When Debussy wrote a *glissando* in his Violin Sonata (a slide executed with either one or two fingers) he wanted it so executed. When he wrote *vibrez et glissando,* he demanded a simultaneous *vibrato* and *glissando.* Ravel and Bartók also wrote, concisely and intentionally, *glissando* effects. This is nothing shockingly new. In the original edition of Haydn's String Quartet, Opus 33, No. 2, there are exactly prescribed *glissando* effects in the Scherzo. They must be executed with much taste and style.

Unlike architecture, which is expressed in terms of space, music is dominated by the inexorable flow of time. To set and maintain the right tempo is one of the most important elements of the artist's task. The question of tempo for Bach's Chaconne has baffled many great violinists. Carl Flesch's metronome reading of =60 is only a general guide for the exposition; the problem is how to keep the tempo throughout the piece when its many moods, reaching from lyricism to majestic power, cause subtle fluctuations within the general tempo. Even the greatest Bach interpreters, among them Pablo Casals and Adolf Busch, argued about the proper Bach tempi, and our ideas about the "right" tempo are constantly changing. (Among the many editions of Bach's solo violin works Busch's, published in 1919, remains closest to the deeper truth.)

A piece of music performed at wrong tempo is like a building erected on a shaky foundation. In either case the structure is bound to collapse. If it doesn't belong there, even an almost imperceptible modification of tempo may break up the flow of the music and the unity of the work. There are artists who have never bothered to become thoroughly acquainted with the classics. They play beautiful phrases and even fine-sounding sections of a movement but they fail, now and then, to understand the overall structure of a composition.

Sometimes a movement of a classical symphony begins with a theme that would be plausible at various tempi if it were detached from the movement and played by itself. Therefore some artists feel that the tempo of the whole movement must be dictated by a "critical" bar, or group of such bars, somewhere in the middle of the movement. Others believe that the fastest element will become the center of the tempo, and the rest of the movement will be built around it. If the speed of the fastest element determines the speed of the entire movement, the artist may vary his tempo a little but never depart from it completely. The listener must not be aware of the subtle modifications, but feel that a constant tempo is being maintained throughout. Any change that becomes obvious is wrong. It is part of a complex process, in which much depends on intuition, to plot and execute any modifications so skillfully that they are virtually imperceptible. Word notations and metronome figures are helpful up to a point, but a Mozart andante is different from a Paganini andante or a Brahms andante. Slow tempi have become slower, and fast tempi faster, than they were when the classical works were written, probably because of the accumulated influence of all the music that has been written in between. We are all influenced by the sum total of all the music we have heard. We help to shape the music and we are being shaped by it. Our reactions to music are very different from those of early nineteenth-century listeners who hadn't heard Wagner, Verdi, Debussy, Mahler, Schönberg, and Bartók.

Musicians have never been able to answer the question, "How fast is a second?" A second seems to last longer when it is filled with good music; that is, when an artist is expressing musically what he wants to say. A second also seems very long when the score indicates that the members of a string quartet or orchestra have a measure of rest, and then all start again at the same time; such a silent second is filled with inaudible tension. "Slow" and "fast" are relative terms in music. People remember Toscanini's "fast" tempi and Furtwängler's "slow" ones, but there was little differencc in actual time. The difference lay in emotional content. (Hans Knappertsbusch's famous "slow" reading in Bayreuth of the first act of *Parsifal* lasted just two minutes longer than the first act under a conductor whose tempi were known as "fast.") Music always provides enough time for an artist to say what must be said. The exact tempo depends on the mood of the artist, the mood of the audience, and the mysterious interplay of performer, audience, and the acoustics of the hall. Though the performer may not be conscious of it, some halls make the performer play faster than others. Whatever the performer does must reflect the spirit of the music, and it must make sense. Schubert is known for his "divine length," Bruckner's length is sometimes quite earthly. If the tempo isn't right, and if the music is not filled with emotional content, divine length easily becomes sheer boredom.

Dynamics pose another problem. Music does not exist without contrast, but if the contrast is overdone the spirit of the music may be annihilated. Everything in music, including crescendo and decrescendo, is a matter of comparative, rather than absolute, value. Casals, for instance, rarely plays passages very loud, but his sense of proportion and balance in relating one sound to another is so subtle and controlled that a Casals *mezzo forte* sounds louder than the ordinary performer's *forte*.

The indispensable attributes of the modern concert violinist are a strong left-hand technique—his fingers must always have complete control—and sustained power in the handling of the bow. Szigeti calls intonation "the basic and all-important question in our art," summing it up: "There is no substitute for perfect intonation." Neither is there a substitute for perfect bowing. In recent times, almost all important violinists have availed themselves of the whole length of the bow—the principal exception being Kreisler, who achieved miracles of sound with only one-third of his bow. Beauty of tone is very important, but sometimes the violin tone must not become too beautiful lest it distract the listener from the content of the music. The experienced performer always listens carefully to the sound he is producing and alters it as the acoustics of the hall require. He must have an instinctive sense of acoustics, and he must adjust to a "dry" hall that softens the tone, or one with sharp, brilliant sound. All performers have their favorite halls (and many which they dislike); most agree on Vienna's Grosser Musikvereinsaal, New York's Carnegie Hall, and Boston's Symphony Hall.

Sound is also a touchstone of the artist's taste. Crimes against good taste are committed by violinists, quite famous ones, who play all music with the same sort of sound. Sound must not only be beautiful, but also fitting to the character of the music. Classical music needs pure, beautiful sound; Tchaikovsky needs luscious sound; Paganini and Brahms need romantic sound. A certain pathos is permissible for Bruch or Saint-Saëns, but not for Mozart. Some violinists are not able to penetrate the mystery of sound; others make a fetish of it at the expense of style and taste. A violinist playing all music with the same sort of sound is no better than a cook who drenches all his dishes in the same sauce. Sound has subtle gradations, from the sober to the sumptuous, and each can be beautiful. Warmth, for example, exists in many nuances: the chaste warmth of Mozart, the sensuous warmth of Tchaikovsky, the noble passion of Beethoven, the distilled emotion of Debussy.

The best artists know that the concert is not the real end of musical performance but the means to the end, which is the totality of the musical impression left by a performance. The artist must always show his ability as a performer and a musician, the one goes with the other. A performer whose technique surpasses his musicality leaves no deep impression. Thanks to radio and television, and to the present high standard of recording, even small-town audiences have considerable musical understanding, Unless the performer creates his own image of the music—unless he is really re-creative—he has failed.

Audiences have matured at a great rate in the past few decades, as shown by the way programs have changed. Nowadays the making of a program is next door to an exact science. Thirty years ago, a violin recital ordinarily began with a sonata, probably an eighteenth-century work, "to warm up with" or "to play oneself in," as the phrase went. Then came a violin concerto with piano accompaniment. After intermission there were a number of small bravura pieces to show off the performer's technique. Finally came the real fireworks as encores.

Since then, taste in programs has much improved, though few of the eighteenth- and nineteenth-century works of the Italian master violinists, that gold reserve of early violin music, are now performed. Corelli's *La Follia,* Tartini's *The Devil's Trill,* and "Vitali's" *Chaconne* remain perennial favorites. (Modern researchers agree that the *Chaconne* was written by an unknown eighteenth-century composer.) But other works by Corelli and Tartini are rarely heard. Important violinists now refuse to perform any of the major violin concertos unless they are playing with an orchestra. Practically all violinists play solid and substantial programs—sonatas by Bach, Brahms, Mozart, Beethoven—and sometimes they play all three Brahms sonatas, or three Beethoven sonatas, during one evening. This can become a strain on the listener unless the performer treats each sonata as a separate musical entity, not all three together. Some violinists carefully build their programs in certain cities, to avoid repeating what they played before, using card indexes. And even the bravura pieces played toward the end of a recital now have considerable musical value, such as Ravel's *Tzigane,* Saint-Saëns' *Rondo Capriccioso,* a Paganini *Caprice,* a Kreisler composition. Flamboyance is out, simplicity is in. (The danger lies in overdoing it and becoming prosaic; a performer should always remain something of a poet.) Artistically, however, the triumph of the new simplicity over the old flamboyance shows progress: instead of giving the audience assorted goodies, the serious contemporary artist now presents his faithful interpretation of large-scale pieces. He expresses his feelings through the music instead of filtering the music through his feelings.

It wasn't always like this. Beethoven, an uncompromising composer and a man who antagonized everybody, nevertheless wrote to his publisher, Ferdinand Ries, about the "Hammerklavier" Sonata as follows:

Should the sonata not be suitable for London, I could send you another one; or you could also omit the Largo and begin straight away with the Fugue, which is the last movement. . . . Or you could use the first movement and then the Adagio and then for the third movement the Scherzo, omitting entirely No. 4 with the Largo and Allegro risoluto. Or you could take just the first movement, the Scherzo, and let them form the whole sonata.

And in 1895, less than a century ago, Fritz Kreisler programed the Cavatina from Beethoven's String Quartet, Opus 130; the Handel Largo; the Bach Gavotte in E; and Paganini's *Moto Perpetuo*. Even after World War I, violin concertos were often played with the piano accompaniment in cities where no orchestra was available. So-called *morceaux de salon* would round out the second part of the program. Today it's the musical substance that matters, not the technical fireworks. Beethoven's less popular sonatas are performed, not only the *Spring* and the *Kreutzer;* Schubert's Opus 162; works by Hindemith and Bartók.

But while the programs are getting musically more mature, the younger violinists performing them often lack the maturity of their predecessors. The contradiction concerns not only violinists, but musicians in general. It is caused by the structure of the modern music business (the emphasis is on business rather than music), which resembles a jungle wherein survival is a matter of ability, timing, and plain luck. Certain instrumentalists become famous less for their musicality or technique than because they filled a demand or had a break; after a while it becomes apparent that they are not really ready for fame. In getting ahead as fast as possible, they had no time for full study of the classics, or to relax and meditate about problems of style and taste; sometimes it is not even clear that they truly love music. Trying to make things easier for them, their teachers often make things more difficult instead. "Labor-saving" devices are introduced into problems of fingering and bowing; effect becomes more important than style. In 1940 Artur Schnabel lectured at the University of Chicago on *Music and the Line of Most Resistance;* Schnabel, a great pianist, claimed that true achievement can be attained only by overcoming its difficulties oneself, never by gimmicks and shortcuts. But that now seems an "old-fashioned" point of view. "A young virtuoso who is offered the chance of recording six contemporary violin sonatas (Ravel, Debussy, Bartók, Enesco, etc.) that the company needs will not have the self-criticism or the self-abnegation to ask the company to wait until these works have slowly matured in him," writes Szigeti, who did not record the Beethoven Sonatas until he was fifty-two. The young virtuoso who would have the moral strength to turn down such a chance would probably be rewarded by seeing a competitor do the recordings. Today's music jungle gives young players little opportunity to mature. Whether or not they feel musically equipped for it, they take a chance in competitions for a prize or a recording contract. Older conductors complain that many young instrumentalists lack musical training, that their teachers have concentrated on technique and neglected problems of theoretical knowledge, style, and taste. Szigeti quotes Georges Szell:

> Instrumentally the most striking common quality is the lack of development of the bow-arm. Everything in their tuition seems to have been concentrated on producing as big a sound as possible and having as swift a left hand as possible. Any subtle function of wrist and fingers of the right hand is practically unknown to them. Therefore while they are able to go through some of the concerti, particularly the cantabile passages, with some semblance of brilliance, they are completely helpless when confronted with, say, a second violin part of a Mozart symphony with its problems.
>
> They have never been told that the bow has to articulate the music. Very few of them know how to play near the frog. Many of them, because of the stiffness of wrist and fingers, have no smooth bow change on either end. Generally speaking, these students are trained and coached solely with a view to a soloist's career, which of course only a very small percentage of them can make anyway, whereas all preparation that would enable them to be relatively happy and not disgruntled members of orchestras or chamber ensembles is completely neglected. They are not taught, or not sufficiently taught, chamber music and ensemble techniques, and moreover they are not stimulated to love music as such, instead of loving only themselves and their careers.

Szell has presented the problem with admirable clarity. He always considered himself music's faithful servant; Szigeti says, "We are more likely to find what Szell calls 'loving music as such' among amateurs than in the ranks of the professionals." We amateurs can afford "to make music" because we love it. We don't depend on music as a livelihood, not in that race that goes to the loudest and the fastest, to the very best technician. The young violinist who hopes to become a soloist probably plays the Paganini *Caprices* well, but his interpretation of Bach and Mozart is disappointing because he fails to feel the spiritual content of the music.

According to orchestra managers, it often happens that available string players are unfamiliar with the repertoire, unable to do advanced sight reading, and reluctant to submit to the necessary orchestra discipline. What Carl Flesch called in 1923 "the tragedy of the orchestra violinist's career," persists and grows worse. There is widespread "mental embitterment." A symphony orchestra is a breeding ground of frustration; some young violinists who aim for a career as soloist indignantly turn down the suggestion that they should play for a few years in a good orchestra. It wasn't always so: as young men, Joachim, Auer, Busch, Ysaÿe, Thibaud, Francescatti, and many others played in orchestras. In his *Art of Violin Playing* Carl Flesch writes that to the aspiring soloist ". . . some time spent in an orchestra, though only as a temporary measure, offers an uncommonly valuable means of extending his musical horizon."

Many young violinists disagree. They hate the dictatorship of the star conductor, and they don't want to give up that part of their inner self that helps create the organism of a great orchestra; for the orchestra too must have its own personality and character, though this offers the line of most resistance to the young instrumentalist. Some prefer to join chamber orchestra groups, touring and traveling and hoping for a lucky break; some actually join an orchestra but feel so harassed by concertmasters and certain conductors that they get out before they lose their love of music.

The growing scarcity of able orchestra violinists who are up to the high artistic standards of current performances creates a serious problem for the important symphony orchestras in the Western world. Orchestras have difficulty finding replacements in their violin sections. A few years ago a famous German orchestra had only sixteen applicants for a first-violin vacancy, compared with almost sixty between the two World Wars. (There seem, however, to be enough young viola and cello players.) In 1965 the Ford Foundation distributed $85,000,000 among the fifty major American orchestras "to advance quality by enabling more musicians to devote their major energies to orchestral performance . . . to attract talented young people to professional careers by raising the income and prestige of orchestra players." The following year, the National Council of the Arts made a grant of $400,000 "to help meet the shortage of qualified instrumentalists."

Pessimists fear that in twenty years there won't be enough able string players, especially violinists, to replace the older generation.

Less than a dozen of the hundred-odd American symphony orchestras are completely professional, and not all of them offer employment all year long. Many have short seasons, and the musicians must earn extra money playing for radio and television, recording companies, or dance orchestras. The situation is quite different in the Soviet Union and the Communist countries, which have a state-sponsored system for the training of young musicians. In Russia, the leading artists are obliged to spend a considerable part of their time teaching; as a result these countries now have a younger generation of able instrumentalists.

Japan, too, is on its way to becoming a major violin country. Western teachers are increasingly impressed by the success of the Suzuki method: since 1958 Dr. Shinichi Suzuki's Talent Education Movement has started training violinists at the age of three. In many Japanese schools musical education is an obligatory part of the curriculum. The Japanese approach string playing with their customary verve. Just as a Jewish mother tries to talk her boy into another half-hour of practicing scales, a Japanese mother goes with her boy to the teacher and watches him during the lesson. The standards of orchestra and chamber-music playing in Japan are rising, and young Japanese men and women are among the prize-winners at international competitions.

The Japanese have grasped the basic truth, namely, that one must start teaching a string instrument very early. "The violin," says Joseph Fuchs, one of the important contemporary teachers, "must be taught early because it requires acrobatics of *both* hands. The interdependence of both left and right hand is important. The left hand is doing one thing while the right hand does another. The beauty of the Suzuki method is that it begins early, rarely goes beyond the age of eleven, and involves the cooperation of the parents."

Japan has already produced a number of technically first-rate violinists. How far they will go as soloists will depend on their ability to understand and re-create the spiritual content of Western music, which may still be alien to many of them. It is a musical, not a violinistic problem. No Japanese violinist has yet reached the level of greatness, —but it may be tomorrow, or a year, or ten years.

ᑢᔆᕀ Chamber Music:
A Passion Fulfilled

Chamber music has always been the domain and the passion of amateurs. It was written for amateurs, was played by amateurs, and is still supported by amateurs who attend the concerts of the famous professional quartets and buy their recordings—deeply happy to hear their favorite music so beautifully performed, deeply unhappy to know they can never do it nearly so well. When "chamber music" is mentioned, some people think of a famous professional quartet, but we chamber-music players know that it is the amateur's special pursuit of happiness. The fiddler, violist, or cellist who once had dreams of glory, and woke up to the gray dawn of reality, often makes his compromise with life in the realm of chamber music.

Famous soloists and harassed members of well-known symphony orchestras may also play string quartets for relaxation. This is pure music for the sake of music. In the early 1940s it was not unusual for a chamber-music player in Hollywood to play one night in a group that included Jascha Heifetz and the next with a violinist working for Paramount Pictures. Both, incidentally, had beautiful Stradivaris.

Some of the greatest composers wrote some of their finest music for string quartet. They were attracted by the enormous challenge—the economy of means, the subtlety of texture, the clarity of expression, and all done with only four voices. Beethoven's late string quartets contain greater music than his greatest symphonies; they are the distilled essence of timeless, eternally modern music. Paul Henry Lang writes in *Music in Western Civilization,* "A new miracle unfolds before us, a new polyphony . . . the dimensions themselves being eliminated, the triumph of pure music over construction."

Chamber music belongs mostly to string players. Its origins go back to approximately 1555, about when the first violins made by Andrea Amati were being played. Chamber music is discussed in *L'Antica musica ridotta alla moderna prattica* by the Renaissance theoretician, Nicola Vicentino. Because "chamber music" grew naturally, we don't know exactly when and where it was first written and performed; opera, of course, is another matter. In the 1580s the *sonata da camera* became popular in Italy. The *sonata* was instrumental music which "sounded." (The *cantata* was sung.) Later the term *sonata da camera* applied to any instrumental music that fell between church music and opera. Characteristically the individual parts in early chamber music were played by single instruments. Chamber music has remained the domain of the individualist. Whether there are two players (a duo) or eight (an octet) they remain musical individualists. Each player plays his part.

After its origin in Italy chamber music flourished in England, France, and Spain (but not yet in Austria and Germany. The countries now associated with the great classical masterpieces did not contribute to the early development). In Italy Salomone Rossi and Biagio Marini wrote trio ("three-part") sonatas; in England many composers (Anthony Holborne and John Dowland, among others) wrote "pavans, galiards, and alemands," and in 1630 Martin Peerson's *Mottects or Grave Chamber Musique* was published; in France Claude Gervaise and Eustache du Caurroy wrote suites for viols in the second half of the sixteenth century; and there was also chamber music in Spain and the Netherlands. Jan Bruegel's painting *The Sense of Hearing,* c. 1620, now in the Prado Museum, Madrid, shows people performing music, and there are instruments of all sorts on the floor. Pieter de Hooch's *Duet for Violin and Lute,* painted in 1667, shows a violin, probably a Cremonese instrument.

During the Renaissance the "chest of viols," a set of six matched instruments—two treble, two tenor, two bass—became synonymous with chamber music. Around the middle of the seventeenth century when the Cremonese instruments, mostly made by the Amatis, became famous, they were highly esteemed by chamber-music players for their sweet tone; so were Jacob Stainer's violins. Both were more expensive than Stradivari's early violins. An Amati remains the ideal chamber-music instrument for amateurs who play at home, where chamber music rightly belongs. Originally this music was written to be performed in the chambers of music-lovers, as Samuel Pepys' *Diary* abundantly documents. The professional quartet came much later.

When the Amatis and young Stradivari wanted to try out their new instruments they probably got together and played sonatas by Corelli, who was justly admired. Trio sonatas and other combinations were written by Vivaldi, Gabrielli, Vitali, Frescobaldi, Purcell, Buxtehude, and later by many others. None of them hit upon the glorious combination of two violins, one viola, and a cello, with each instrument playing an individual part; Joseph Haydn was the genius who invented it.

In 1755, when Haydn was twenty-three, he wrote his first string quartet, Opus 1, No. 1, in a country house in Weinzierl, near Vienna. Andrea Amati had created the first Cremonese violins almost exactly two hundred years earlier, and Vienna did for the string quartet what Cremona had done for its instruments. Young Haydn knew, of course, about earlier developments in chamber music: in Mannheim members of the Stamitz family, F. X. Richter, and Giuseppe Toeschi had experimented with the form; in Vienna there had been Georg Christoph Wagenseil, Georg Matthias Monn, and Franz Asplmayr. But it was Haydn who brought out clearly the individuality of the four instruments, each speaking its own voice, and the four together forming an artful ensemble. There has been much guesswork about how he hit upon the great idea: perhaps it was by accident. He was immensely gifted, he had listened to much music, and he had time at the country home of Carl von Fürnberg; there he wrote his first quartets, which he called *cassations, notturni, divertimenti*. He soon freed the quartet from the domination of the first violin and treated all four instruments on equal terms. By the time he wrote his quartets Opus 20, with their astonishing fugues in the last movement, he must have created quite a stir at the home of his then patron, Prince Nicholas Esterházy. The time was now 1772. Haydn even made the cello sing out the opening theme, which had never been done before. (Beethoven later did it too, in his first Rasumovsky Quartet, Opus 59, No. 1.)

From then on until he died in 1809, at the age of seventy-seven, Haydn developed this noble art form to perfection. Most of his later quartets are masterpieces, rich in invention, with emotions ranging from noble pathos to wry humor, always vibrant with feeling; in all, there are eighty-three string quartets by Haydn. Many contain hidden surprises, and over the years one discovers still another subtle touch of beauty, a haunting harmony, a reflection of the composer's genius. Between 1784 and 1803 Haydn wrote thirty-nine wonderful string quartets, each one captivating with its mysterious development, mood, and rhythm, and its refined balance. His latest works, written when he was in his seventies, have touches of wisdom and smiling at the follies of mankind, as charming as treasured moments in Verdi's *Falstaff,* another old man's masterpiece. There is never a lack of invention despite his old age; often one is astonished by the depth of feeling and passion. The more often one plays these quartets, the more one loves them—the test of tests.

Haydn played the violin, and probably quite well—he played the first violin part of his own quartets that contain technical problems and hidden traps. Michael Kelly, the Irish singer who was Don Curzio, the stuttering notary, in the first performance of Mozart's *Le Nozze di Figaro,* tells us in his *Reminiscences* that he heard Haydn and his fellow players, and calls them "tolerable." "Not one of them excelled on the instrument he played but there was a little science among them, which I daresay will be acknowledged when I name them." The players were: Haydn, first violin; the composer Karl Ditters von Dittersdorf, second violin; Mozart, viola; and the composer Jan Baptist Wanhal, cello. Haydn played a Stainer violin.

The classical string quartet composers are Haydn, Mozart, and Beethoven. In analogy with the great Cremonese makers, Haydn reminds us of Andrea Amati, the inventor; Mozart resembles Stradivari, the perfectionist genius, a man for all musical seasons; and Beethoven shares much with Guarneri del Gesù—going his own way, breaking the rules, often misunderstood in his titanic struggle, and always very great.

The violin and chamber music are both children of the Renaissance, but the string quartet is a creation of Vienna's classicism. Violins and string quartets were first appreciated by aristocratic patrons who understood beauty and could afford beautiful things. Feudal patronage was still important in Vienna around 1800; members of the Habsburg court, princes, counts, and cardinals commissioned chamber music works, and often played an instrument. The names of Prince Schwarzenberg, Prince Lobkowitz, and Prince Nikolai Galitzin today live on in the quartet dedications of Beethoven; the three beautiful Rasumovsky Quartets, Opus 59, have given a certain immortality to Count Andreas Rasumovsky, the Russian ambassador in Vienna, one of Beethoven's long-suffering friends. (In Berlin, King Frederick William II commissioned Mozart to write six string quartets and Carl Gotthard Langhans to build the Brandenburg Gate. Mozart completed three, K. 575, 589, and 590, with prominent cello parts for the King. They will outlive the Brandenburg Gate.)

Count Rasumovsky again made chamber-music history in 1808 when he asked Ignaz Schuppanzigh, the prominent Viennese violinist, to form a quartet of professional musicians for his musical soirees. (Beethoven admired Schuppanzigh, and earlier had "three times a week lessons" from him.) Count Rasumovsky played second fiddle in the Schuppanzigh Quartet: they couldn't turn him down since he paid for the music, the musicians, and the refreshments. But he soon dropped out, and so did Prince Lichnowsky; to play with professionals never works. Composers began to expect their quartets to be played by professionals and wrote difficult parts, far too difficult for amateurs. Gradually chamber music, once the exclusive domain of the amateur, moved away from the "chamber" into the concert hall, where it was performed by technically superior pros. More people hear it now, but some purists still feel that chamber music should begin and end at home. Yet Beethoven in his later years, and many composers after him, wrote some of their finest works in this genre for the pros.

These great professional quartets are often miracles of musical ensemble work. They are so perfectly integrated that they seem even to breathe in the same rhythm. Their bow pressure and vibrato seems synchronized, yet their playing has wonderful spontaneity. They float above the music but they float together; the slightest *rubato* by one player is instinctively followed by the other three. And although the four instrumental voices are perfectly blended, the individual voices are clearly discernible. In a great string quartet no player may be superior to the others; ideally, they should be equal. Their togetherness is never mechanical but musical, intellectual, and emotional, often the result of hard work and team discipline. Before the Budapest Quartet —the world's finest professional quartet in the 1940s and 1950s— began performing in public, the players worked several hours every day, Sundays included, for six months; sometimes it took them a whole day to get half a dozen bars into shape.

Playing chamber music is different from either playing as a soloist or as a member of an orchestra. The soloist is his own master, and also his own servant. Chamber-music ensembles made up of celebrated soloists (often at the suggestion of a recording firm, because this can be big business) rarely last for a long time, and even more rarely are they completely integrated. Great soloists often find it difficult to subdue their artistic personalities. They try, often instinctively, to dominate the group—and thus wreck it. Solo playing is diametrically opposed to quartet-playing. But we owe beautiful recordings to the supertrio of Heifetz–Primrose–Piatigorsky and the Stern–Rose–Istomin trio is the best of its kind—proof that there are always exceptions.

The orchestra player, on the other hand, may be an outspoken individualist in his life and his philosophy but as a player he is a member of a tightly integrated group under the absolute command of the conductor. A great orchestra cannot be an experience in democracy; it is a dictatorship. No wonder that many able orchestra players escape into the wonderland of chamber music, where they can be individualists as well as members of a group. If they coordinate them with their fellow players, they may express their own ideas; chamber music is a salutary experience in regimented individualism. The player's personal taste and style must not be contrary to his fellow players', otherwise the mixture won't work. Chamber music is give-and-take, and above all listening to the others. The first violinist, a *primus inter pares,* must not act like a miniconductor, waving his bow like a baton. His eyes may convey the needed leadership, and sometimes that leadership switches to another member of the group, depending on the music. Beating time with the foot is frowned upon in better quartet circles. Ideally, each player should know the entire score. (No orchestra player is expected to know the entire score; it's enough if he studies his own part.) Bowings are important, and whenever possible the players should use similar bowings because this enhances style and articulation. The same phrase must not be played by one player in *staccato,* the other in *spiccato,* the third in *détaché.*

The members of some successful professional quartets rarely see each other except at rehearsals and concerts, making out a powerful case against togetherness. Some players say the reason they are still together after several years is that they try to be together as little as possible. String players are often sensitive people who get on each others' nerves, and good string quartets have burst apart under the stress of wild disagreements—artistic, financial, personal, sexual. It seems to work out best when the players have separate friends, hobbies, and ways of life—and when their wives are discouraged from excessive mingling, though they cannot help meeting at concerts and backstage afterward. The wives should never be allowed to attend rehearsals, and the players should rehearse in an auditorium or hotel room, not in the home of a member.

Once the members of a quartet start fighting about women, politics, food, or anything else, they are in trouble as a group. Musical arguments, on the other hand, are necessary and healthy: these should be thrashed out and the final decision based on the majority or on compromise. The balance of sound often creates arguments. One player may say he didn't hear himself when the other three heard him very well indeed, maybe too much. When one player ruins a phrase, the others lambaste him in the forthright and colorful language of quartet players. Responsibilities should be as equally divided as to money. Arguments about tempo, fingering, bowing, phrasing, rhythm, and so on, should be settled by majority vote; if the vote is two to two the players negotiate and compromise, and if they have similar musical tastes a compromise will be reached. Otherwise they won't stay together for long. They should include in their repertoire mainly works that all four members are enthusiastic about; this goes especially for modern works. They should be flexible; quartet players know that nothing is definitive in music or life. As they become older and more mature, tempi may change and so will the mood of a movement.

There have been many professional quartets since Schuppanzigh's: the four Koella brothers; the four Mueller brothers, who performed Haydn, Mozart, and Beethoven all over Europe in the 1840s; the famous quartets called after their first violinists—Joseph Hellmesberger, Joseph Joachim, Arnold Rosé, František Ondříček. There was the fine Bohemian Quartet (Karel Hofman, Josef Suk, Oskar Nedbal, Hanuš Wihan); the early (and original) Budapest Quartet which Brahms liked very much; the Flonzaley; the Kneisel, that disbanded in 1917 after thirty-two years of performances, spreading new enthusiasm for chamber music in the United States from coast to coast. Since then, many fine quartets have come, and some have already gone: the Kroll, the Busch, the London, the Gordon, the Kolisch, the Léner, the Coolidge, the Perole, the Roth, the Amadeus, the Smetana, the Claremont, the Curtis, the Hungarian, the Végh, the Paganini, the Griller, the Juilliard, the Hollywood, the Alard, the LaSalle, the Loewenguth, the Knoeckert, the Barylli, the Wiener Konzerthaus, the Janáček, the Czech, the Ostrava, the Weller, the New Music, the Pro Arte, the Fine Arts, the Musical Art, the Italiano, the Budapest, the Guarneri— and the list is not complete.

Chamber music devotees are a frankly prejudiced and wildly contentious breed, split into more factions than the old Chamber of Deputies in Paris. Nearly everybody has his favorite, though many agree on certain great quartets. My favorite one was the Budapest (Joseph Roisman, Alexander Schneider, Boris Kroyt, Mischa Schneider), which at its best had everything that one can hope for in the ideal quartet. To hear them play the late Beethoven quartets was complete fulfillment; they made this greatest music come alive. Occasionally, to show their virtuosity, they performed a musical stunt; they recorded Milhaud's Quartets Nos. 14 and 15, separate compositions but so written that they can be played simultaneously to form a string octet. After recording No. 14 the players put on earphones and, while listening to the playback, recorded No. 15. Afterward engineers superimposed the two recordings. Boris Kroyt, the violist, who had earlier been a soloist with both the violin and the viola, figured that theoretically he might have recorded the first and the second violin parts and the viola parts of both quartets, playing a total of six different parts, and let the engineers put them all together. (Viola-players often have fascinating ideas: Mozart, Beethoven, and Dvořák, and Hindemith, among others played the viola.)

Some quartets have performed the real stunt, playing by heart. The Kolisch Quartet played Schönberg by heart—terribly difficult. But even playing an early Haydn by heart is a special strain for the two middle voices—second violin and viola—who may have to pom-pom for, say, twenty-nine bars. Playing by heart impresses a segment of the audience, but it may give the musicians a somewhat uncomfortable feeling. String quartets were not written to be played by heart. They were written for each player to play his part and know the entire score.

The division between the few highly skilled professionals in the concert hall and the many well-meaning but less proficient amateur players at home has not been inimical. On the contrary, the finest professional quartets (not necessarily the most famous) have something of the dedication and spontaneity of good amateurs. We amateurs need the professionals' inspiration and the encouragement; we always hope against hope that we may bring off some works almost as they ought to sound. Almost. And we are grateful to the pros for letting us hear the modern quartets we can never hope to play ourselves.

The pros, on the other hand, have a need of us. Our loyalty and enthusiasm support them. The audience at a symphony concert has few people who would be able to play the music they've come to hear, and among operagoers still fewer would dare sing one of the parts. But in the audience at a chamber-music concert, a considerable number of enthusiasts have played much of the music or at least tell themselves they've played it. This establishes a warm, intimate, yet critical relationship between performers and listeners that is unique in today's cold, businesslike world of music. It's just as well that chamber music ceased to be the privilege of the select friends of an aristocratic patron; otherwise it might have died out with the aristocrats.

Chamber music is not synonymous with string quartet; the term includes various groupings. Two players are the minimum though sonata teams, strictly speaking, are not considered chamber-music players. But Mozart's duos for violin and viola are certainly very great chamber music. The maximum is nine or ten players. Quartets, quintets (usually with two violas), and trios (violin, viola, and cello) are the most popular combinations. To play a string trio is a very delicate task; the absence of the second violin puts a greater responsibility on each player. Music is basically mathematics, and a trio is as different from a quartet as a triangle is from a square. The most beautiful string trio of all, Mozart's Divertimento in E flat, K. 563, poses problems of balance, tone, and cooperation surpassing those in his string quartets.

Nearly everybody seems to agree that the string quartet is the finest combination in chamber music. No wonder most chamber-music literature is written for it. But the string quintet can also be very beautiful; Mozart's G minor Quintet, K. 516, for two violas, is probably his greatest chamber-music work. Hans Keller calls the G minor Quintet "as great as the G minor Symphony, whence it is greater: the same wealth of feeling must needs be expressed yet more economically in the chamber work," and he defines the string quintets as "the greatest and most original structures of Mozart, chamber-musical or otherwise."

Flutists, oboists, clarinetists, and horn players occasionally join the string players in some rarely performed, very beautiful works. Pianists sometimes create a problem. There is fine chamber music for strings and piano but even great pianists often consider them written for the piano with string accompaniment. Pianists are by nature often self-sufficient and independent, whereas the principle of chamber music is interdependence. No matter how sensitive a pianist, a piano remains a mechanical instrument: its sound is produced by hammers. In chamber music with piano it is difficult to achieve a blend and balance between the keyboard instrument and the strings. Again the finest piano quartets were written by Mozart, who opposes the piano to the string trio and creates magnificent beauty. Still, Keller rightly calls the combination "a problematic genre." It is a truism that piano and the strings are not an ideal mix. (Even when a great violinist plays with a great pianist, there remains a physical divergence of the quality and color of sound. The pianist, sure of his intonation and envious of the string player's "soulful" tone, bangs away; the violinist (or cellist) tries to overcome his inferiority in volume by exaggerating the expressivo and vibrato passages, because the pianist cannot do this—though some great pianists almost give the impression that they can.

Mozart's great piano quartet, K. 478, in G minor, demonstrates his incredible sense of balance. With the seeming facility that characterizes his greatest masterpieces Mozart solves the almost insoluable problem, creating piano sound with, rather than against, string sound. He managed to blend both.

The secret of good chamber-music playing is to listen. Many players just perform their parts, hoping that by some mysterious process the others will play theirs in roughly the same manner and tempo and that all will arrive at the end at approximately the same time. The better the quartet player, the more he listens to his fellow players. A good amateur should divide his effort into seventy-five per cent playing and at least twenty-five per cent listening. (Professional quartets achieve the fifty-fifty balance.) Unfortunately the adverse ratio is more frequent, and no wonder; only when one knows one's own part well can one afford to listen to the others. The quality of an amateur quartet should be judged by its lightness and transparency, not its volume and emotion. When four amateurs manage to play together softly yet clearly, so that the texture of the music becomes transparently audible, they've got something. They are no longer four players but a string quartet, which perhaps could be called the most sensitive of all musical instruments.

At the concert hall and in the opera house there is now the dictatorship of the star, whether conductor, virtuoso, or singer. Playing chamber music is a civilized form of the pursuit of happiness, and an exercise in humility; it also offers an ideal democracy. The four players must reach a subtle psychological rapport. Their relative positions in life are unimportant; when they sit down, they are first or second fiddles, violas or cellos. The intricate relationship among them is based on mutual respect in musical matters. A member who is out of step with the others in any question of style or taste will break up the inner unity of the group. Technical proficiency is of lesser importance

—amateurs have learned to live with their imperfections—and technical mistakes are forgiven, but not mistakes against the spirit of the music. A *staccato* run that fails doesn't matter so much; a wrongly conceived phrase does. False notes may have to be tolerated; false tempi are impermissible. Above all, enthusiasm is taken for granted. Chamber music is noncompetitive but never lukewarm.

Naturally there are always problems, as among close friends, and a string quartet suffers from its grouping. Two members play the same instruments: to make matters worse, one is called "first" violin and the other "second" (even in modern quartets, where both violin parts have comparable difficulties). No one likes playing second fiddle in life, and not in a quartet either. It is immaterial whether the second fiddler alternates with the first (which never works out), or "sacrifices" himself so there will be a quartet—or because the first-violin part is too difficult, though he may never admit it. Who will play the second fiddle remains the quartet's most delicate human-relations problem. It is sad to spend one's chamber-music life in the shadow of the first violin, endlessly repeating pom-poms while the first violin plays lyrical melodies. After a few years some second fiddlers become resigned; others rebel.

Owing to the law of supply and demand, viola-players and cellists are well aware of their rarity value and may take advantage of it. Some assume prerogatives that endanger the democratic structure; they explain in their musical opinions and indicate that their suggestions should be followed. The viola-player should not be an ex-violinist who didn't quite make the grade and seeks refuge behind the viola's thicker strings and the easier viola part. Rather, he should play the viola because he loves it, with its enchanting alto timbre. The cellist should not have delusions of grandeur. Musically, he is the foundation of the string quartet but that does not give him the right to ignore a *pianissimo,* or play *rubato* for his own delight whenever he has the melody. He must always remain a member of the group with his duties as well as rights.

The "literature," as we chamber-music players call our repertory, though not large, is very beautiful. Bad operas and inferior symphonies have been written, but relatively few quartets didn't come off: composers have always given their best to this demanding genre, intrigued by the challenge of using the bare essentials to express their musical ideas. In a symphony score the tone colors of the woodwinds and the magnificence of the brass can cover up a great deal; in a string quartet the composer's thought must be absolutely clear and honest to succeed.

Possibly three hundred string quartets exist, but most amateurs play only a certain number of these and as they grow older they grow to love the best quartets and play them time and again: the great quartets by Haydn, the "Ten Famous Quartets" by Mozart (who wrote twenty-six), and all Beethoven's seventeen quartets. (Discoveries in this field are rare; the "famous" quartets are usually also the best, and that's why they became famous. In his early works even Mozart can be a bore.)

There is a popular mystique that Haydn is good "to play oneself in with," as though his masterpieces were glorified warm-up exercises. Haydn was a genius, and must be approached with devotion. Some of his quartets have been given names, like some famous violins: the "Lark," the "Rider," the "Frog," the "Bird," the "Emperor," the "Rising Sun." Some Mozart quartets also have names, the "Hunt," or the beloved "Dissonance." To bring off any of these, all four players must have taste, style, musicality, and a certain technique. Even a famous professional quartet is occasionally grounded by Mozart's deceptive simplicity and graceful perfection: if Mozart isn't done exactly right, things may go very wrong.

The titanic greatness of Beethoven awes everybody, and playing certain Beethoven quartets is as exhilarating an experience for a string quartet as playing Hamlet must be for an actor. There is a widespread, mistaken belief that Beethoven's six early quartets, known as "Opus 18," are "relatively easy": they are extremely delicate, presenting difficult problems of technique and style. Beethoven was almost thirty when he started working on them and he meditated long and hard before composing them. He said he'd learned much from Haydn and Albrechtsberger and from his friend Aloys Förster, and he filled sixteen pages of his sketchbook for only the opening phrase of Opus 18, No. 1.

In 1806 he wrote the three "Rasumovsky" quartets, Opus 59, and began a new era in chamber-music history. They are technically demanding, rhythmically complex, and almost symphonic works, with great power and deep emotion. Beethoven wrote bravura passages into the first violin part, knowing that Schuppanzigh would bring them off. They have since been the downfall of many first fiddlers who are no Schuppanzighs. The next two quartets, the "Harp," Opus 74, and that in F minor, Opus 95 (which Beethoven called *quartetto serioso*), are somewhere in between Opus 59 and the late quartets, and often enigmatic. In 1824 (four years before his death) Beethoven was commissioned by Prince Nicolai Galitzin, a Russian amateur cellist living in Vienna, to write three quartets. Galitzin, a man of vision, wrote to Beethoven, "Your genius is centuries in advance." The composer worked on Opus 130, 131, and 132 all at the same time, though it approaches the impossible to conceive of this. No written analysis can convey the greatness of this absolute music. Opus 131 in C sharp minor, a gigantic work, is the greatest and noblest expression of Beethoven's genius. It consists of numbers instead of movements, and must be played through without pause. The difficulties are no longer technical, but there are formidable musical problems that must be approached with understanding and patience and dedication. In Opus 135 Beethoven writes into the last movement *"Muss es sein? Es muss sein"* (Must it be? It must be). The Great Fugue, Opus 133, is so complex that it is rarely successfully performed even by the best professional groups. Beethoven's last composition before he died was the Finale of Opus 130 in B flat major. His friends asked him to write it to replace the Fugue. Now Opus 130 ends on a note of absolute happiness.

As one gets deeper into the spirit of chamber music, nothing else quite comes up to the greatness of the classic masterpieces. Some people find Schubert a little repetitious, but the music is beautiful when it is performed right. It takes time to discover the melancholy hidden behind Schubert's singable melodies; even his chamber music is full of *Lieder*. The contradictions of his strange genius are apparent in the Quartet in A minor, Opus 29, his only chamber-music work to be printed during his lifetime. There is great beauty in his long, exhausting G major Quartet, Opus 161. It is considered an "ungrateful" work but it is quite rewarding when well played. Schubert's chamber-musical masterpiece, the String Quintet in C major, has been compared to the last quartets by Beethoven (whom Schubert admired so much) in its scope and depth of feeling.

Mozart, in his string quintets, loved the tonal warmth of two violas; Schubert, like Boccherini before him, used two cellos. The C major Quintet shows Schubert's complexity: the Adagio is almost terrifying in its haunted melancholy; in the finale Schubert regains his love of life, yet a trace of sadness lingers on.

Chamber-music players have their own secret code. When they speak of the "A minor" it is taken for granted that it's the Schubert A minor Quartet, not the Brahms A minor. But Schubert's A major Piano Quintet is known simply as the "Trout" Quintet, not by its key or opus number. There are two Smetana quartets but only one is played, the autobiographical masterpiece known as "From My Life" with the most important viola part in the whole literature. One can speak of "the" Verdi, "the" Debussy, "the" Ravel: each composed only one quartet. "Opus 96" refers to Dvořák's "American," but "Opus 95" means Beethoven. All this belongs to tradition; chamber-music players are great believers in tradition.

Then there are the "problematic" quartets by Brahms and Schumann, composers who were thinking of the piano even while writing for strings. And there are all the others: Mendelssohn, César Franck, Saint-Saëns, Tchaikovsky, Borodin (the D major is not "coffeehouse music" if played with restraint and taste), Grieg, Hugo Wolf, Richard Strauss. And somewhere there begins the era of the "moderns": Reger, Dohnányi, Hindemith, Prokofiev, Milhaud, Bloch, Shostakovich, Křenek, Villa-Lobos, Martinů, Vaughan Williams. And great works by Schönberg, Janáček, Bartók, Kodály; these pose problems of intonation, rhythm, and ensemble playing that few amateurs can master. The British musicologist A. Hyatt King correctly concludes, "The technical standards of atonal and microtonal chamber music are severe, being, in fact, beyond the range of all save professional musicians or highly skilled amateurs."

Teachers and Students

It is no exaggeration to say that a teacher can make or break a violin student. For every talented pupil whose career is furthered by a good teacher there are scores who are ruined by a bad one. Many years ago Alberto Bachmann wrote, "Teachers who make light of scale study, chord practice, the use of exercises and études, but who substitute a slovenly system of easy pieces or 'recreations' are to be avoided." Today that still goes, although many people now realize that a good violin teacher must be both a good violinist and a good musician. He must be strict and avoid all shortcuts. "It is a curious fact," Szigeti wrote, "that those variation works which treat technical problems from many angles, and aim at a certain comprehensiveness, are on the way out, from the point of view of publishers and teachers between whom there undoubtedly exists a certain interdependence." Today the general idea is to make things easier, to digest and condense difficult exercises. All serious artists agree that this never works. In art there is no substitute for conscientious study and hard work.

Violinists (and singers) never get tired of arguing about the merits of their teachers, and about the alleged miracles the teachers are said to have achieved. Alas, in teaching, one man's poison may be another man's meat; few teachers produce similar successes with several students, but if they do they may become great teachers.

Although much has been written about certain "schools" of playing, the scope and influence of a school can never be clearly defined. We speak of the classical Italian school when Corelli, Locatelli, Tartini, and Pugnani were teaching, but doubtless each had his own method, preferences, idiosyncrasies. Often the "school" is arbitrarily determined by time and place. When Baillot, Kreutzer, and Rode were teaching in Paris, people talked of the French school. Then the phenomenon shifted to Belgium, where Hubert Léonard (1819–1890) from Liége (who had studied under Habeneck in Paris) began teaching: his *Études Classiques* and *The Violinist's Physical Training* are still being used. One of his best students, Joseph Marsick, later taught Carl Flesch, who became one of the important teachers of the early twentieth century. Does that make Flesch a member of the "Belgian school"? Each prominent teacher develops his own "system" based on his experience and pedagogic wisdom (or lack of it). Other pupils of Léonard and Marsick were Jacques Thibaud, César Thomson, and Henri Marteau; all were excellent musicians. Another Belgian, Joseph Massart, was a pupil of Kreutzer and spent fifty years teaching at the Paris Conservatoire; he had among his pupils Wieniawski, Franz Ries, František Ondřiček, and Fritz Kreisler—a pretty good batting average.

The complex relationship between teacher and pupil is psychologically delicate. Probably there is the right teacher for every serious student on earth but the problem is to get them together. A teacher may perform a miracle with one gifted pupil and fail completely with another equally gifted. The real miracle is when a pupil finds the teacher who is just right for him, psychologically and musically. Such a relationship is an even greater rarity than a successful marriage.

The city of Vienna contributed three great epochs to the history of music. The first was classicism, which began with Gluck, continued with Haydn, reached its apotheosis with Mozart and Beethoven, and was reflected by Schubert. The great era of musical Romanticism came to it in the second half of the nineteenth century, when Brahms, Bruckner, Johann Strauss, Hugo Wolf, and Gustav Mahler lived there. Early in our century Vienna made musical history once more, when Arnold Schönberg, Alban Berg, and Anton von Webern evolved there an entirely new musical idiom. No other city on earth has such a record, but Vienna could not compete violinistically with Italy, France, Belgium, or Russia. Vienna had good instrumentalists, such as Schuppanzigh and Clement, and able teachers—Joseph Böhm, Joseph Mayseder, Jakob Dont, the Joseph Hellmesbergers, father and son, and Arnold Rosé—but the "Viennese School" was not important for the development of violin-playing. The only Vienna-born violinist to reach the very top, Fritz Kreisler, owed more to his training in Paris than in his hometown. Perhaps the best teacher Vienna ever knew was Leopold Mozart, the composer's father, who came there from Augsburg. His violin method is still considered a standard work.

During the early twentieth century the two most important violin teachers were Otakar Ševčik and Leopold Auer. Ševčik (1852–1934), from the small Bohemian town of Písek, began as a virtuoso but switched to teaching. His *School of Violin Technique* is masterly, a system of scientific exercises for scales, double stops, changes of position, bowing, and so on. Ševčik taught his system in Kiev, Prague, and Vienna, later in America, and finally he returned to Písek, where he had a carefully selected small group of acolytes. Undoubtedly Ševčik's system gave the average student the possibility of acquiring a sound technique. (I happen to be one of its beneficiaries.) But the idea of the system also limited its scope. Ševčik taught his advanced students to break up the difficult passages in the great violin concertos into exercises for scales, double stops, and bowings, but the great concertos are not a sequence of technical problems; they are great music. At the highest level Ševčik's system was still concerned with technical points rather than with musical values. Not surprisingly his star pupils were mostly celebrated for their technique. Ševčik created virtuosos: Kubelik, Kocian, Ondříček.

Leopold Auer, born in 1845 in Veszprem, Hungary, began as soloist and concertmaster, and had an important string quartet, but later he too devoted himself to teaching. At the Conservatory at St. Petersburg he founded what might be called the classical Russian school, and became almost a legendary personality. On a visit to Vilna in 1907, Auer heard from his friend Elias Malkin, of the Imperial School of Music, about a six-year-old *Wunderkind* named Jascha Heifetz. Auer didn't like prodigies and refused to listen to the boy, but somehow Malkin persisted: little Jascha played the Mendelssohn Violin Concerto and Paganini's last *Caprice*. Auer embraced the child and asked Papa Heifetz to bring the family to St. Petersburg—but by the time the family arrived from Vilna, much later, Auer had forgotten all about the boy: eventually Heifetz began studying with Auer. In 1918 Auer came to America and became the teacher of Heifetz, Elman, Zimbalist, Milstein, Francis Macmillen, Kathleen Parlow, David Hochstein, Cecilia Hansen, and many others. He died near Dresden in 1930, at eighty-five; he was buried in Ferncliff, New York.

All Auer students were said to have common characteristics, especially the so-called Russian bowhold. This was contradicted by Auer himself; in his *Graded Course of Violin Playing,* Auer demanded the old Campagnoli bowhold. (Bartolomeo Campagnoli, a pupil of Nardini, had demanded that the fingers be kept close together on the stick.) Auer became involved in a cause célèbre in 1878 when he refused to give the first performance of the Tchaikovsky Violin Concerto. Tchaikovsky had asked him to play it; Auer thought it unplayable, and according to Tchaikovsky's letters, Auer also persuaded Emile Sauret not to perform it. (Sauret, 1852–1919, a friend of Liszt, had developed a style close to Sarasate's.) Later Auer changed his mind and his pupils studied the Tchaikovsky Concerto, but he made numerous editorial changes "because some of the passages were not suited to the character of the instrument." Today the modern Soviet school has brought back the original edition. At the important Tchaikovsky Competition in Moscow the violin concerto is obligatory, and must be played in the original version.

Great teachers are never dogmatic. "The most dangerous thing in a teacher is dogma," says Ivan Galamian who taught in Moscow since he was fourteen, then for many years in Paris, and came to New York during World War II. He is one of the great teachers of our time, demanding of his students but giving them a great deal in return. A great teacher doesn't try to apply his "method" to every student; he treats each differently, for no two are alike. The teacher's art is to make the best of a pupil, despite the pupil's weaknesses. Louis Persinger, of the San Francisco Symphony Orchestra, followed no dogmatic method in teaching a six-year-old boy, Yehudi Menuhin. Naoum Blinder, also with the San Francisco Symphony (a pupil of Adolf Brodsky, Auer's colleague in St. Petersburg, and of Ševčik), accepted a ten-year-old boy, Isaac Stern, and worked with him for the next eight years; Stern never had another teacher. Blinder recognized Stern's natural talent and taught him to think independently, to rely on himself. "We often talked about art and music rather than fingering and intonation," Stern remembers.

Some of the great violinists possess what is called a natural technique, as opposed to a learned one. These lucky people seem to be born for the violin—or, more accurately, the violin seems invented for them. By instinct they do everything right. They may use different fingerings for the same scale, depending on the composition, and the tone color they want to achieve; yet they know that in each case only one fingering is right for them. Adolf Busch, a great artist and teacher, explains in the introduction to his edition of the Bach sonatas and partitas that the fingerings are based upon the principle of expressing the "inner polyphony" as well as the melodic line, even in monophonic movements, by giving each "inner voice" its own string. He treated the four strings of the violin as a "quartet of strings" and the structure became transparent. A fine example is the Presto of the Sonata No. 1, in G minor.

A great artist's left hand is dictated by his mind, not his fingers. A violin-player who cannot overcome a certain weakness of his fingers and arms may be a good musician but will never be a great violinist. Of a serious artist who was much esteemed by his fellow violinists and played Bach with deep understanding, it was said that he behaved on the platform as though he were playing in a telephone booth; and one couldn't overhear the scratching noise of his bow. The finest violinists never worry about technique as such. They practice logically, concentrating on special problems of intonation, speed, dynamics, bowing, and fingering. Even the greatest have their problems (though they won't always admit it). Many of them accept no one else's fingerings, not even from famous teachers or famous editors, but always devise their own. Fingering must not be a matter of the muscles but of the mind.

Violinists may ask one another, "How long do you practice?" but the very question proves their ignorance of what is not merely a problem of technique. Some fiddlers need more or less practice than others; some also need more or less sleep, and their preferences for food are as individual as for the music which they perform. Eventually every violinist develops his own system of practice and knows how much he needs. We read that young Paganini was forced by his father ". . . to play his violin at least ten hours a day." If this were true it is a miracle that Paganini survived the ordeal to become the greatest violinist. Heifetz, the greatest violinist in our time, needs "relatively" little practice; Auer, his teacher, told his students to practice three hours if they were any good, four if they were a little stupid, and "If you need more than four hours, try another profession." Galamian has said, "Four efficient hours of practice is best." The emphasis is on "efficient."

Most leading violinists dislike discussing their systems of practice and methods of work. They feel, with Paganini, that each man should have a few secrets. So there are probably as many methods of practice as there are fiddlers, and each has his own warm-up exercises. But many noted artists agree that when they study a new work, they first approach it in its totality. They may play it accompanied by their pianists, to get acquainted with the musical structure and the melodic line. Music is melody, though in some forms of modern music it may be difficult to hear and perceive it. Only after the artist has a clear conception of the whole work does he begin to study it technically, working out the details of bowing and fingering, phrasing and interpretation.

The rest is up to the artist's conscience. He must decide if and when he is ready for the performance. Years ago, when Isaac Stern performed at the Casals Festival in San Juan, Puerto Rico, he took along the score of the Stravinsky Violin Concerto, a very difficult work. For the next four days he rehearsed during the day, performed at the Festival in the evening, and studied the Stravinsky Concerto with intense concentration at night. After working on it for about fifteen hours in all, he flew to Hollywood and recorded it, with the composer conducting the orchestra.

All violinists agree that to get a musically fine performance of a concerto, it is necessary to work closely with the conductor of the accompanying orchestra. Nowadays it's strictly fifty-fifty. The days are gone when either a celebrated conductor or a famous violinist would tell the other artist what to do. The better the conductor, the easier it is to work with him. A great conductor is always willing to consider suggestions that make sense. It is far more difficult for the violinist to get the members of the orchestra on his side—especially the violinists, most of whom are would-be Heifetzes; the leading performers agree that it is best to try to persuade the orchestra, that it's hopeless to order them around, particularly when it is a celebrated orchestra. Demands should be specific; the reason should always be explained; sometimes the soloist should show them how a certain detail should be done. The musicians should know what they are doing, and should love doing it; an antagonistic or even indifferent orchestra can spoil the soloist's flawless performance.

The relationship between a famous violinist and his permanent accompanist—provided he has one—is delicate. It may be threatened by personal or musical differences. Ideally, the accompanist should be on the same musical level as the soloist, for his job is no longer to play only the relatively easy accompaniment of brilliant violin pieces by Paganini, Sarasate, Wieniawski, Kreisler; at a recital today he usually plays the sonatas of Mozart, Beethoven, Brahms, Debussy, and Franck, which demand as much of the pianist as of the violinist. But no matter how accomplished the pianist, he always plays second fiddle to the fiddler. It is rare that a great violinist and a great pianist team up permanently. Carl Flesch and Artur Schnabel were an exception, so were Casals and Cortot. In such cases both artists have similar beliefs in musical and artistic matters. Both Flesch and Schnabel were convinced that art comes from the emotions of the unconscious; both distrusted mechanical perfection, and were more interested in interpretative than technical matters.

At best the two artists will respect each other—which is more than mere liking one another—and they will agree that there is always room for disagreement. Tomáš G. Masaryk said that "democracy is discussion"; so is musical cooperation. And the pianist, no matter how

prominent he is, must at certain moments take second place to the violinist. During the Brahms Sonata he is almost a senior partner, but he
becomes a junior partner during the encores at the end of the recital,
and that's the impression most people take home.

Most of us no longer believe in the superiority of a certain "school" of
violin-playing. Any "school" means rules, and rules mean limitations.
Our aesthetic principles demand that the only limitations should be
those imposed by taste and style. Artistic beauty can never be the result of a "school." Beauty is planned balance, style, and taste, and
every man has to discover it for himself.

Most of the basic rules of violin-playing make sense. Doubtless the
best way of playing the fiddle is the natural way. Easy as it sounds,
this is as difficult to achieve as the "natural" style of singing. Caruso
had almost a natural technique—he overcame a brittle spot through
iron discipline in his youth—and seemed to sing almost effortlessly,
but when other singers tried to imitate his methods the results were
disastrous. A good violin teacher shows his pupil the mechanics of
right-hand and left-hand technique, but the violinist who has problems with his advanced technique must work them out himself. Even
the best teacher can only guide him.

The most difficult thing to teach is *vibrato*—in fact it is almost un-
teachable. Each great violinist has a characteristic *vibrato* just as
the voice of a great singer has a characteristic timbre. *Vibrato* is
much more than the result of muscular movement. The *vibrato* of
Heifetz, of Oistrakh, of Primrose, or of Casals reflects the artist's
entire personality, his musicality, his whole approach to music.
(Casal's noble *vibrato* perfectly expresses his ethical approach to
music.) Such things cannot be taught. What makes the matter still
more problematic is the fact that the violinist's ears are insensi-
tive to his own *vibrato*. Some violinists, including famous ones, play
everything with the same *vibrato*—a uniform emotion for Bach and
Paganini, Mozart and Vieuxtemps. This is stylistically wrong; the true
artist adapts his *vibrato* to the spirit of the music.

One can teach a gifted student the secret of good bowing, for it is es-
sentially a matter of muscular concentration, of balancing the weight
of the bow. But some prominent violinists have a "bow problem"

with, for instance, their down-bow *staccato* runs, and never solve it completely. One can also teach the student the so-called secret of the left hand, i.e., to develop equal strength of all four fingers and never apply pressure from the wrong angle. That, too, is a matter of using the muscles the "right" way though it is much more difficult to do it than to explain it.

But one cannot teach the student that the fingers should be guided by the musical phrase, not by the consideration of avoiding a technical problem. Here we enter the realm of metaphysics. In *A Violinist's Notebook* Szigeti demonstrates how he solved for himself many such problems after years of trial-and-error. Most of the great violinists feel they have to play scales every day. "No violinist in his senses would dream of substituting anything for scale practice," Szigeti writes. Some believe that playing Bach may be more useful than playing scales or études, *if* one plays Bach correctly. Some say that they practice at least one movement of a Bach solo sonata every day. Some practice Carl Flesch's *Urstudien,* perhaps the best manual of basic daily exercises.

Again, singers may provide a valid comparison. (The singer's vocal cords are comparable to the strings of the violin, the singer's resonators—certain bony cavities in the mouth, throat, and nose—to the violin's body. The singer uses his breath, controlled by various sets of muscles, somewhat as the violinist uses his bow.) No matter how beautiful the singer's "natural" voice, he must also become so sure of his technique that he takes it for granted. In principle "technique" means perfect control of one's muscles—which sounds easy and is very difficult. Only a few artists are able to do it. Practicing scales seems to be one way of keeping control of one's muscles, and many great violinists agree on that. Paganini told young students who came to ask for advice that they must "not neglect even for a day to practice scales," and Heifetz has bewildered young violinists after they played a movement from a concerto when he said, "And now let's hear a few scales."

Paul Hindemith wrote, "One would expect every musician to have the urge to hand on what he has achieved to pupils who understand it." Many great violinists throughout the centuries have considered it their duty to share the wealth of their experience with young students. It is not only altruism: often the artist-student relationship adds another di-

mension to the teacher's art. Ideally, both student and teacher will
benefit. But great artists are not always great teachers. Sivori, a young
violinist from Genoa who studied with Paganini in Paris, later told
David Laurie that Paganini was "probably the worst teacher of the violin who ever lived." He had no patience; when Sivori tried to play
some exercises which Paganini had quickly written for his lessons, Paganini would walk up and down "with a mocking smile on his face
and uttering a depreciatory remark now and then." He would stare at
his pupil—Paganini was over six feet tall and Sivori quite short—and
ask Sivori why he couldn't do better. Poor Sivori would stammer that
he didn't have Paganini's ability. Paganini got furious—this was not a
matter of ability, he said, but of steady work, and he accused Sivori of
being lazy, but then, he said, he would try once more. And "Paganini
would seize the violin like a lion seizing a sheep," and play the exercise without even looking at the music, walking around and playing it
so incredibly well that Sivori got completely depressed. Perhaps it
didn't occur to Paganini that no one else had his ability.

Exactly the same happened to me with Jascha Heifetz, our latter-day
Paganini. In Beverly Hills, one afternoon, during a discussion of violin matters, Heifetz picked up his beautiful Guarneri del Gesù and, by
way of explaining his point, played a couple of terrifying passages. His
fingers were faster than my eyes; I had no idea how he'd done it. I
asked him to do it once more. Again I failed to perceive the exact execution. Heifetz seemed quite surprised, but I know to this day that
very few violinists would have been able to see and understand how
he'd done it.

It is no secret that great artists doubling as teachers have a large
percentage of casualties among their students. Exceptions only confirm
the rule: Viotti, Vieuxtemps, Kreutzer, Marteau, and Ysaÿe were great
violinists *and* great teachers. In the Soviet Union, where the famous instrumentalists, all state-trained, are required to teach part of the time,
David Oistrakh and Mstislav Rostropovich, two very great artists, seem
to have the teacher's knack, judging by the caliber of their students.
The great artist-teacher can transform routine study into inspiration;
he can widen the student's horizon and make him see further than a
teacher can who doesn't perform. Yet inspiration is only for those who
are musically, intellectually, and technically ready for it, or the great

artist's effort to inspire may create inhibitions, almost fear. The student, like poor Sivori, realizes that he will never be able to join the teacher on his flight to the stars, and gets depressed.

The good teacher knows that the gifted student must have freedom to make good music—emotional and intellectual freedom, freedom of musical understanding and of technique. The artist-teacher tells his student that freedom comes from discipline. Perhaps he explains to the student that the performing artist cannot reach the stars unless, paradoxically, he has his feet firmly planted on the ground. He is aware of the obligations which artistic freedom give him, and he disciplines himself scrupulously. When something goes wrong he faces it, trying to discover why it went wrong.

Once in a thousand cases, a great artist is able to give his technique, his sense of discipline, his working method, his whole philosophy to a gifted pupil just at the moment when the pupil is ready for it. It's a blessed moment. And if all goes well, the pupil will become a great violinist.

INDEX

Names of instrument makers are in italics; names of instruments in quotation marks.

217
227
234
247, 8

251
252
253 (2)
254
262

264
265
266